EXPLORING THE

C-SPAN

ARCHIVES

Advancing the Research Agenda

EXPLORING THE
C-SPAN
ARCHIVES

Advancing the Research Agenda

edited by
Robert X. Browning

Purdue University Press, West Lafayette, Indiana

Cataloging-in-Publication data available from the Library of Congress.

Paper ISBN: 978-1-55753-734-8
ePDF ISBN: 978-1-61249-440-1
ePUB ISBN: 978-1-61249-441-8

To the memory of my sister,
Barbara Browning

CONTENTS

THE C-SPAN ARCHIVES AS THE POLICYMAKING RECORD OF AMERICAN REPRESENTATIVE DEMOCRACY: A FOREWORD

Almost two centuries ago, the idea of research libraries, and the possibility of building them at scale, began to be realized. Although we can find these libraries at every major college and university in the world today, and at many noneducational research institutions, this outcome was by no means obvious at the time. And the benefits we all now enjoy from their existence were then at best merely vague speculations.

How many would have supported the formation of these institutions at the time, without knowing the benefits that have since become obvious? After all, the arguments against this massive ongoing expenditure are impressive. The proposal was to construct large buildings, hire staff, purchase all manner of books and other publications and catalogue and shelve them, provide access to visitors, and continually reorder all the books that the visitors disorder. And the libraries would keep the books, and fund the whole operation, *in perpetuity.* Publications would be collected without anyone deciding which were of high quality and thus deserving of preservation—leading critics to argue that all this effort would result in expensive buildings packed mostly with junk.

To make matters even more confusing, the critics turned out to be right: Most research libraries today are predominantly filled with publications that interest no one. To take one example, more than half the books in the libraries at my own university have not been checked out even once. Yet, the central benefit of these hugely important institutions has turned out to come from collecting the exhaustive record of human thought and activities in some area or areas, making it possible for future scholars to make discoveries from this material that could not have been foreseen at the time. And the progress since has been spectacular.

Such must have been the case three decades ago when Robert X. Browning and his colleagues were trying to set up the C-SPAN Archives. You can almost hear the arguments: C-SPAN is not exactly the most popular TV network, even when it runs live debates of current interest, and now Browning is planning to preserve in perpetuity the 17th hour of a Senate filibuster being taped at 2 a.m., with three senators in the chamber watching?

It is a good thing for society and American democracy that Browning won those arguments. We now have more than 214,000 hours of videos constituting the primary, and in most cases the only, visual and audio record of the policymaking process in the world's leading representative democracy. With the vision we now all have with hindsight, we can see that it is a true shame that the visual record of prior policy and politics in America is now lost forever. Fortunately, this is no longer the case, and perhaps will never be the case from here on out.

The C-SPAN Archives has produced obvious benefits for the public in understanding governmental debates and policies through the many hundreds of thousands of these videos watched and studied every year. But, just like research libraries, the most important benefits of the C-SPAN Archives are those which were unknown when the Archives was formed. And that is the point of this important volume—to record, explain, and build on the fast progress being made in the fields of research that have grown up around, as a result of, or coincident with the Archives.

I am especially interested in the progress in research turning text, audio, and video into actionable research data. Few could have imagined in the 1980s that the VHS tapes being filed on shelves and in boxes in West Lafayette,

Indiana, would eventually be digitized. Fewer still could have understood that developments in methodology, statistics, machine learning, and data science would turn this digitized treasure trove into informative research data capable of producing insights and measures crucial to social science inquiry. These include automated measures of emotion, nonverbal behavior, crowd counts, interactions, and numerous other crucial indicators valuable for a wide range of social and political research.

The C-SPAN Archives not only has a bright future, but it has helped create one for us all as we shed light on how democracy works in America. The research benefiting from the Archives, and well represented in this impressive book, is teaching us a great deal. In this sense, the original vision of the founders of the C-SPAN Archives is having a bigger impact now than it ever has. We should all be glad that this book is being printed and copied, and is due to be stored in the world's libraries in perpetuity.

Gary King
Albert J. Weatherhead III University Professor
Director, Institute for Quantitative Social Science
Harvard University

PREFACE

I t has been my pleasure to edit and now present the second volume of papers from the November 2014 Advancing the Research Agenda conference. At that conference, 16 scholars presented pathbreaking research conducted using the C-SPAN Archives. The conference exceeded our expectations. Scholars from a wide range of disciplines undertook research that addressed issues in rhetoric, communication technology, African American congressional representation, the portrayal of the First Lady, presidential debates, and image bite analysis. In addition, three papers pioneered ways to study congressional behavior using video resources.

When we established the C-SPAN Archives almost 30 years ago, we anticipated it would be valuable for research, teaching, and civic understanding. The latter two uses have really had an impact. Teachers from K–12 to college use C-SPAN video clips to illustrate points in a variety of courses. Lesson plans are created for K–12 teachers at the C-SPAN Classroom website (http://www.c-spanclassroom.org/). College professors select their own clips to illustrate processes and concepts in their lectures. In the first volume in this series, Professor Glenn Sparks describes using clips of authors of books his students were reading.

Journalists, politicians, and elected officials clip and post videos from the C-SPAN Archives' online Video Library in a national virtual debate on public policy. Each year more than 2 million clips, with more than 13 million views, are hosted in the Video Library. This is in addition to the full-length programs, which garner more than 15 million views each year. So, the C-SPAN Video Library has raised the public debate on political and policy issues as the public engages in a clipping and posting debate.

But it is the academic research on which the conference, and subsequently this volume, focuses. That research takes time and commitment from scholars. First, they must undertake the research and fit it in the context of previously published work. And developing data from video records is time consuming and tedious. Data need to be collected, coded, and analyzed from the video record. The level of innovation and amount of time spent, as presented in the chapters of this volume, are truly impressive.

The intellectual work that went into the conference and this volume demonstrate how far the C-SPAN Archives has come over the past nearly 30 years. Sixteen scholars each approached a topic in their area of expertise and turned to the C-SPAN Archives to find data to shed light on their topic. They advance our knowledge in each of their fields as well as demonstrate for others how the C-SPAN Video Library can be used for a wide range of research.

This volume is organized around four themes. Theme 1, Making Sense of Recorded Events and Re-Collected Memories, comprises two chapters. In Chapter 1, Katherine Cramer Brownell uses the C-SPAN Video Library to examine the 1960 Kennedy–Nixon and 1976 Ford–Carter debates and how our collective memory of these debates has evolved in the current day. As a historian, she uses the Archives as primary source material to demonstrate that beliefs that people cite during C-SPAN–covered forums may not reflect what really happened. She mines much information from comments by principal actors who reflect on the events that Brownell examines.

In Chapter 2, Alison N. Novak and Ernest A. Hakanen examine the future of technology as presented on the weekly C-SPAN series *The Communicators*. They performed a very thorough and systematic analysis of this series, which features half-hour interviews with industry leaders and legislators. Their work is important in helping us understand the ways in which technology and our technological future are discussed and presented. Communicators include industry leaders and analysts talking about the latest communication technology issues. How these participants frame technology policy issues helps us understand the way that technology issues are interpreted and affect our collective memories.

Theme 2, Changing Ways of Searching and Analyzing Data, comprises three chapters. In Chapter 3, Erik P. Bucy and Zijian Harrison Gong examine presidential debates, focusing on what they term "image bite analysis." This important contribution uses C-SPAN to examine nonverbal behavior in the Romney and Obama presidential debates. President Obama's poor performance in the first debate can be traced to his poor nonverbal behavior, which had a greater influence on the audience than what he actually said. Bucy and Gong also discuss how to tie this research to tweets and the possibility of future automated coding. Research in nonverbal attributes in public debates and elite interaction are an important developing area that the C-SPAN video collection makes possible. We expect to see others build upon Bucy's and Gong's research.

In Chapter 4, stonegarden grindlife takes a novel approach to measuring polarization in Congress, examining volume levels in the U.S. House of Representatives and using these levels to measure inflection and anger in debates. This is not a new topic, but one that has never before been studied in this way. Stonegarden brings technical sophistication to measuring audio levels and correcting for systematic changes so that the underlying variation due to conflict can be analyzed.

In Chapter 5, David A. Caputo's contribution is based on the keynote lecture he gave at the November 2014 Advancing the Research Agenda conference. In it he discusses the phenomenon of Massive Open Online Courses (MOOCs) and how these courses can use C-SPAN and the Archives in a new approach to education. He also discusses the idea of advocacy MOOCs, particularly those involving campaigns. His chapter causes us to reflect on the ways that this video collection can be used in teaching, especially in a large-scale way.

Theme 3, Contributing Engaged Scholarship, comprises one chapter in which Mary L. Nucci uses the search function of the C-SPAN Video Library to explore how issues in science and technology are evidenced in C-SPAN programs. The C-SPAN Video Library houses all congressional floor debates, many congressional hearings, and public policy forums. Searching this collection reveals a wide variety of scientific topics. Future scholars can build upon

Nucci's research to explore in further detail ways that science and technology are debated. Patrice Buzzanell also talks about engaged scholarship in the final reflection chapter. Understanding and assisting practitioners in using this vast collection is a challenge we expect that many other scholars will take up.

Theme 4, Celebrating Difference, Telling Our Stories, comprises five chapters. In Chapter 7, Nadia E. Brown, Michael D. Minta, and Valeria Sinclair-Chapman examine the oral histories of members of the Congressional Black Caucus. From the words of the CBC members themselves, we learn about the history of the founding of the Caucus and the motivations of the founding members, and about differences in the agendas of Black political women who sought to advance issues specific to women and African Americans. This chapter contributes to our understanding of the concept of representation among Black leaders and how members from minority majority districts have sought to provide representation to Black constituents from other districts who did not have Black representation. This chapter is unique in that the authors use oral histories originally collected by the Congressional Black Caucus Avoice Virtual Library Project.

In Chapter 8, Ray Block Jr. and Christina S. Haynes look at the presentation of the First Lady, Michelle Obama, who has developed the theme of "Mom-in-Chief." Block and Haynes effectively use clips from the C-SPAN Video Library to illustrate how Mrs. Obama uses this theme in speeches. Their work will be reviewed by others who want to approach both the topic of diversity as well as how others such as Nancy Reagan, Barbara Bush, Hillary Clinton, and Laura Bush chose to present themselves as First Ladies. C-SPAN has dedicated an entire series and book to studying the history of First Ladies (*First Ladies: Presidential Historians on the Lives of 45 Iconic American Women* [PublicAffairs, 2015]).

In Chapter 9, Christopher Neff takes advantage of the way senators announce their votes in the Senate to examine the order in which they vote, using information known after the vote to present an interesting analysis of those who vote first and those who hold back on their vote during the Senate roll call. Others have begun to notice that the way in which senators vote allows research into cue taking, taking cover, and personal interactions.

In Chapter 10, which looks at the representation of women in STEM disciplines, Lauren Berkshire Hearit and Patrice M. Buzzanell use C-SPAN video to examine how debates and speeches in the C-SPAN Video Library characterize these women. Their approach differs from others in the book but serves as example of how the C-SPAN Video Library can reveal and expose communication analysis.

In Chapter 11, Bryce J. Dietrich examines how members of the U.S. House of Representatives interact with each other on votes both with and without bipartisan cosponsorship. By examining pixel changes as members gather in the well during House roll call votes, Bryce is able to demonstrate that there is more bipartisan mixing following votes on bills with bipartisan cosponsorship. Taken together with stonegarden grindlife's work, these two chapters show the way that innovative use of video and audio technology can expose underlying political phenomena that have heretofore not been studied in this way.

Patrice M. Buzzanell closes the book with a reflective essay on the research presented in this volume, demonstrating the depth of the varying approaches by examining how they help us understand our collective memory, how they illustrate different ways of searching and analyzing C-SPAN video, how they advance the idea of the engaged scholar, and what they tell us about ourselves. Patrice challenges us to think about future research possibilities.

These chapters illustrate the different ways that scholars across different disciplines can approach the C-SPAN collection to answer their research questions. Each of the contributing authors presents research that advances our understanding of political science, communication, history, Congress, and science. They also help us understand how the C-SPAN Video Library can be used in ways we may not have previously considered. My hope is that others will follow in their footsteps and expand upon these studies and the methods presented.

ACKNOWLEDGMENTS

A book like this does not come together without the help of a lot of people. Brian Lamb, Susan Swain, and Rob Kennedy of C-SPAN continue to encourage the development of research using the C-SPAN Archives. Their financial support through the C-SPAN Education Foundation research grants is instrumental in making the Purdue conferences and subsequent books a success. Joanne Wheeler, executive director of the Foundation, helps make that happen. Purdue President Mitch Daniels office has provided the Purdue funds to allow us to hold the conferences. David Reingold, the Justin S. Morrill Dean of the College of Liberal Arts, has been an enthusiastic supporter of the C-SPAN Archives and our research efforts. The heads of my two academic departments, Rosie Clawson of political science and Marifran Mattson of the Brian Lamb School of Communication, help in so many ways with the conferences and provide such sound advice and counsel along the way. Professor Jay McCann of political science helped review the conference proposals that shaped the contributions in this volume. Josh Scacco, Rosie Clawson, and Howard Sypher graciously agreed to chair the conference panels. All the authors were a pleasure to work with, and through working with them I learned so much about the potential of the Archives that I had never thought of.

Three people have been essential in making this book a reality. First, Nita Stickrod of my C-SPAN staff skillfully handled all the conference planning and worked with the authors and conference staff to keep everything running smoothly. Patrice Buzzanell, my Purdue communication colleague, helped with reviews, advice, and encouragement and provided countless ideas at each stage of the process. None of this would be possible without her intellectual contribution and friendship. Kelley Kimm of the Purdue University Press provided such skillful editing of the manuscript. Her editing produced a much stronger book as she guided us all on style, substance, and presentation. Thanks to all of you.

David A. Caputo has been a colleague, mentor, and friend for over 30 years. He was the one who have me the support to initially create the Archives and so willingly gave the insightful keynote for the conference that is printed in this volume. The entire staff of the C-SPAN Archives—especially my two managers, Steve Strother and Alan Cloutier—provided necessary support to the authors and me by maintaining the Video Library that makes this research possible. Two other Purdue colleagues, Howard Sypher of communication and Ed Delp of engineering, provided many ideas and assistance for research and technology that underlie this volume.

Finally, my family and friends, especially Andy Buck and those of Tecumseh Bend, are vital for their friendship and encouragement. While this book was in production I lost my sister, who was closest in age and personal support. I miss her keen wit, humor, and insights, and this book is dedicated to her lasting memory.

Robert X. Browning, Editor
Summer 2015

CHAPTER 1

GOING BEYOND THE ANECDOTE: THE C-SPAN ARCHIVES AND UNCOVERING THE RITUAL OF PRESIDENTIAL DEBATES IN THE AGE OF CABLE NEWS

Kathryn Cramer Brownell

On January 13, 1992, Janet Brown, the executive director of the Commission on Presidential Debates, led a discussion of the history of presidential debates with students at the Washington Center for Internships and Academic Seminars Symposium on "Campaign '92: In Pursuit of the Presidency." The broader symposium offered participants an insider look at multiple facets and pressures surrounding the planning of the upcoming presidential debates. Pointing to polling data and research in political science on the impact of the debates on voter support of a particular presidential candidate, William Burke, the president of the Washington Center argued that "the majority of people make their decision based on these debates" (C-SPAN, 1992a). The symposium that followed brought in campaign strategists, political party leaders, journalists, and organizers of the debates to discuss with students and the broader viewing public the centrality of the event to the democratic process.

And yet, while Janet Brown shared her experiences in organizing the 1988 debates and the negotiations underway for the time, format, and structure of the 1992 debates, she left out a significant change that had taken place. Committed to providing a forum for voter education, the League of Woman Voters had sponsored the 1976, 1980, and 1984 debates but gave up sponsorship in 1988. Angry that by 1988 the Republican and Democratic Parties had formed a new commission to reach agreements on the debate ground rules, format, and moderators without consulting with the League of Women Voters, its president, Nancy M. Neuman, withdrew sponsorship a week before the scheduled vice-presidential debate. Neuman articulated a strong critique of these pre-debate arrangements, as she declared. "We have no intention of becoming an accessory to the hoodwinking of the American public" (Rosenbaum, 1988). Refusing to give its "stamp of approval on a shoddy product," the League argued that agreement between the two parties to permit only short answers and brief rebuttals without "follow-up questioning" made the debates merely another campaign event that was good for the candidates, but not for informing the electorate about the issues at hand.[1]

In the aftermath of the 1988 election, a national "debates over the debates" occurred as the Commission on Presidential Debates moved to institutionalize the event in presidential campaigns. Did presidential debates "hoodwink" or inform the American public? While these campaign events drew high ratings, what role did they play in the democratic process? For more than half a century, political pundits and journalists have grappled with this question. And yet, as the historian David Greenberg (2011) argues, expecting the "debates to be grandly edifying" and then "berating them for not rising to such a lofty standard," misses the point (p. 138). Rather, Greenberg views the debates as important political rituals which "thicken our commitments to political life" (p. 153). In this capacity, debate anecdotes about presidential success and failure reveal shared assumptions about the presidency and political power. Analyzing their origins and trajectory illuminates how and why certain practices and values have become ingrained in American electoral politics, especially in making on-camera performances a central qualification for holding a public office while also heightening the power of media consultants, pollsters, and "spin doctors" in American political life (Brownell, 2014).

Though beginning in 1960 (remember the famed Lincoln–Douglas debates pitted two would-be senators, not presidents, against one another), the resurrection of presidential debates in 1976 coincided with the dramatic changes in electoral politics and media structures. Party reforms following the 1968 election moved the nomination process from backrooms of convention halls, where party bosses negotiated with one another, to the primary trail (Brownell, 2014). Though any candidate could make a presidential run and the selection process was opened, successful contenders for the nomination needed media publicity, which frequently involved hiring professional consultants to navigate an increasingly expansive media terrain. At the same time, television programming expanded. Cities were wired for cable television, a fourth broadcast network, FOX, appeared in 1986, and satellite technology increased viewers' access to coverage of live events. The 1980s brought new cable networks, particularly the Cable-Satellite Public Affairs Network (C-SPAN), which opened to viewers the proceedings of the House of Representatives in 1979 and then the Senate in 1986, offering unprecedented coverage of political events. The Cable News Network (CNN) followed in 1980 to offer 24/7 news coverage and expanded political commentary on the news that had begun to reshape network news programs in the post-Watergate era.

These changes raise an important research question for historians: What was the political and cultural influence of these transformations in the media landscape? In the age of broadcast television, the U.S. Federal Communications Commission (FCC) required news programs to uphold the public interest by covering political contenders and public policy issues in an "equal" and "fair" presentation. Not only did the FCC overturn the Fairness Doctrine in 1987, but also the expansion of cable television and satellite technology held the promise to promote diversity, the free market, and individual choice through the expanding dial. But, did it promote democracy, fashion new opportunities for political professionals to hoodwink the public, or, perhaps, create alternative political rituals?

The C-SPAN Archives' online Video Library can help answer these questions. The Video Library includes not only presidential speeches, debates, and congressional activities but also analyses of electoral trends and panel discussions on shifting campaign strategies. Even educational events like the Pursuit of the Presidency symposium offer an unparalleled window into how candidates, journalists, consultants, public officials, and the public experienced, discussed, and understood the dramatic changes in the media environment that took shape around them. Whether through viewer call-in programs, televised conferences of the professional political consultants, or programs about recent political history, the Video Library offers a range of political commentary from this rapidly changing media environment. During these discussions, professional campaign operatives frequently set the parameters and terms of discussion in ways that media scholars have called an "echo chamber"—a cultural environment in which anecdotes of Washington politics "gives a special resonance" to particular political practices to make them more powerful than they in fact are (Schudson, 1995, p. 141). The threat, argues media historian Michael Schudson, is that this self-enclosed world can taint objective journalism and popular history narratives, especially as they circulate on television.

Historians have often neglected television programming in their historical analysis because of both a proclivity to prioritize written documents and the difficulty of accessing video material (Greenberg, 2012). As such, few have examined the origins and the implications of "the echo chamber," a concept about which media scholars and political scientists frequently reference and theorize (Jamieson & Capella, 2010).[2] Since Neil Postman (2004) famously wrote in 1985 of the dire situation facing American democracy as Americans choose entertainment over information in his landmark book, *Amusing Ourselves to Death,* political analysts and scholars have sought to quantify how the decreasing size of the sound bite, the increase of negative advertisements, and the distraction offered by more programming choices have contributed to voter apathy and disenchantment with the electoral process (Iyengar, 1994; Iyengar & Kinder, 1989; Mann & Ornstein, 2013). Television debates, argues Postman, reflect how Americans consume the image rather than engage with the substance of policy discussions.

And yet, this notion that style and substance are mutually exclusive binaries overlooks deeper cultural, economic, and political changes during the 1980s. Journalism ethics and corporate media structures changed during that decade. Gary Hart's failed bid for the presidency in 1988 showed how personal sex scandals became fodder for news coverage. That same year CNN's Bernard Shaw shocked the Democratic candidate, Michael Dukakis, during a debate by asking how the Massachusetts governor would respond to his wife, Kitty, being raped (Bai, 2014). While scholars have begun to examine the output of changing electoral strategies, political rhetoric, media coverage, and professional standards, how these new practices resonate among viewers, the origins of these shifts, and their impact on American civic life and the presidency more broadly remain unclear (Jamieson, 1996; Ponce de Leon, 2015, Troy 1991).

The C-SPAN Video Library holds a wealth of material to help historians fill this void and ascertain how Americans grappled with these dramatic political changes during the age of cable television. It provides an opportunity to go beyond the popular anecdote about John F. Kennedy's 1960 campaign or Ronald Reagan's communication skills to place presidential history within the broader cultural context. By focusing on media discussions of presidential debates in particular, this chapter will provide an initial exploration into these broader questions while offering examples of how to use new sources to recapture a more nuanced history of the American presidency by using an interdisciplinary framework. During the 1992 symposium about presidential debates, Janet Brown used two specific historical anecdotes to justify the organization, assumptions, and actions of the debate commission as it prepared for upcoming campaigns: the Kennedy–Nixon debates in 1960 and Ford's comment about Eastern Europe not being under the Soviet Union's control during the 1976 election. Brown contended that Kennedy's superior television performance in 1960 and Ford's "gaffe" in 1976 proved how the debates had contributed to the development of a modern political environment in which entertainment had transformed the nature and content of news because "we are used to being enlivened" (C-SPAN, 1992a).

But, the debates alone did not simply create this environment, as Brown's anecdote implied. The same strategists who shaped campaign tactics—from Nixon to Clinton—by putting a premium on entertainment and television appearances, also generated the norms of political analysis and commentary on cable news programming. In doing so, they created a political echo chamber about the importance of performative politics—a restrictive "style versus substance" analysis of politics—that eventually alienated many voters from the entire process. Though promoting a flawed history, political actors, from Janet Brown to Roger Ailes and George Stephanopoulos, the latter political operatives, reiterated iconic moments from presidential debates that further enhanced their political power. Beginning with the perceived devastating blow of Nixon's sweaty brow in the 1960 election, political consultants convinced political contenders that televised debate performances won or lost elections. The expansion of political commentary with around-the-clock news shows further brought these consultants and pollsters into the public eye as they then reshaped public dialogue. With its extensive programming collection, the C-SPAN Video Library illuminates how and why the "debate over the debates" became a way for the public to grapple with, and frequently critique, the implications of a changing 24/7 news cycle and the emergence of the presidency as the "entertainer-in-chief."

THE KENNEDY TAN VERSUS THE NIXON SHADOW: MYTH, FACT, OR SOMETHING ELSE?

After declaring the 1988 debates "successful" (C-SPAN, 1992a), Janet Brown worked diligently over the next four years to institutionalize the key points of success that she, scholars, journalists, candidates, and other experts deemed essential to a fair format for the next presidential election. In its pursuit of an unbiased programming format, before, during and after the debates, the Commission on Presidential Elections reminded the public of the central importance of the debates in American elections. No one anecdote better sums up the power of format and image in helping turn an election than the story of the first televised debate between Nixon and Kennedy. The 1960 election, many journalists and political pundits contend, stood as a revolutionary moment in which television transformed the electoral process and created the modern celebrity presidency in which Kennedy's television image and style precluded the substance of the Nixon campaign effort (Donaldson, 2007; Gould, 1996). During the symposium about the organization of the 1992 debates, this interpretation came up not from Brown but from a younger audience member. The forum showed how the crowd accepted this story as a fundamental truth.

A young woman raised her hand during the event and asked, "With the Kennedy–Nixon debates isn't it a fact that anyone who watched it on TV when polled said that they thought that Kennedy was a stronger candidate, but the people listening to it on radio thought that Nixon was a stronger candidate" ultimately showing that the debates were all about optics not issues(C-SPAN, 1992a). Janet Brown responded that the questioner was "absolutely right about 1960, and this was one of the very interesting aspects of that election" (C-SPAN, 1992a). This story of Kennedy's victory on television and Nixon's alleged victory on radio reaffirmed the notion that the formatting of the debate and the visual image presented on television changed the way the public received the electoral messages. As a result, it clearly highlighted that the medium of television distinguished style from substance in that election.

Despite the power and longevity of this interpretation, scholars have argued that this story is more a myth than a reality (Brownell, 2014; Greenberg, 2011; Schudson, 1995; Vancil & Pendell, 1987). The "public opinion poll" that showed Nixon winning on radio and Kennedy on television came from a survey taken by a small Philadelphia research firm; it was not a nationally recognized or scientifically sound poll. Moreover, this narrative assumes that radio listeners were influenced only by the content of each candidate's statements and not by inflections of voice or Kennedy's prominent Boston accent, both stylistic factors (Schudson, 1995). Nevertheless, this interpretation continues to pervade popular history, especially as it has played out on television, so the question emerges: Why has it had such resonance? This narrative reflects an interpretation and memory of the event that started to take root in the 1960s as political contenders, like Nixon himself, came to believe that media mattered more than any other component of the electoral process (Brownell, 2014). This is not necessarily what happened in the 1960 debates, but rather, what political experts came to believe happened, and this perception has shaped the growth and trajectory of presidential debates, particularly when cable programming provided an opportunity for the expansion of such political commentary during the 1980s.

Expectations were high for the presidential debates in 1960. In his coverage of the campaign, Theodore White called them "a revolution in American presidential politics." He penned with excitement how "American genius in technology" promised to allow "the simultaneous gathering of all tribes of America to ponder their choice between two chieftains in the largest political convocation in the history of man" (White, 2009, p. 279). Media coverage at the time proved to be very evenhanded, and actually focused more on the content of debate itself, as well. One headline read: "Nixon, Kennedy Clash in TV Debate over Ways to Spur Economic Growth, Finance Medical Care, Aid Schools" as the story discussed the nuances of the policy discussions. Perhaps a more compelling observation emerged with the article's statement, "The all important question of 'who won' may never be conclusively answered even on Election Day…but there was nothing in the show to indicate clearly it would overwhelm other phases of the campaign" (Staff Reporter, 1960).

Originally published in 1961, Theodore White's account, *The Making of the President 1960,* concludes that despite the "revolutionary" democratic potential, the debates were "an opportunity missed" for an in-depth discussion of the issues at hand during the election, a popular analysis during the election year. White emphasizes how both mediums that broadcast the debates, television and radio, missed this opportunity. According to White, this came from not merely the difficulties that Nixon had with the debate—from his makeup problem to his adherence to the suggestion of his running partner, Henry Cabot Lodge, that he use the opportunity to "erase the 'assassin image'"—but rather the structure of the debates, which allowed only "two-and-a-half-minute answers back and forth" (White, 2009, pp. 285–292). The *New York Times* published an array of editorials from newspapers across the country to highlight the diversity of opinions American television viewers held. Responses ranged from "it was a weak and wish-washy piece of history" to it was a successful "experiment that demonstrated that politics may be waged intelligently, even urbanely" (Excerpts From Editorials, 1960).

After the election, scholars immediately started researching the impact of the televised debates in a more statistical manner, hoping to offer concrete evidence of how they may or may not have influenced the election. One study of 95 New York voters observed that Kennedy may have had a stronger performance that resulted in an "improvement of the Kennedy image" but that "this improvement was not accompanied by shifts in the voting intentions" (Lang & Lang, 1961, p. 278). The debates, this study argued, crystallized and confirmed voter decisions rather than changing them. Moreover, many participants in the study—both Kennedy and Nixon supporters—reported a "deep-seated distrust about the spontaneity of [Kennedy's] performance" (Lang & Lang, 1961, p. 286).

Though television mattered during the 1960 campaign, it remained a controversial tool—one that could incite as much criticism as it could support. Daniel Boorstin's (1962) landmark book *The Image: A Guide to Pseudo-Events in America* framed Kennedy's television strategy, with its emphasis on "pseudo-events" and use of image, as a threat to the future of representative government. The son of a former Hollywood studio executive, John F. Kennedy understood the potential of television performances to create excitement and enthusiasm about his candidacy. He approached the television debates not as a contest against a political opponent but as media events where, such as during his appearances on the *Jack Paar Show* or *Meet the Press,* he sold his personality, appealing to voters as "media consumers" first and foremost.[3] Because he had personally hired the film producer Jack Denove to follow him on the campaign trail and capture his performances to later use in advertisements, Kennedy appeared vibrant as he was taking action and communicating with the large crowds his campaign had built. Kennedy embraced an innovative yet controversial media strategy, a "showbiz politics" rooted in California politics, and the motion picture industry in particular, as his campaign prioritized the media and used his celebrity status to win votes (Brownell, 2014).

And yet, on the primary trail and during the national campaign, Kennedy faced constant criticism from his reliance on television performances, frequently undergoing attacks that he had style but lacked experience and leadership. As he pursued a media-driven primary campaign, prominent Democrats critiqued his reliance on money and celebrity to gain fame. Hubert Humphrey referred to the candidate as "Jack who has Jack" (Wehrwein, 1960), while Eleanor Roosevelt (1958) publicly admonished the senator for trying to "influence through money." During the national campaign, Vice President Nixon continued to advance this critique as his campaign warned against the use of "cheap publicity" to gain political points (Buchwald, 1960). Instead, Nixon used the camera to promote his experience as a statesman, a "New Nixon" who was a respectable and deserving public servant capable of succeeding President Eisenhower.[4]

Both candidates approached the debates in ways that reflected their broader campaign strategies. Kennedy saw the event as another opportunity to get viewers "interested in his personality," a tactic which had helped him win the Democratic nomination against the powerful Senate majority leader in the party, Lyndon Johnson (Reinsch, 1960). On the other hand, Nixon viewed the debates as an opportunity to show his intimate knowledge of world affairs, and, thus his executive capability. As the lesser known candidate, Kennedy had to assert constantly his credibility, and the debates provided a national stage to present himself as an equal to the man who had occupied the office of the vice presidency over the past eight years and had already proved his ability to negotiate before cameras on the world stage.

And yet, despite this more complicated historical reality, the simplistic narrative that the debates "changed everything" has persisted. Many of the tropes that shape popular memory—Kennedy's confidence and tan, Nixon's poor health and five o'clock shadow—first appeared in White's *Making of the President.* Presidential scholar Robert Dallek argues that White's book provided a window into America in 1960. He also notes how White was known for not just covering events but attempting to influence them (Dallek, 2009). This first analysis of the debates did both. It reflected a post-WWII hope for the democratic potential of television that existed alongside a concern that image consciousness would undermine democratic discussions (Greenberg, 2004). Though only 16 pages of the 384-page book, this section has become its most famous, promoting an easy interpretation of the 1960 election that not only overlooks the broader narrative of the election but simplifies the ways in which journalists like White, citizens, and politicians grapple with and discuss the opportunities and limitations of television in politics. Almost 50 years later, the producer of the television debates, Don Hewitt, remembered that the night of the first debate was the moment when politicians looked at television and declared, "That's the only way to campaign." The evening, he recalled, was a "great night for John Kennedy, and the worst night that ever happened in American politics" (Daitch, 2009, p. 31).

Hewitt's memory, like subsequent news coverage that remembered Kennedy's victory during the 1980s, conveys the notion that the deep-seated apprehensions that Americans had toward a new political style that prioritized media messaging and political performances faded away overnight (Brownell, 2014). This skewed memory of the debates even influenced historical discussions by scholars in programs C-SPAN aired in the middle of the 1992 election from the series *Road to the White House.* The program replayed the 1960 debates (see C-SPAN, 1992b, 1992c, and 1992e) and offered historical lessons and analyses of them for viewers to use the past as insight into the contemporary election. It featured interviews with two guests: Joel Swerdlow, an author of a new book about presidential debates, and Stephen Wayne, a Georgetown political science professor who made clear what instruction the debates provided for modern politics. Swerdlow emphasized the impact of Nixon's "shifty eyes" as he kept shifting his view from the clock that counted down his time allotted for answering questions and the camera. Swerdlow argued that though Nixon's "shifty eyes" may seem "shallow" when "you get into a big mass media phenomenon; those are the type of things that become important." Swerdlow agreed with Wayne's narrative, as he reiterated the story about how television viewers believed Kennedy had won the first debate with his "smooth appearance and his matter of fact answers," but those who "did not have to look at Nixon" and instead simply heard his "smooth voice" on the radio, perceived Nixon as the winner (C-SPAN, 1992b).

A range of programming in the C-SPAN Video Library reveals that by the 1992 election, journalists, scholars, students, and politicians had all accepted this simplified narrative as a fundamental fact of American history in ways that heightened the public's perception of the media's power in American politics. Since 1960, this memory has validated a new multimillion dollar industry—political consulting—by reinforcing the message that candidates needed to hire expensive consultants, pollsters, and media advisers to craft messages and help them navigate the media terrain if they wanted any real chance at winning an election. During the 1960s, newcomers to the political scene—figures such as Roger Ailes and Pat Buchanan—convinced Richard Nixon that his political defeats came at the hands of the television debates. These media consultants first shaped political strategies behind the scenes in the 1968 election, and then set the parameters of political commentary over the next two decades.

LIBERATING POLAND AND LAUNCHING THE "SPIN" INDUSTRY

As Nixon planned his presidential comeback eight years later, he surrounded himself with campaign advisers and professional media men who reinforced this specific memory of the 1960 election. As a result, not only did the former vice president revamp his campaign to follow in Kennedy's footsteps by making media and advertising central to his campaign, but he also refused to debate his opponents in 1968 (Bernstein, 1968) and in 1972. By the time the unelected president, Gerald Ford, agreed to a series of debates in 1976 with the Democratic challenger, Jimmy Carter, this legacy of 1960 shaped the candidates' approaches. Each side prepared texts, discussed images, and even introduced real-time focus groups to chart the strengths and weaknesses of each moment during the debates for post-debate analysis. Fearful that any unscripted moment of the debate could cost the incumbent the election as it had Nixon in 1960, Ford's and Carter's teams prepared thoroughly.

If the memory of the 1960 debates validated the centrality of television performances to win presidential elections, the legacy of one moment in the

1976 debates would continue to accentuate the perceived power of the media in American politics and, as a result, influence political practices and even an entire new media profession in the 1980s: the spin doctor. During the second debate in 1976 against Jimmy Carter, Gerald Ford made the statement, "There is no Soviet domination of Eastern Europe and there never will be under a Ford administration." This comment, or "gaffe," by the president has become another infamous moment in presidential debate history, and its memory, as told especially by Janet Brown during the 1992 symposium and by journalists since then, has come to validate the importance of media spin, and the post-debate production process.

Media analysis of Ford's statement, contended Janet Brown (C-SPAN, 1992a), lost the debate and possibly the election for Ford. The public did not care about the statement, Brown explained, until reporters made it an issue and declared Carter the winner. This interpretation has had a profound impact on political strategy. Throughout the 1980s, campaign professionals saw debates as especially important electoral events that were open to interpretation, and this example from the 1976 debate helped to make the case for the importance of spin. When Gerald Ford made the statement that Eastern Europe was not dominated by the Soviet Union, it did not influence the polls until the next day. This, Brown asserted, is evidence of the effective way in which the media influenced the post-debate spin process by setting the news agenda (C-SPAN, 1992a). Television viewers did not respond to the statement as Ford made it, but they did the following day when reporters told them of this misstatement and exaggerated its implications.

Over the next decade Ford's misstep in the second debate became fodder for understanding the incumbent's defeat by Jimmy Carter that year, resulting in a debate anecdote in which massaging of the media message among reporters became as important as the message itself. According to one 1992 story from the *Wall Street Journal* on the "debatable debates," Ford's gaffe "established the enduring principle that media interpretation of the debates can prove every bit as important as the encounters themselves" (Harwood, 1992). That same year, as the C-SPAN series *Road to the White House* historicized the impact of the 1960 elections, it also replayed the three debates from the 1976 campaign. In the first one, aired on October 20, 1992 (see C-SPAN, 1992f), the program noted the date and the moderators of the debate before airing the footage. The third debate, aired on October 21, 1992 (see C-SPAN,

1992g), followed the same format. The second debate, however, not only aired first on October 16, 1992 (see C-SPAN, 1992d), but also included an introduction with Joel Swerdlow, who outlined why Johnson and Nixon had not debated since 1960, and Professor Stephen Wayne's argument about Ford's Eastern European comment. Wayne contended that Carter did not call out the president after his misstatement, but the media did in the aftermath of the debate, ultimately influencing voter perceptions of Ford's competency in foreign policy matters. With the interpretation of the performance as central to the debate itself, subsequent campaigns and presidential administrations hired media consultants to influence reporter perceptions so they would not lose the spin battle as Ford had.

"Spin," as it became known during Reagan's administration (Greenberg, 2016), had been a part of presidential administrations over the previous century, as figures from Theodore Roosevelt, Herbert Hoover, Franklin Roosevelt, and John F. Kennedy worked assiduously to nurture relationships with the press to ensure favorable coverage of their presidential administrations and to set the news agenda. The Vietnam War and Watergate scandal revealed the willingness of presidents to lie to the press, resulting in the emergence of investigative reporting that transformed the nature of press–presidential relationships (Greenberg, 2016). And yet, as reporters searched beyond official statements and even into the personal lives of candidates for stories, Reagan's administration employed an effective news operation to institutionalize lessons learned from Ford's mistake. In fact, each White House press announcement took on the characteristics of the post-debate spin analysis that Ford had allegedly neglected. Larry Speakes, a press spokesman for Reagan, proudly displayed a sign on his desk stating, "You don't tell us how to stage the news, and we don't tell you how to cover it" (Kurtz, 1998, p. xxii). By the 1988 election, journalists unabashedly referenced the activities of "spin alley," a behind-the-scenes hallway where staffers from each campaign argued why their candidate won the debate to reporters (Greenberg, 2011).

By focusing on the art and power of spin during the 1980s, political commentary accentuated the power of these spin doctors. Though critics again pointed to their existence as style triumphing over substance—proof of what Walter Cronkite called the "unconscionable fraud that our political campaigns have become"—the story of the 1976 debate deemed them a necessary part of politics in the age of 24/7 news. (Greenberg, 2011, p. 146). But, this media anecdote also overlooks two other components of the debate. First, despite the popular narrative, Jimmy Carter capitalized on the issue during and after the debate by stating, "I would like to see Mr. Ford convince the Polish-Americans and the Czech-Americans, and the Hungarian-Americans that those countries don't live under the domination and supervision of the Soviet Union behind the Iron Curtain" (C-SPAN, 1992d). During the debate and later on the stump, it was the Democratic presidential candidate who paved the way for the broader media criticism. Carter linked this statement to broader concerns at the time about Ford's competence as an international leader and his unwillingness to speak openly with the American people about his foreign policies. On October 8, two days after the debate, the *New York Times* noted that Carter, "choosing to ignore the Ford, Kissinger, and Scowcroft attempts to clarify, called the President's statement 'ridiculous.'" According to Carter, the statement reflected Ford's "confusion about our people, about the aspirations of human beings, about human rights, about liberty, about simple justice" (King, 1976).

Moreover, both Carter and Ford competed for a demographic group very much at play for both the Democratic and Republican Parties during the era of dramatic political realignment for both parties: White, blue collar ethnic voters. Carter's Protestantism had alienated many Roman Catholic voters, and this issue became another way to keep this traditional voting bloc in the Democratic Party, despite their earlier allegiance to Nixon as part of his appeal to the "silent majority." Moreover, grassroots organizations, including chapters of the Polish American Congress, used this moment as opportunity to gain leverage in the national political conversation. During a campaign in which Ford's own campaign had acknowledged "foreign policy and national defense are low priority issues," Polish Americans used this misstatement as an opportunity to inject their voices into the national dialogue (Chanoc, 1974). Following the debate, both Ford and Carter took to the campaign trail to speak to White ethnic organizations. Ford argued that "his policy had been too literally constructed and that he had meant to say that such domination existed in much of Eastern Europe but that his policy was not to acquiesce in it" (Mohr, 1976). In a foreign policy speech, Henry Kissinger (1976) reinforced the message, and overwhelmingly the press paid substantial attention to Ford's clarification. By the final debate, the Ford campaign continued to relish in the "large advantage" the president had over Carter because of "the perception that [Ford is] experienced in foreign policy and that [he] will keep America strong enough to maintain peace." Though a setback, his misstatement is not what cost Ford the election.

POLITICAL COMMENTARY IN THE AGE OF 24/7 NEWS

This narrow legacy of both the importance of television performance in the 1960 debates and the role of spin in 1976 permeated media narratives of the debates and electoral strategies during the 1980s with very dramatic implications for shifting the realities of campaign structures and organizations by 1992. A *New York Times* article asked what the presidential debates actually had accomplished over the previous 40 years and argued that they did not inform people about the candidates or the issues at play, but rather that "these glitzy confrontations have converted the choice of a President into a Hollywood high-noon shootout" (Wicker, 1991). After the 1988 election—during which Gary Hart withdrew from the Democratic primary because of accusations of an extramarital affair and Michael Dukakis had to answer questions about the hypothetical rape of his wife—criticism of the superficiality of the political process ran high.[5] The debates, which allowed for such personalized discussions to occur, underwent intensive criticism for "including more grandstanding than substance," and Janet Brown explained that she had worked with the Commission on Presidential Debates to restructure the format to allow moderators to ask candidates harder, more penetrating questions (Ayres, 1991). In her discussion with students in January of 1992 at the Washington Center, Brown asked the students for their feedback and ideas on how to make the debates more about the issues at stake and less about the image of the candidate.

But, as the 1992 election played out, media images, "sound bites"—a term coined during the 1988 campaign—and political punditry on news shows centered on the candidate's personality while emphasizing the importance of the spin team to political success. Democratic consultant James Carville and Clinton staffer George Stephanopoulos became media celebrities themselves for their ability to shape the news for the Democratic contender, the Arkansas governor Bill Clinton. Before Clinton's first debate with President

George H. W. Bush was even over, Stephanopoulos raced through Clinton's war room headquarters to put out press announcements about how "Bush was on the defensive" (Cutler, Ettinger, Pennebaker, Hegedus, & Pennebaker, 1993). As D. A. Pennebaker filmed the campaign team for his documentary film *The War Room,* it became clear that if the Clinton campaign won the spin competition—slogans, advertisements, and most importantly interpretation of events—it would win the election. As the film documents, the team accomplished both feats and cemented the place of spin in presidential campaigns and even in the daily function of the White House.

By the 1992 campaign, the debates had become a certain type of ritual: a media-driven form of entertainment with its own history that reinforced the power of the media and its practitioners in American politics. But this popular history of presidential debates, similar to popular history of the American presidency more broadly, depends on anecdotes that promote a superficial understanding of deeper changes in American culture. Iconic moments—Nixon's sweaty brow, Ford's liberation of Poland, or Ronald Reagan's humor—became reduced to clichés that simplified broader changes in campaign trends and American history while also creating an echo chamber in which stories of success or failure are constantly recirculated, but seldom understood (Hess, 1981; Jamieson & Capella, 2010; Sabato, 1991; Schudson, 1995).

Programming from the C-SPAN Video Library provides sources to study the American presidency from an alternative lens that goes beyond the anecdote. Studying the concerns debates have generated provides a window into how journalists, viewers, and politicos themselves have grappled with broader changes in civic life as new media technology has altered the political terrain. During the 1980s, the emergence of 24/7 cable news facilitated opportunities for a deeper exploration of the candidates and issues but did not necessarily produce more informed voters. In many cases 24/7 coverage heightened the power of consultants themselves, validated their expertise, and in the process deepened the skepticism of Americans, many of whom felt frustrated and powerless in a political process that seemed tied to media productions and reliant on staging of events for media consumption rather than generating discussions of how to govern (C-SPAN, 1992a).[6]

Consider, for example, the trajectory of one man in particular: Roger Ailes. The successful producer of the *Mike Douglas Show,* Ailes met Richard Nixon in 1967 as the presidential hopeful prepared to go on the show as a guest. As Nixon chatted with the producer, he sighed with frustration that "gimmicks like this" were required to be elected. Understanding the potential of television to reach voters and communicate through images, Ailes shook his head and told Nixon, "Television is not a gimmick" (McGinniss, 1969, p. 63). Determined to have a new approach toward the medium that haunted his memories of the 1960 election, Nixon hired Ailes to round out the media strategy team that had convinced Nixon that he lost in 1960 in part because of his poor performance during television debates.[7]

When Nixon won the 1968 election, Ailes launched his career as a political consultant. By the 1980s Ailes had founded Ailes Communications Inc., and he ran George H. W. Bush's media campaign in 1988. He also appeared as a commentator on C-SPAN programs, from a panel that examined news, politics, and ethics in November 1987 (C-SPAN, 1987) to one in 1989 that discussed the connections between the entertainment industry and the political process (C-SPAN, 1989).

In 1968 Ailes contended that politicians forever more "would have to be performers" (McGinniss, 1969, p. 155). Two decades later, after organizing Bush's successful media campaign, he became known as "a political celebrity himself" with his public commentary on electoral strategies in the 24/7 news era in the aftermath of that election (C-SPAN, 1989). Ailes justified media scrutiny and performances as central to American political traditions where "candidates have to run a gauntlet…which requires a degree of physical and emotional stamina" (C-SPAN, 1989). In this environment, argued Ailes, debate performances were even more important as content for political advertisement and to shape the media narrative around the presidential contenders (both of which Ailes Communications Inc. was hired to create and monitor). A decade later as the president of Fox News, Ailes became a new type of Republican Party boss—his support has become essential for conservative presidential hopefuls, many of whom use electoral campaigns to try out for not just the presidency but a place as a political commentator on his programs (Hemmer, in press; Sherman, 2014).

The C-SPAN Video Library provides a wealth of sources for scholars to understand this echo chamber and thoroughly explore how and why campaign professionals such as Roger Ailes gained power, authority, and influence in both constructing electoral campaigns and justifying new media strategies behind the scenes and in the public eye.

NOTES

1. For a broader exploration of the 1988 election, see Germond and Witcover (1988) and Bai (2014).

2. See for example work done by Kathleen Hall Jamieson, including Jamieson and Capella (2010), *Echo Chamber: Rush Limbaugh and the Conservative Media Establishment,* and Hemmer (in press), *Messengers of the Right: The Origins of Conservative Media.*

3. The term *media consumers* as a definition of this outreach objective originally appeared in Kelley (1956), *Professional Public Relations and Political Power,* on p. 50.

4. Discussion of the various stages of the "New Nixon" can be found in Greenberg (2004), *Nixon's Shadow.* His look specifically at the New Nixon of the 1950s during Nixon's vice-presidential career can be found on pp. 36–72.

5. For criticism of the 1988 election and its superficiality, see also Troy (1991), *See How They Ran: The Changing Role of the Presidential Candidate.*

6. In the discussion with college students on the history of presidential debates for the Pursuit of the Presidency forum (C-SPAN, 1992a; http://www.c-span.org /video/?23775-1/history-presidential-debates), students ended the symposium by expressing deep frustrations with this modern media landscape.

7. This interaction between Nixon and Ailes is described by McGinniss (1969) in *The Selling of the President, 1968,* on p. 63.

REFERENCES

Ayres, D. B., Jr. (1991, September 26). Networks seek presidential debate overhaul. *New York Times,* p. 22.

Bai, M. (2014). All the truth is out: The week politics went tabloid. New York: Knopf.

Bernstein, R. M. (1968). *Public relations analysis of particular areas* [Report] (Folder, "Public Relations, General," Box 79, Topical File 13 of 29, Len Garment 1968 Campaign File). White House Central Files, Nixon Presidential Library and Museum, Yorba Linda, CA.

Boorstin, D. (1962). The image: A guide to pseudo-events in America. New York, NY: Atheneum.

Brownell, K. C. (2014). *Showbiz politics: Hollywood in American political life.* Chapel Hill: University of North Carolina Press.

Buchwald, A. (1960, October 22). Stars turn noses up, aid campaign. *Los Angeles Times,* p. B6.

Chanoc, F. (1974, October 1). *Re: Polling information on foreign policy/national defense* [Memo to M. Duval] (Folder, "Second Debate: Polling Information," Box 2). White House Special Files Unit Files, Gerald R. Ford Presidential Library, Ann Arbor, MI.

C-SPAN (Producer). (1987, November 6). *News, politics, and ethics* [online video]. Available from http://www.c-span.org/video/?420-1/consumer-v -political-advertising

C-SPAN (Producer). (1989, December 5). *Entertainment industry representatives talk politics with AAPC pros* [online video]. Available from http://www.c-span.org /video/?10454-1/entertainment-industry-politics

C-SPAN (Producer). (1992a, January 13). *History of presidential debates* [online video]. Available from http://www.c-span.org/video/?23775-1/history -presidential-debates

C-SPAN (Producer). (1992b, October 11). *Presidential candidates debate* [online video]. Available from http://www.c-span.org/video/?33073-1/presidential -candidates-debate

C-SPAN (Producer). (1992c, October 15). *Presidential candidates debate* [online video]. Available from http://www.c-span.org/video/?33149-1/presidential -candidates-debate

C-SPAN (Producer). (1992d, October 16). *Presidential candidates debate* [online video]. Available from http://www.c-span.org/video/?33210-1/presidential -candidates-debate

C-SPAN (Producer). (1992e, October 17) *Presidential candidates debate* [online video]. Available from http://www.c-span.org/video/?33218-1/presidential -candidates-debate

C-SPAN (Producer). (1992f, October 20). *Presidential candidates debate* [online video]. Available from http://www.c-span.org/video/?33353-1/presidential -candidates-debate

C-SPAN (Producer). (1992g, October 21). *Presidential candidates debate* [online video]. Available from http://www.c-span.org/video/?33391-1/presidential -candidates-debate

Cutler, R. J. (Producer), Ettinger, W. (Producer), Pennebaker, F. (Producer), Hegedus, C. (Director), & Pennebaker, D. A. (Director). (1993). *The war room* [Motion picture]. United States: October Films.

Daitch, V. (2009). Oral history interview with Don Hewitt. In D. T. Critchlow & E. Raymond (Eds.), *Hollywood and politics: A sourcebook* (pp. 30–35). New York, NY: Routledge.

Dallek, R. (2009). Foreword. In T. H. White, *The making of the president 1960* (reissue ed.; pp. xi–xv). New York, NY: Harper Perennial.

Donaldson, G.A. (2007). *The first modern campaign: Kennedy, Nixon, and the election of 1960.* Lanham, MD: Rownan & Littlefield Publishers.

Excerpts From Editorials. (1960, September 28). *Excerpts from editorials on TV debate. New York Times,* p. 24.

Germond, J. W., & Witcover, J. (1989). *Whose broad stripes and bright stars: The trivial pursuit of the presidency, 1988.* New York, NY: Warner Books.

Gould, L. (1996). *The modern American presidency.* Lawrence: University of Kansas Press.

Greenberg, D. (2004). *Nixon's shadow: The history of an image.* New York, NY: W. W. Norton.

Greenberg, D. (2011). The debate about the debates. In M. Bose (Ed.), *From votes to victory: Winning and governing the White House in the 21st century* (pp. 136–155). College Station: Texas A&M Press.

Greenberg, D. (2012). Do historians watch enough TV? Broadcast news as a primary source. In C. B. Potter & R. C. Romano (Eds.), *Doing recent history: On privacy, copyright, video games, institutional review boards, activist scholarship, and history that talks back* (pp. 185–199). Athens: University of Georgia Press.

Greenberg, D. (2016). *Republic of spin: An inside history of the American presidency.* New York, NY: W. W. Norton.

Harwood, J. (1992, September 21). Debatable debates: Sometimes, they're not so great, but this year could be different. *Wall Street Journal,* p. 8.

Hemmer, N. (in press). *Messengers of the right: The origins of conservative media.* Philadelphia: University of Pennsylvania Press.

Hess, S. (1981). *The Washington correspondents.* Washington, DC: The Brookings Institution.

Iyengar, S. (1994). *Is anyone responsible? How television frames political issues.* Chicago, IL: University of Chicago Press.

Iyengar S., & Kinder, D. (1989). *News that matters: Television and public opinion.* Chicago, IL: University of Chicago Press.

Jamieson, K. H. (1996). *Packaging the presidency: A history and criticism of presidential campaign advertising* (3rd ed.). New York, NY: Oxford University Press.

Jamieson, K. H., & Capella, J. N. (2010). *Echo chamber: Rush Limbaugh and the conservative media establishment.* New York, NY: Oxford University Press.

Kelley, S. (1956). *Professional public relations and political power.* Baltimore, MD: Johns Hopkins Press.

King, S. (1976, October 8). Ethnic groups score Ford on Europe view. *New York Times,* p. 1.

Kissinger, H. A. (1976, October 15). Press Conference by Secretary of State, Harvard University, Cambridge, Massachusetts (Folder, "Third Debate: Issue Papers—Foreign Policy," Box 3). White House Special Files Unit Files, Gerald R. Ford Presidential Library, Ann Arbor, MI.

Kurtz, H. (1998). Spin cycle: Inside the Clinton propaganda machine. New York, NY: Touchstone.

Lang, K., & Lang, G. E. (1961). Ordeal by debate: Viewer reactions. *Public Opinion Quarterly, 25*(2), 277–288. http://dx.doi.org/10.1086/267020

Mann, T., & Ornstein, N. (2013). *It's even worse than it looks: How the American constitutional system collided with the new politics of extremism.* New York, NY: Basic Books.

McGinniss, J. (1969). *The selling of the president.* New York, NY: Trident Press.

Mohr, C. (1976, October 8). Ford, trying to bind up wound, backs freedom for Eastern Europe. *New York Times,* p. A18.

Ponce de Leon, C. L. (2015). *That's the way it is: A history of televisions news in America.* Chicago, IL: University of Chicago Press.

Postman, N. (2004). *Amusing ourselves to death: Public discourse in the age of show business* (20th anniv. ed.). New York, NY: Penguin Books.

Reinsch, J. L. (1960, September 26). *RE: TV* [Memo to Robert F. Kennedy] (Folder, "Media Campaign: Democratic National Committee, 8/22/60–10/28/60," Box 37). General Subject File, Pre-Administration Political File, Rose Fitzgerald Kennedy Personal Papers, John F. Kennedy Presidential Library and Museum, Boston, MA.

Roosevelt, E. (1958, December 18). [Letter to Senator John Kennedy] (Box 32, Roosevelt, Eleanor). President's Office Files, Special Correspondence, John F. Kennedy Presidential Library and Museum, Boston, MA.

Rosenbaum, D. E. (1988, October 4). Women voters' league drops backing of debates. *New York Times,* p. D31. Retrieved from http://www.nytimes.com/1988/10/04/us/women-voters-league-drops-backing-of-debate.html

Sabato, L. (1991). *Feeding frenzy.* New York, NY: Free Press.

Schudson, M. (1995). *The power of news.* Cambridge, MA: Harvard University Press.

Sherman, G. (2014). *The loudest voice in the room: How the brilliant, bombastic Roger Ailes built Fox News and divided a nation.* New York, NY: Random House.

Staff Reporter. (1960, September 27). Nixon, Kennedy clash in TV debate over ways to spur economic growth, finance medical care, aid schools. *Wall Street Journal,* p. 3.

Troy, G. (1991). *See how they ran: The changing role of the presidential candidate.* New York, NY: Free Press.

Vancil, D., & Pendell, S. (1987). The myth of viewer-listener disagreement in the first Kennedy-Nixon debate. *Central States Speech Journal, 38,* 16–27. http://dx.doi.org/10.1080/10510978709368226

Wehrwein, A. C. (1960, February 21). Wisconsin battle one of contrasts. *New York Times,* p. 55.

Wicker, T. (1991, May 22). High noon, low hype. *New York Times,* p. A25.

White, T. H. (2009). *The making of the president 1960* (reissue ed.). New York, NY: Harper Perennial.

CHAPTER 2

FRAMING TECHNOLOGICAL INFLUENCE THROUGH C-SPAN

Alison N. Novak
Ernest A. Hakanen

In this chapter we present an analysis of *The Communicators,* a weekly C- SPAN program in which government, policy, and industry experts discuss the future of technology.[1] This is the first project to explore how these focused, televised interviews frame technological potential and impact. The results of this project hold implications for media studies, sociology of invention research, and political communication. Through knowing how issues are framed over long periods of time, researchers can gain an understanding of how leaders view the future of technology and its impact on society as well as insight into policy change and public reaction to developments in technology.

C-SPAN began airing *The Communicators* in early 2005. It is a weekly series featuring half-hour conversations designed to bring journalists, politicians, and technology leaders together to discuss current events, trends in the media industry, and the future of public policy, particularly with regard to technology in America's future. Each week, guests comment on salient and growing global and local issues, focusing particularly on how their organization plans to approach the topic in the future.

Compared to other interview-based news shows, *The Communicators* offers insight into how the future of media technology is voiced and addressed by those who seemingly have the most power over its direction. Programs such as this offer insight into the relationship between government, industry, and the public, as well as how each of them views intersecting roles in technology creation. Such programs grow popular as a "culture of fear" is identified and investigated by academics, who suggest that society generally has anxiety regarding the use of technology in the future (Jeffries, 2013). The public turns to programs like *The Communicators* to gain perspective and calm anxieties.

This study combines a frequency and descriptive frame analysis to provide in-depth analysis of 434 episodes of *The Communicators* housed in the C-SPAN Archives' online Video Library—every episode from the October 2005 premiere through August 2014. It is only through the Video Library that this project is possible.

The frame analysis required both researchers to watch the all 434 videos and develop a list of frames (see Appendix A) that fit the featured descriptions of technology. Each video was assigned a series of frames: past/present/future technologies, the public, policy, and policymakers. This provided insight into the many perspectives (and combinations of perspectives) on technology offered on the show. The project also included a descriptive frame analysis featuring examples of frames and insight into the way each frame was invoked and used.

BACKGROUND

Technology as a force for change has incurred a long-standing debate among academics, public opinion leaders, and mass society over the past century. Differing perspectives on the development of communication and media practices have encouraged discourses within popular and critical debates. Many scholars have argued that technological developments are a source for good—improving global communication, advancing information access, and reducing international political stress (Brooks, 2006; Levy, 1997). Other researchers have argued that recent technological advances have endangered basic interpersonal connections and limited our capacity to connect with others (Twenge, 2006). Still others have argued that these effects are actually secondary to the discourses surrounding our perception of the influence of technology on modern society (Turkle, 2012). As a result, it is often not only the technologies that influence mass society but also the discourses surrounding the technologies (Chandler, 2014). Group opinion leaders, developers, and consumers, furthering and fueling the debate over the future of communication and media technology, support each of these different perspectives.

Among the causes and effects of these three perspectives is the uncertainty that new technological developments often bring (Goldsbourough, 2004; Jeffries, 2013). While technology is commonly branded and marketed as a solution to life's great problems (e.g., e-mail as a way to stay in touch from afar), critics often suggest that it carries a societal price (e.g., e-mail diminishing our ability to communicate interpersonally) (Ball & Holland, 2009). Uncertainty, fear, and the desire to predict the future to minimize that fear become hallmarks of new technological developments (Jeffries, 2013; Mordini, 2007). Even years after technologies gain acceptance and popularization in mass society, the debate goes on, amplified by more recent inventions and updates. This culture of uncertainty has certainly not hindered the momentum of progress; however, it becomes omnipresent and reflected in other future-centered discourses (Jeffries, 2013; Wilson, 2014).

For example, this uncertainty manifests in conversations and discourses related to the development of children and younger generations (Novak, 2014). Due to its close proximity to and use of these new technologies, society reflects uncertainty as to how it is affected (in long- and short-term contexts). Recent research has shown that discourses over the fear of technology's influence in mass society and fears over the changing social practices of the millennial generation are closely related and frequently simultaneously appear in news broadcasts (Novak, 2014).

Perhaps most important to this study is the way these conversations are translated to an audience. Research analyzing audiences of political and news debate programs suggests that the public is particularly vulnerable to mass media effects in these conversation and debate formats due to the perception of equal representation of both sides of a controversial technological issue (Paulus, Lester, & Britt, 2013). These interview and conversational formats encourage viewers to learn about an issue, but they also reinforce an agenda of uncertainty. As the audience becomes more aware of an issue, they also become more aware of the culture of fear surrounding it. Further, because these formats rarely resolve any debates, the viewer is left with the impression of uncertainty (Paulus et al., 2013). It is through this process that the fear and uncertainty surrounding new technology is translated from developers, opinion leaders, and academics to the mass audience (Jeffries, 2013).

While more research is needed to determine whether this process occurs specifically within C-SPAN's series *The Communicators,* the program does offer an opportunity to study how these discourses appear within this program format, which is arguably a critical first step in the effects-based research process. Featured guests on *The Communicators* have included Martin Cooper, inventor of the modern cell phone, Michael Powell of The National Cable and Telecommunication Association (and former U.S. Federal Communications Commission [FCC] chair), and Dan Glickman, then head of the Motion Picture Association of America. Each week the moderator asks the guest questions, such as "Has technology plateaued?" "What are the implications of net neutrality on file sharing?" and "What is the largest risk to children in digital media today?"

These questions are emblematic of the larger culture of uncertainty and fear surrounding the future of technology. In an effort to calm or address these fears, predictions are made by guests. However, because many of these guests are also politicians and policymakers, these discourses are also a facet of the political process. The discussions of fears and uncertainties lend insight into the mindsets that produce many of the regulations, laws, and political debates surrounding technology. As a result, it is even more important to explore these discourses in full in studying media and technology regulation.

FRAMING AND METHODS

A frame analysis allows researchers to consider the way media producers select and present information to an audience (Goffman, 1986). Specifically, it sheds light onto recurring patterns of content, style, and formatting (Chong & Druckman, 2007). When interviewees discuss the future of technology, they adopt a frame that is used to depict their point of view. When making choices about words, examples, sentence structure, and even humor, the speaker employs a frame. By analyzing the frequency of frames, as well as information about the speaker and context of the interview, researchers gain insight through statistical information about how the future of technology is framed within *The Communicators.*

For this study we both watched and analyzed the previously mentioned 434 episodes of *The Communicators,* which is the complete corpus of the series from its premiere in October 2005 through August 2014.[2] The show airs on C-SPAN on Saturdays at 6:30 p.m. EST and features a different interviewee each week. It frequently covers current events, favoring guests that have a relationship with salient topics. For example, during Comcast's takeover of NBC, Comcast executives were interviewed on the show. While each episode usually features one guest, prominent journalists who have a history of covering the topic are asked to guest moderate or help build the discussion. The journalists often ask redirecting questions as a means of steering the conversation toward the salient issue or to help prompt for more information.

We used an inductive framing process to develop the set of frames for this study (Thomas, 2006). Although previous research has studied how the public frames the future of technology, few studies have looked at how this debate unfolds within a mediated space, such as television. As a result, it was critical to develop a unique and tailored set of frames from this series. To do this, we selected and watched a 10 percent random sample of episodes (43 episodes). While watching, we independently created a list of recurring themes and frames that were employed and simultaneously took notes on other categorical items, such as gender, position, or career. After watching the 10 percent sample, we collaborated and developed a list of several categories: gender, current type of employment, technological effects (past, present, and future), public, policy, and government/policymakers (see Appendix A to this chapter). Within each category we developed and contextualized frames and then assigned numbers to each frame for later statistical analysis. Each frame is exclusive and exhaustive of the types of discourses appearing within each category.

After we developed the 10 percent sample, one researcher watched the entire corpus of the 434 episodes, assigning a frame to each of the categories for each episode. For reliability purposes, a third individual was asked to watch a 5 percent (21-episode) random sample and assign frames to each. This 5 percent sample matched the researchers' analysis 90 percent of the time, with a Cohen's kappa of 84 percent. For increased validity, each finding included quotes from the transcripts of each of the episodes.

FINDINGS

Here we present the findings of the frequency of frames, as well as some data on which frames were frequently used together. While an exhaustive set of findings would be too lengthy for one book chapter, these results help address and analyze how guests appearing on *The Communicators* framed the future of technology. We will discuss four of the eight categories (technological effects—past, present, and future; public; policy; and government/policymakers) in the following section and provide examples and quotes to support each of the analyses. We will also discuss connections between the four categories, which we selected for their statistical significance and relevance to the future of technology within C-SPAN.

Technological Effects

Our study divided the framing of technological effects into three subcategories: past, present, and future. We did this because we discovered that when responding to a question about the effects of technology on society, guests often prefaced their response with a time period or referenced timing in their response. As a result, this study holds implications for the past, present, and future of technological influence.

Past Technologies

The majority (68 percent) of guests on the show opined that past technology was slow, weak, or hurting productivity. Often these conversations revolved around examples of technologies and media resources that have been replaced by newer models or technologies. A common example was the slow speed of information transmission when newspapers were a primary information resource. Guests framed technologies of the past as being out-of-date and no longer a mainstay within the industry—problematic for their inability to compete with today's faster channels and modes. For example, in a 2005 interview, Vinton Cerf (vice president and "chief Internet evangelist" for

Google) compared the technologies of the past to those that might be available in the future:

> With holographic projection devices, it may be possible to actually produce what we see in the science fiction shows in the past where [a] real three-dimensional image is viewable because the holographic projection unit presents it to you. I think that's not impossible in the next 10 years. (C-SPAN, 2005)

Cerf's quote illustrates the comparative quality that often accompanied discussion of technology's influence on the past. Technologies in the future were thus framed as a way to solve earlier problems (such as 3-D replication), emphasizing the weaknesses and issues of technologies in the past.

Future Technologies

Technologies of the future were discussed as being more efficient and often easier to physically handle than technologies of the past. For example, in an interview with Aereo founder and CEO Chet Kanojia, newer antennas were compared for their portability and feasibility in everyday life:

> Over the air antennas in the past, they were large. We miniaturized them through a lot of sophisticated technology. And the purpose of miniaturizing them was so we can [someday] build hundreds of thousands of these things into a very small room. (C-SPAN, 2013)

Kanojia's quote is emblematic of the vision that most guests shared on the future of technology's effects in everyday life. The majority (53 percent) of guests framed technology as being faster, stronger, or making a more efficient society in the future. Roughly 65 percent of guests who opined that technologies in the past were weak similarly identified future technologies as being strong or making society better. This is particularly important to this study as it suggests that there is a relationship between the way technologies of the past and technologies of the future are viewed. While more research is necessary before a cause and effect relationship can be stated, it is clear that there is a relationship between the past and future of technology, particularly when guests compare one to the other. For example, if past technologies are framed as idyllic, then it is likely that future technology is framed as problematic. This is also combined with only 11 instances of interviewees voicing concern that technologies in the future will be corrupt or unsafe. The low appearance of this frame combined with the high appearance of the more optimistic frame of future technologies making society better reinforces the prominence of the latter view among participants in the program.

Present Technologies

When discussing the current state of technology, many guests (43 percent) voiced concerns of corruption or a lack of safety. Particularly emphasized was the need for more regulation of current technologies so that they could, someday, be helpful for citizens. It is important to note that there was a relationship (60 percent) between those who were politicians (Republican, Democrat, and Independent) and those who viewed technology today as corrupt and unsafe. These guests often used examples of specific companies or industries that create and sell technologies with potential negative effects on both individuals and overall society. For example, Representative Zoe Lofgren (D-CA) particularly noted that technology currently being used by the U.S. government is invasive of people's privacy and larger freedom:

> Everything you do, not only does it deal with the Fourth Amendment, but it also has an impact on the First Amendment. Under our Constitution, citizens have a right to speak their mind, to say what they think is right, if they feel they are being watched or intimidated. It is a very serious assault on our structure of government. Obviously, there are technology issues that I care about. The real issue is rooted in American freedom. (C-SPAN, 2014i)

Lofgren's comments reflect that it is not the technologies themselves that are dangerous in present circumstances; rather, it is those who use the technologies for unethical or corrupt purposes that are to blame. Politicians such as Lofgren then relate this current state of technology to their own actions and congressional votes on related issues. By framing current technologies as corrupt or problematic, these politicians demonstrate their own political motivations and set themselves up as public protectors or defenders.

• • •

Overall discussions on the role of technology presents one larger discourse regarding how technology's effects in the past, present, and future are viewed. Throughout the 434 episodes, the following narrative was constructed: Technologies of the past were slower, less efficient, and thus potentially harmful to mass society, and while current technologies may be viewed as corrupt or unsafe, through government regulation (like that voiced by politicians) these technologies can grow to make a better society through efficiency, speed, and strength.

This largely expands the information we have about how the culture of fear is articulated. As demonstrated in this analysis, the future of technology is viewed as positive and helpful; however, it is the current state that draws the most anxiety and fear. This will be more fully explored in the coming sections.

Public

When discussing the public, the majority of guests framed them as collective and without independence, lacking agency, or totally influenced by technology. In a 2010 interview with two former FCC staffers, the public was referred to as needing protection from corrupt technological systems. As such, Richard Mirgon and Edmond Thomas addressed the FCC's lack of resources and its inability to help consumers with current safety issues, thus framing the public as weak and needing protection: "The FCC greatly underestimates the current and future capacity needs of public safety when it assumes that 10 megahertz of broadband spectrum is adequate for mission critical high-speed data" (C-SPAN, 2010b). Further, when Craig Vogelstein described the adoption of Microsoft software in the 1990s, he noted, "People started using Windows because everybody else started using Windows, what in the economic literature, is called network effects" (C-SPAN, 2014d). Thus, it was not an individual's choice to use Windows, but rather just the effect of the technology on the larger public.

Often, the public is viewed as lacking the resources or the knowledge to protect themselves from the problems or safety issues present in technology. Mirgon's and Vogelstein's quotes suggest that the public needs the help of agencies like the FCC to keep people safe. This reinforces the view that the public is vulnerable to media effects and people need external help to defend themselves against corruption.

Guests also have suggested that the public is problematic for the industry and market design of their companies. For example, in his 2007 interview, Dan Glickman, then chairman and CEO of the Motion Picture Association of America, noted:

> We also engaged in some litigation against people who download movies[,] and the music industry has done the same thing on their side. We are engaged with an active education campaign with universities. A lot of piracy starts at the university level. Also the recognition that we must offer consumers alternatives where they can get material online [in] reasonably priced hassle[-]free ways. If they believe that they can get the material [in an] easy fashion, [e]specially online…they will be less likely to download it illegally. (C-SPAN, 2007a)

Here, Glickman demonstrates the tension that exists between those who head technology-centered companies, with their desire to protect profits, and the public, with its desire to obtain media content easily and at a reasonable price.

In an interview with Larry Downes, coauthor of *Big Bang Disruption: Strategy in the Age of Devastating Innovation* (Penguin, 2014), the relationship between the public and technology market is highlighted:

> When the Kindle came and it was right, the market said, this is what we've been waiting for, we've been hearing about this, somebody has cracked the code, and the uptake is essentially a vertical line. It's not about customer segments arriving in this nice sequential way we use[d] to think about it, it[']s now complete: what we call catastrophic success. All your customers arrive, could be in days if it's a game app, it could be in years if it[']s a piece of hardware, but it's a very compressed period of time. Straight up! (C-SPAN, 2014g)

As Downes points out, the market is the place where industry and the public meet and therefore becomes the mechanism for selling goods. Interviews such as this one suggest that the public's interest is moderated by the product. This again showcases a tension between the public and technology's influence. The industries represented on *The Communicators* rely on the public's adoption of their technologies, thus they recognize the public as the ultimate consumer. However, they also view the public as particularly vulnerable to technology's influences and thus under industry's control. This is one possible explanation for why the public was often framed in two ways.

This relationship is further addressed in an interview with Alan Paller, director of research for the SANS Institute, while discussing cybersecurity and hacking of company databases and banks:

> I call it the awakening of this public knowledge and it may be what was needed to stop the historical pattern of security [breaches] that people write about…and not do anything about. We can raise the bar a lot higher without damaging operations. Let's spend our money on making systems more secure. (C-SPAN, 2011)

Here, the public is viewed as an important force with regard to both the industry and the supporting cybersecurity agencies and government. The public (and its attention) becomes the reason for later reform and future policies regulating technology. This is an important finding when considered with the earlier finding that although present-day technologies are viewed as corrupt, future technologies are viewed as a positive force for change. This further illustrates how this change from present to future technology influence is discursively framed to occur. It is through public awareness and concern that regulations and policy changes can be made to de-corrupt the issues within current technology.

Policy

Perhaps the most complicated category in this analysis is the public policy's role in technological innovation. The most common frame (33 percent) of public policy stated that policy is currently dysfunctional because it's too weak, not regulatory enough. However, just a few percentage points behind, the second most common frame (26 percent) is that policy is harmful and hurting the public. These two frames combined indicate a complex relationship between technological innovation and public policy.

Guests commonly spoke of policy as negatively affecting the development of helpful future technologies. Particularly, policy was associated with government or politicians. For example, Verizon Communication Executive Vice President for Policy Thomas Tauke noted his recommendations for government policy changes.

> Administration has essentially followed since then, that the government is really the light regulatory presence on the Internet, espousing a policy through the world—not a policy throughout the world. It raises a question about whether or not there should be a change from that policy. (C-SPAN, 2010a)

Tauke's interpretation of policy in 2010 was that it was hindering the ability of technology to address different cultural climates and of technological developments to evolve to fit the needs of society. Tauke was not the only industry leader who believed the government's policies on technology hindered development. Patricia Harrison, then CEO of the Corporation for Public Broadcasting, argued that other offices within the government often worked against the interests of corporations through an exchange program allowing companies to provide services to each other, thus hindering their ability to serve the public:

> We are not going to wait for the government to fix it[. I]t could be a long wait[. W]e will take action ourselves. What happens when they [companies] observe average people doing this? They think, I can do this. I see it time and time again. As we started bringing [the] exchange program, they went back and decided to be a catalyst for a positive action. (C-SPAN, 2006)

Echoing Tauke's interview, Craig Silliman added:

> Policy is the way the world should be, politics is the way the world is. (C-SPAN, 2014e)

It is important to note that interviews such as Tauke's, Harrison's, and Silliman's were common among the series, possibly reflecting the overall mission of *The Communicators* to blend commentary regarding politics, communication, and technology. However, what such interviews make clear is the tension in the relationship between the U.S. government and industry. That such interviews occurred throughout the 434 episodes viewed (an eight-year span) suggests that this tension exists regardless of which party is in political control.

Some members of government say that issues in technology regulation stem from politicians not being willing to act or work on larger problems. FCC Commissioner Michael Copps noted in his interview that in his experience, one of the barriers to having technology be more representative of American diversity is that Congress is not willing to act or make policy changes to encourage diversity in media ownership:

> Let's put the focus where it should be, television [and] radio stations, and open up some opportunities and create some incentives for minorities to do that. We have fallen down on the job. We have a diversity committee at the FCC and it sen[t] dozen[s] of recommendations to the chairman's office well over a year ago. And they sat there until very, very recently. And they've been put out kind of grudgingly because they can't get media ownership until they have this in the public domain. But I'm not going to settle. Gee, we're asking so many questions, so let's vote on listing media ownership. This problem has been there for years and years and years. We've got to deal with it. The members of Congress are waiting for this, and they say do not vote on this until you have addressed diversity. (C-SPAN, 2007b)

However, politicians also have noted their issues with current policies and regulatory reform, saying they stem from the industry itself. Often these individuals have cited industry as the problem, pushing back against policies that could help make technologies better. In an interview with Representative Joe Barton (R-TX), the congressman noted that it was industry that delayed changes in technological function, not pressures from government or the public:

> Long story short, we are about a month away from that [eliminating antennae television signals]. 97% of American families know that it is coming. 93% of every household has a television set [that] is ready for it. And based on coupon redemption, we think that there are a

hundred thousand households that are not prepared. That is significantly less than 1%. The question is, if 94.5% of America is ready,
why delay it? Mr. Waxman asks that there [be] a delay and I said I
would not do that. We were prepared to offer a number of amendments and chairman Waxman talked to me and said that maybe we
could do something that would not require a delay. (C-SPAN, 2009)

The larger trend of blaming other groups for issues with policy is demonstrated by a recurring pattern within the data. Less than 25 percent (combin-
ing categories) of guests believed that current policies were doing positive
things for the industry, the public, or the government itself.

Regardless of their profession, guests believed that policies needed to
change to make technology the positive force they believed it could be. This
again provides insight into why so many guests believed present-day technologies were unsafe or corrupt: They believed that it is the policies currently in
place that caused many of the earlier issues.

It is important to note that throughout the interviews, policy was addressed
as a unique and somewhat autonomous force within technological regulation.
While policies were often described as being created in the past by a group
of politicians (as with the Telecommunications Act of 1996), in their current
state these policies were described as being mismanaged or neglected. Like the
findings regarding the public as a force for change, updates or new sets of policies were viewed as a potential means of enabling technology to have a positive place in the future. Many guests addressed the needed updates to some
of the foundational regulatory laws in media and communication; again, reinforcing the view that while bad/outdated policy was responsible for current
negative effects, good/modern policy would bring about future positive effects.

Government/Policymakers

Like the public, government and policymakers were framed as being outdated
and behind the times when it came to technology. The Telecommunications
Act of 1996 has been a major focus of the series and was often cited as an example of policy that had fallen out-of-date. Many industry leaders interviewed
noted the need to update the regulatory laws and were critical of Congress's
current inability to do this. Policymakers and government were viewed as

being behind the times and not aware of the full spectrum of technological needs. Christopher Harrison, vice president of business affairs for Pandora Music, stated that

> publishers have all voiced some concern about the current state of licensing and the Department of Justice is currently reviewing those. They have asked for public comment. I anticipate that when they come out, they will take an active role in reviewing those and voicing our opinions. (C-SPAN, 2014f)

Later that same month, Jot Carpenter, the Vice President for CITA added,

> What is really important is, we think, in a vitally competitive industry, you don't need a lot of regulation....The fact of the matter is, companies keep each other honest....They launch at each other pretty aggressively in the marketplace to win business, and I think the last six months have been great evidence of that. All of which is to the benefit of the consumer. (C-SPAN, 2014c)

U.S. Representative Steve Scalise (R-LA) also concluded that the government lags behind technological innovation:

> Technologies move so fast, government ha[s]n't figured out how to slow things down. (C-SPAN, 2014a)

Interviews such as these underscore the perception that politicians alone are not capable of making the changes to technology-centered policy. Instead, it is both the industry leaders such as Pandora and the public who are needed to move things forward.

During an episode featuring vendors from the Consumer Electronics Show in 2014, Jennifer Bernal, Google's policy analyst, noted that Congress was now turning to industry specialists to help it design and rewrite policy:

> Also, technology is so important to policy now....We're learning about new technology to support the community but also we understand how technology is impacting the way we live. (C-SPAN, 2014i)

When asked about the potential for public and government cooperation in the regulation process, ICANN Executive Officer Fadi Chehadé added:

> And we ensure that the stakeholders have a seat at the table and guide us along the way. And the stakeholders here are businesses, governments[. W]e have over 130 governments sitting on ICANN committees, we have civic society, we have technical organizations, we have academics[. A]ll of them we have sitting on an equal footing and making sure these identifiers serve the planet well. (C-SPAN, 2014b)

As analyst Bernal and executive officer of ICANN Chehadé point out, this is one way that industry and policymakers come together to shape the impact of technology in the future. This is particularly emphasized by the fact that policymakers were framed as helpful and responsive only 7 percent (29 of 434 episodes) of the time.

This may also suggest that guests framed the future of technology as being cocreated by the public, government, and industry leaders. Rather than just asserting that one of those groups has control over it, guests viewed the process as being supplemented by a variety of perspectives, efforts, and contexts.

REFLECTION

This chapter only begins to detail the ways that the future of technology was framed in the C-SPAN series *The Communicators.* The overall narrative regarding how technology has played a role in everyday life and how it will do so in the future is mediated through a variety of perspectives and voices. Clearly noted is the view that technology in the past was slow, problematic, and unsafe and that future technology will make society safer and more efficient. Despite this view of the future, today's current technology is looked at as corrupt and unsafe, potentially damaging to an easily influenced public. Guests argued that through regulation and cooperation between the public, government, and industry leaders, the future of technological influence would be brighter.

The major takeaway of this chapter regards the culture of fear that accompanies the development and uncertainty of new technology. This culture of fear has been critically examined by academics; however, few studies have examined how this culture manifests in the discourse and frames used by industry leaders and politicians responsible for the future implications of technology. Our study suggests that although the culture of fear is often thought of as relating to the future of technology, it more centrally manifests in the way current technologies are viewed and explained—as having a negative influence on society.

There are many possible explanations for why negative frames are used to describe current technologies. First, as the culture of fear theories point out, the anxiety surrounding the influence of technology co-occurs with the popularization of new technologies, particularly those adopted by younger generations or youth. As identified in this study, the public is often viewed as being easily influenced and lacking agency, as well as fearful of what those new, popularized technologies may do.

It is also important to consider the context of these interviews. *The Communicators* is one of the longest running series featured on C-SPAN. It provides guests with an audience to share their views and inspire public support. Thus, many guests may treat this as a time to carefully craft a publicly acceptable message, rather than voice their real opinions. Nevertheless, it is still important to analyze the messages found in this series because they are widely disseminated.

While this study presents some of the most important and topical findings on the subject, there are other areas that require further exploration and examination. For example, data on gender and current types of employment should and can be studied for their correlation with any of the other six categories. Brief statistical analyses show that there are relationships among a politician's party and his or her views of policy and policymakers; however, this lies outside the scope of this study. It is also important to note that 70 percent of the guests on the show were male, reflecting norms of the technology industry and American politics, and also encouraging the study of how women may articulate their relationship to technology differently than their male colleagues.

Finally, future studies should explore the topic of the public as it is framed and described within the series *The Communicators*. While in this analysis the public was conceptualized as anyone outside government or industry, it is clear that there is a fluid definition used within the series by guests to address the various needs and behaviors of those who engage with technology in their everyday lives. Even linguistic differences such as referring to publics as "consumers," "stakeholders," or "markets" should be considered with regard to how these industry leaders address and describe the people to whom they sell their products.

As new episodes of *The Communicators* air, research should continue. This series provides a gateway for viewers to understand the mindsets and backgrounds of industry professionals and policymakers as they engage with current events and growing global issues. As such, its research value is critical to academic understanding of how technological fears and influence are framed and communicated to the public.

NOTES

1. All episodes of *The Communicators* are available at http://www.c-span.org /search/?searchtype=Videos&sort=Newest&seriesid[]=15.

2. Although data collection concluded in August 2014, the program continues to air regularly.

REFERENCES

Ball, W., & Holland, S. (2009). The fear of new technology: A naturally occurring phenomenon. *The American Journal of Bioethics, 9*(1), 14–16. http://dx.doi .org/10.1080/15265160802617977

Brooks, A. (2006). Dispelling HR's fear of technology takeover. *Employee Benefit Plan Review, 60*(10), 6.

Chandler, D. (2014). Technological determinism. Retrieved from http://www.aber .ac.uk/media/Documents/tecdet/tecdet.html

Chong, D., & Druckman, J. N. (2007). Framing theory. *Annual Review of Political Science, 10,* 103–126. http://dx.doi.org/10.1146/annurev.polisci.10.072805.103054

C-SPAN (Producer). (2005, December 24). *Impact of the Internet on communications* [online video]. Available from http://www.c-span.org/video/?190322-1 /impact-internet-communications

C-SPAN (Producer). (2006, October 21). *Public broadcasting issues* [online video]. Available from http://www.c-span.org/video/?194905-1/public-broadcasting -issues

C-SPAN (Producer). (2007a, September 20). *Film piracy* [online video]. Available from http://www.c-span.org/video/?201096-1/film-piracy

C-SPAN (Producer). (2007b, November 2). *Media ownership rules* [online video]. Available from http://www.c-span.org/video/?202027-2/media-ownership-rules

C-SPAN (Producer). (2009, January 22). *Digital television transition* [online video]. Available from http://www.c-span.org/video/?283576-1/digital-television -transition

C-SPAN (Producer). (2010a, April 3). *Broadband communications policy* [online video]. Available from http://www.c-span.org/video/?292796-1/broadband -communications-policy

C-SPAN (Producer). (2010b, July 24). *Public-safety communications bandwidth* [online video]. Available from http://www.c-span.org/search/?searchtype =Videos&query=richard+mirgon

C-SPAN (Producer). (2011, August 11). *Communicators with Lewis, Paller, and Lotrionte* [online video]. Available from http://www.c-span.org/video/?301013-1 /communicators-lewis-paller-lotrionte

C-SPAN (Producer). (2013, December 23). *The future of television, part 1* [online video]. Available from http://www.c-span.org/video/?315552-1/future -television-part-1

C-SPAN (Producer). (2014a, February 27). *Communicators with Representatives Polis, Scalise, and Blackburn* [online video]. Available from http://www.c-span.org /video/?318046-1/communicators-technology-legislation

C-SPAN (Producer). (2014b, March 8). *Internet domain name* [online video]. Available from http://www.c-span.org/video/?317453-1/communicators-fadi-chehad

C-SPAN (Producer). (2014c, May 5). *Communicators with Jot Carpenter* [online video]. Available from http://www.c-span.org/video/?318741-1/communicators -jot-carpenter

C-SPAN (Producer). (2014d, May 24). *Communicators with Fred Vogelstein* [online video]. Available from http://www.c-span.org/video/?316848-1/communicators -fred-vogelstein

C-SPAN (Producer). (2014e, May 31). *Communicators with Craig Silliman* [online video]. Available from http://www.c-span.org/video/?319568-1/communicators -craig-silliman

C-SPAN (Producer). (2014f, July 23). *Communicators with Christopher Harrison* [online video]. Available from http://www.c-span.org/video/?320590-1/communicators -chris-harrison

C-SPAN (Producer). (2014g, June 7). *The communicators with Larry Downes* [online video]. http://www.c-span.org/search/?searchtype=All&query=downes

C-SPAN (Producer). (2014h, July 15). *House session* [online video]. Available from http://www.c-span.org/video/?320421-2/us-house-legislative-business

C-SPAN (Producer). (2014i, August 16). *Communicators at the Consumer Electronics Show, part 1* [online video]. Available from http://www.c-span.org /video/?319121-1/communicators-ces-hill

Goffman, I. (1986). *Frame analysis: An essay on the organization of experience.* Boston, MA: Northeastern Press.

Goldsbourough, R. (2004). The benefits, and fear, of cookie technology. *Black Issues in Higher Education 21,* 23.

Jeffries, F. (2013). Mediating fear. *Global Media and Communication 9*(1), 37–52. http://dx.doi.org/10.1177/1742766512463039

Levy, P. (1997). *Collective intelligence: Mankind's emerging world in cyberspace.* Paris, France: Helix Books.

Mordini, E. (2007). Technology and fear: Is wonder the key? *Centre for Society, Science, and Citizenship, 25*(12), 544.

Novak, A. (2014). Millennials, citizenship, and *How I Met Your Mother.* In J. Zenor (Ed.), *Parasocial politics: Audience readings of cultural politics in pop culture* (pp. 117–132). Lanham, MD: Lexington Books.

Paulus, T. M., Lester, J. N., & Britt, V. G. (2013). Constructing hopes and fears around technology: A discourse analysis of introductory qualitative texts. *Qualitative Inquiry, 19*(9), 639–651. http://dx.doi.org/10.1177/1077800413500929

Thomas, D. R. (2006). A general inductive approach for analyzing qualitative evaluation data. *American Journal of Evaluation, 27*(2), 237–246. http://dx.doi .org/10.1177/1098214005283748

Turkle, S. (2012). Alone together: Why we expect more from technology and less from each other. New York: NY, Perseus Books.

Twenge, J. M. (2006). *Generation me: Why today's young Americans are more confident, assertive, entitled, and more miserable than ever before.* New York, NY: Simon and Schuster, Inc.

Wilson, J. (2014). Nothing to fear but fear itself. *Learning and Leading with Technology, 41*(6), 7.

APPENDIX
List of Frames

- ◄ Gender
  - ▪ Male (1)
  - ▪ Female (2)
- ◄ Current type of employment
  - ▪ Republican politician (1)
  - ▪ Democratic politician (2)
  - ▪ Independent politician (3)
  - ▪ Private sector CEO, VP, ranked title (4)
  - ▪ Industry analyst (5)
  - ▪ Journalist (6)
  - ▪ Scholar (7)
  - ▪ Retired (8)
- ◄ Technological effects: past
  - ▪ Fast, strong, making a better or more efficient society (1)
  - ▪ Unsafe or corrupt (2)
  - ▪ Slow, weak, hurting productivity (3)
  - ▪ Uncertain (4)
- ◄ Technological effects: present
  - ▪ Fast, strong, making a better or more efficient society (1)
  - ▪ Unsafe or corrupt (2)
  - ▪ Slow, weak, hurting productivity (3)
  - ▪ Uncertain (4)
- ◄ Technological effects: future
  - ▪ Fast, strong, making a better or more efficient society (1)
  - ▪ Unsafe or corrupt (2)
  - ▪ Slow, weak, hurting productivity (3)
  - ▪ Uncertain (4)
- ◄ Public
  - ▪ Smart, educated (1)
  - ▪ The ultimate stakeholders of the market; able to make demands and cause change in the industry (2)

- Dumb, lacking agency, totally affected by technology (3)
- Fearful, reactive, scared of technology or innovation (4)

◄ Policy

- Harmful, preventing industries from making technological advancements (1)
- Harmful, hurting public (2)
- Good, protective of small companies (3)
- Good, protective of consumers/public (4)
- Needing reform for more regulation (5)
- Needing reform for less regulation (6)
- Dysfunctional because it's too big, pervasive, or invasive (7)
- Dysfunctional because it's too small, not regulatory enough (8)
- No discussion (9)

◄ Government/policymakers

- Controlling, powerful (1)
- Behind the times (2)
- Innovative, helpful, responsive (3)

CHAPTER **3**

IMAGE BITE ANALYSIS OF PRESIDENTIAL DEBATES

Erik P. Bucy
Zijian Harrison Gong

Presidential debates provide an ideal setting in which to observe and document the nonverbal behavior of political candidates in a competitive context. Because debates are televised, they present viewers with an extended opportunity to evaluate candidates not only for their issue positions, which are widely reported and available from a multitude of sources, but also for their communication efficacy and nonverbal communication style, from which viewers may infer a variety of politically relevant traits and associated evaluations. The use of the continuous split-screen presentation format by C-SPAN and other cable and broadcast networks during the 2012 general election debates between Barack Obama and Mitt Romney (Peters, 2012) highlighted the role of nonverbal behavior to an extent never before seen, as both candidates were in view continuously throughout each 90-minute encounter whether speaking or not. Indeed, the considerable consternation expressed by Obama supporters over the president's subpar performance in the first debate stemmed largely from his nonverbal communication, which was criticized for seeming at times evasive, unconcerned, and disengaged (Nagourney, Parker, Rutenberg, & Zeleny, 2012).

Analyzing the nonverbal dimension of presidential debates requires a markedly different approach to derive meaning than does rhetorical or textual analysis. First, there is no nonverbal "transcript" that can be easily examined for recurring themes, rhetorical tropes, oratorical flourishes, memes (pithy statements), or other language-based devices or strategies. The analyst must look to completely separate literatures—on emotion, expression, and even biobehavior—for inspiration and theoretical grounding (for a review, see Bucy, 2011). Fortunately, a set of validated nonverbal categories now exists for the coding of political debates and other televised messages, including news, advertising, press conferences, presidential addresses, and other communication genres (see Grabe & Bucy, 2009). Second, nonverbal analysis encompasses not just facial expressions and bodily gestures but also tonal elements, eye gaze and "shiftiness," blink rate, head orientation, and other behaviors. Production features that affect candidate presentation, such as camera angles, shot lengths, vector orientation, and lead room, can be carefully coded as well (see Bucy & Ball, 2010; Tiemens, 1978).

Regardless of variable selection, as a form of content analysis, nonverbal coding should proceed from a firm conceptual foundation rather than represent an atheoretical exercise in merely generating data. While there is no need to reinvent categories for coding, as a plethora of useful variables already exist for this purpose (see Grabe & Bucy, 2009, 2011), there is a definite need for work to proceed with solid conceptual grounding.

Notwithstanding the range of possible variables that could be coded, nonverbal analysis of political communication recognizes a distinction between *sound bites*, defined as video segments in which candidates are shown speaking, and *image bites*, defined as video segments in which candidates are shown but not heard (Bucy & Grabe, 2007). Nonverbal behavior occurs in both, but in a presidential debate setting a sound bite denotes the utterances of the candidate who is speaking while an image bite denotes the visual portrayal of the candidate who is listening, or shown in a reaction shot. Because political discourse requires dedicated attention and a cognitive framework or schema for efficient processing of political information (see Ferejohn & Kuklinski, 1990), the effects of nonverbal displays are sometimes more pronounced for image bites, or reaction shots, than are candidate statements.

As shown in the analysis that follows, evidence from the 2012 presidential debates corroborates the general finding that viewers respond more to the candidates' nonverbal displays than to their verbal arguments. Given the popularity of the split-screen format among the television networks (Peters, 2012), it is more important than ever for candidates to be aware of the nonverbal signals they are conveying.

In the sections that follow, we present a framework for "image bite" analysis of the 2012 U.S. presidential debates, highlighting the role of nonverbal behavior in political communication. C-SPAN's footage of the 2012 presidential debates, which used a split-screen format and persistent camera shot in the first and third debates, is used to contrast the performances of Barack Obama and Mitt Romney. We review the major categories of nonverbal display behavior used in image bites analysis then present three applications of the approach to illustrate the utility of the coding scheme. First, the results of a detailed content analysis of the candidates' nonverbal communication, including facial expressions, evocative gestures, and voice tone, are presented. In particular, particular emphasis is placed on the communicative style of President Obama, whose performance in the first debate represented a low point in the campaign and gave Mitt Romney momentum in the polls. Next, we show how memorable moments during debates can be utilized as conversation starters in focus groups to address broader questions about the appropriateness of candidate nonverbal behavior and how communication style affects viewer interpretations of leadership ability. Finally, we discuss how our biobehavioral coding of debates can be used to predict the valence and volume of candidate mentions on the social media platform Twitter. Issues in coding, including coder training, techniques to ensure accuracy, and achieving intercoder reliability, as well as future directions of image bites research, are also considered.

THE IMAGE BITES APPROACH

Though mentioned by Barnhurst and Steele (1997) in the 1990s, the image bite concept was not elaborated and systematically measured until Bucy and Grabe (2007) documented the ratio of image to sound bites in a longitudinal study of major network news coverage of presidential elections from 1992 to 2004. They found, perhaps not surprisingly, that candidates were being *shown* more than they were being *heard* and that as average sound bite time was shrinking, the cumulative time that the broadcast networks (ABC, CBS, and NBC) were dedicating to visual coverage of the candidates per campaign story was increasing. Building a conceptual case for studying the content of image bites begins with an appreciation for the social information that non-verbal displays express. Facial expressions in particular are reliable indicators of a communicator's emotional state and simultaneously serve as the basis of myriad judgments about politically relevant traits, such as competence, integrity, dominance, and appropriateness (Bucy, 2011). Indeed, inferences of competence from photographs of candidates' faces alone can predict electoral outcomes at a rate significantly better than chance (Todorov, Mandisodza, Goren, & Hall, 2005).

Unlike verbal pronouncements and written communication, facial displays and other nonverbal modes of communication require no textual literacy to process and are not dependent on linguistic and syntactical modes of sense making (see Messaris & Abraham, 2001). They are readily recognized and, for the most part, understood by viewers regardless of educational level, socioeconomic status, or political sophistication (see Grabe & Bucy, 2009; Prior, 2014). This endows nonverbal communication with a universal quality that spoken words lack. Because of this accessibility, political nonverbals are arguably more important to study than rhetorical strategies because they are comprehended by a much broader segment of the electorate—the mass audience, basically, as opposed to the politically motivated and educated audience. Recent findings by Prior (2014) reinforce the importance of political visuals to the average citizen. When traditional political knowledge questions are accompanied by a related visual image for illustration, the sizeable differences normally observed for gender, age, and education dissipate dramatically in national samples. Prior concludes that visual knowledge is as indicative of civic competence as is verbal knowledge.

Beyond its equalizing potential, visual processing is also much more efficient than verbal processing. Facial expressions are accurately recognized within milliseconds of exposure, even sometimes outside of conscious awareness. During speeches and other televised events, viewers are even influenced by microexpressions—rapid and subtle displays of facial emotion lasting less than a second. In a study of President George H. W. Bush's speech following Iraq's invasion of Kuwait, participants exposed to Bush's microexpressions of happiness/reassurance reported significantly less anger and threat compared to an experimental group shown the same speech with the microexpressions removed (Stewart, Waller, & Schubert, 2009). Thus, nonverbal variations of even very short duration can affect emotional responding to a political speech. Consistent with the evolutionary preference for visual processing, political nonverbals are also better remembered than verbal information (Grabe & Bucy, 2009; Prior, 2014), and they are more reliable indicators of information acquisition during televised events than measures of verbal recall.

Coding Nonverbal Behavior

When coding nonverbal behavior, it is important to prioritize those gestures and displays that are politically consequential. For this, one must consult the research literature in human ethology, evolutionary psychology, and behavioral biology—branches of the life sciences interested in the interaction between social behavior and biology—to identify the nonverbal display repertoires that play the largest role in social organization, including politics. Fortunately, the first generation of empirically oriented scholars in politics and the life sciences, notably the political scientists Roger Masters and Dennis Sullivan, along with psychologist John Lanzetta (all colleagues at Dartmouth College in the 1970s and 1980s), synthesized the extant literature and carefully derived a set of enduring facial display categories with exacting, behaviorally derived definitions that lend themselves to continued use and application across both observed and televised settings (Lanzetta, Sullivan, Masters, & McHugo, 1985; Masters, Sullivan, Lanzetta, McHugo, & Englis, 1986). These categories have been used since their introduction in the mid-1980s in experimental and content analytic work involving television news, debates, and other televised political appearances (see Bucy & Grabe, 2007, 2008; Grabe & Bucy, 2009; Masters, 2001; Masters & Sullivan, 1993).

For our image bites research the 2012 presidential debates were recorded from C-SPAN's telecast and the digital files were used for content analysis, focus group discussion, an eye-tracking experiment, and a public opinion study of social media expression during the first debate. To track the timing of candidate comments, we relied on the C-SPAN Archives' online Video Library of the debates. C-SPAN's consistent use of a two-shot split-screen technique and maintenance of a medium shot length throughout the first and third debates was advantageous for purposes of analysis. (The second debate followed a town hall format and featured a moving camera perspective that was much less uniform.) In split-screen presentations the screen is divided into two equal-sized boxes. Each candidate occupies half of the screen, and two different cameras are used to feature each candidate continuously. This dual visual presentation allows viewers (and researchers) to assess the performance of one candidate without overlooking the reactions of the other.

Consistent with earlier visual analysis of political debates (e.g., Tiemens, 1978), an individual shot, defined as an uninterrupted piece of video between the beginning and ending of a camera change, was used as the unit of analysis. In our coding, shots less than 30 seconds in duration were regarded as single segments, while shots longer than 30 seconds were divided into 30-second increments for analysis. Once candidate introductions and opening statements commenced, shot changes were almost nonexistent. Thus, we identified 177 codable segments for the first debate and 180 codable segments for the third debate. Since both of these debates were broadcast uninterrupted, with a split screen featured throughout, we were able to capture the nonverbal behavior of both candidates for virtually the entire 90 minutes in each case.

CODING SCHEME AND KEY VARIABLES

To provide a sense of the more consequential nonverbal behaviors on display during presidential debates, we focus on categories for analysis that drive viewer response in predictive modeling (see Shah, Hanna, Bucy, Wells, & Quevedo, 2015). In particular, we code the candidates' facial expressions, evocative gestures, and tone of voice. The following sections describe how these behaviors were operationalized and coded in the 2012 debates.

Facial Displays

In the biopolitics literature, at least four different categories of facial displays are associated with social dominance and subordination: happiness/reassurance, anger/threat, fear/evasion, and sadness/appeasement (Masters et al., 1986; Stewart, Salter, & Mehu, 2009). Of these, the two most common and, arguably, most consequential in political communication are happiness/reassurance and anger/threat. Because there was considerable concern among partisans and the press about President Obama's lack of engagement in the first debate (Alexander, 2012; Nagourney et al., 2012), we also consider fear/evasion. Each expressive category draws on research from primate and human ethology, which has found that different patterns of display behavior are associated with distinct roles in rivalry for dominance (see Bucy & Grabe, 2008). As composite terms, these emotion/display pairs reflect the duality of the emotion being expressed (e.g., happiness or anger) and the social signals communicated (e.g., reassurance or threat). On an interpretive note, it is worth appreciating that content analysis of nonverbal display behavior can only measure the visible display observed and cannot assume that the associated emotion was genuinely felt while being expressed by the communicator.

Happiness/reassurance displays, characterized by a smile or relaxed mouth position, are relatively fluid, smooth, and flexible. In these expressions, the eyes may be wide open or just slightly closed. Also evident are raised eyebrows and visible upper, or both upper and lower, teeth. Eye contact may be brief, followed by a cutoff or change of gaze to avoid staring. In addition, "crow's feet" wrinkles may appear around the eyes, and the communicator's head might be tilted to the side, back, or in a nodding position. Functionally, happiness/reassurance displays facilitate a hedonic or friendly mode of social interaction and in most situations lower the probability of an aggressive or competitive encounter. The exception is counterempathy, in which case a smile or other hedonic signal conveyed by a disliked other (e.g., a reviled politician or tormenting superior) may evoke a negative response in the observer (see Bucy & Bradley, 2004). As a sign of subordination, fearful smiles should be coded as an instance of fear/evasion.

Anger/threat displays evidence a more rigid pattern of facial expression, including a fixed stare, vertical head orientation, raised upper and tightened lower eyelids, brows that are pulled down and drawn together, lower or no teeth showing, and lowered mouth corners. When expressing anger/threat, the lips may be pressed firmly together or squared and tightened. The expression overall has a negative or tense quality and is coupled with a hostile communicative intent. Functionally, anger/threat displays are associated with competitive or hostile (agonic) encounters, aggressive behavior, and challenges to dominance hierarchies. Whereas political challengers and rivals are frequently aggressive, "the leader is usually the focus of attention, often engaging in hedonic or reassuring behavior" (Masters, 1981, p. 64). As Howard Dean learned after his infamous "scream" during the 2004 primaries, excessive exhibitions of anger/threat on the campaign trail may attract intense media attention and quickly become characterized as nonpresidential.

Fear/evasion displays feature furrowed brows and gaze aversion, a lowered head position, abrupt movement, and, at times, side-to-side head turning. In some cases, the emitter's eyelids will be raised: the "deer caught in the headlights" look. Other times, the brows might be slightly furrowed and wrinkles may form in the middle of the forehead, suggesting worry; the lips may also stretch horizontally and the chin may be lowered. An evasive expression communicates an intention to avoid confrontation. Functionally, fear/evasion displays are also associated with agonic encounters, but instead of indicating aggression they signal subordination, avoidance, and inferior status—the social outcomes of effective aggression. Candidates who are forced to respond to allegations or difficult questions, who are caught in a contradiction or misrepresentation, or who are asked to justify contradictory statements might exhibit fear/evasion.[1]

Figures 3.1 and 3.2 present screen captures of the candidates' expressive variability in debate 3 across the prototypical display categories discussed above. Also included are images of both candidates' neutral expressions, which characterize their reaction shots while not speaking and serve as reference points for determining when a prototypical display of happiness/reassurance, anger/threat, or fear/evasion is occurring.

Evocative Gestures

Evocative gestures were coded as body language that signals affinity or defiance (see Grabe & Bucy, 2009). *Affinity gestures* consisted of hand, body, or facial movements that suggest a friendly relationship or attempt at bonding between the candidate and the audience, moderator, or opponent. Examples included waving or giving a thumbs-up; winking or nodding knowingly to the camera, moderator, or other candidate; or using an open palm when referencing a policy, making a point, or appealing to the audience or opponent on a topic of mutual agreement (rather than a closed fist or pointed finger).

Defiance gestures consisted of hand, body, or facial movements that suggest a threatening or antagonistic relationship between the candidate and his or her opponent. Examples include finger pointing, wagging, or shaking; fist

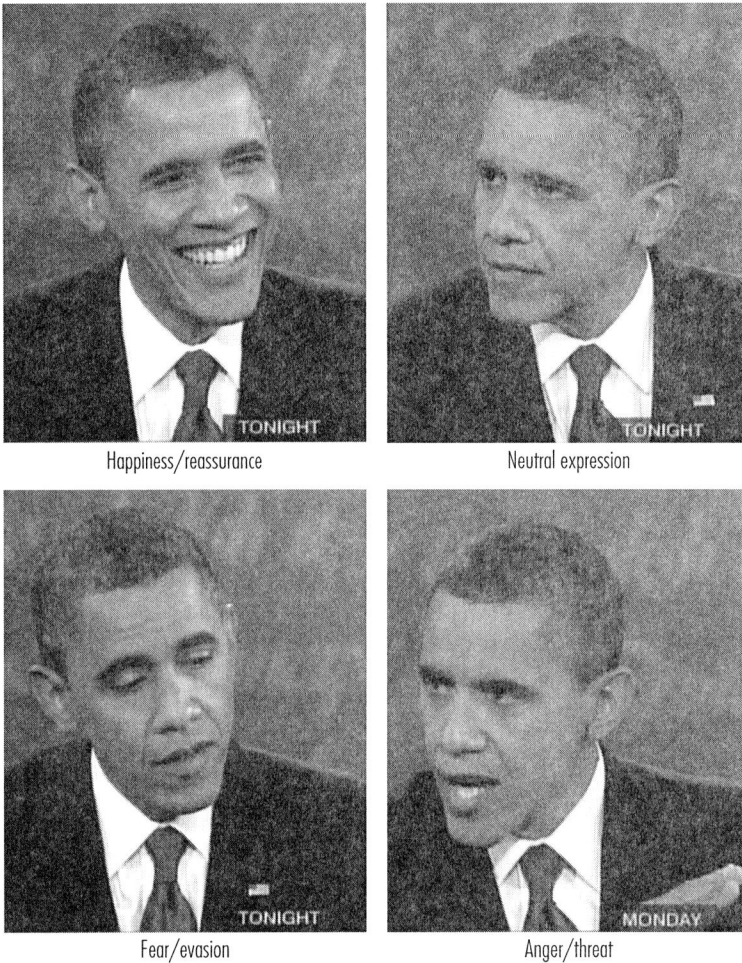

FIGURE 3.1 Obama's expressive variability across prototypical displays, debate 3.

raising; head shaking in disagreement; negative expressions accompanied by prolonged stares; and other behaviors signaling aggression.

From analysis of network news general election coverage we know that trailing candidates and debate losers are shown more often exhibiting anger/threat and making defiance gestures in news segments than are frontrunners and debate winners (Grabe & Bucy, 2009). Debate winners, by contrast, are more likely to be shown engaging in affinity behaviors that imply bonding, compassion, or friendship. While less nuanced than facial expressions, gestures typically work in unison with expressions and can amplify their effect.

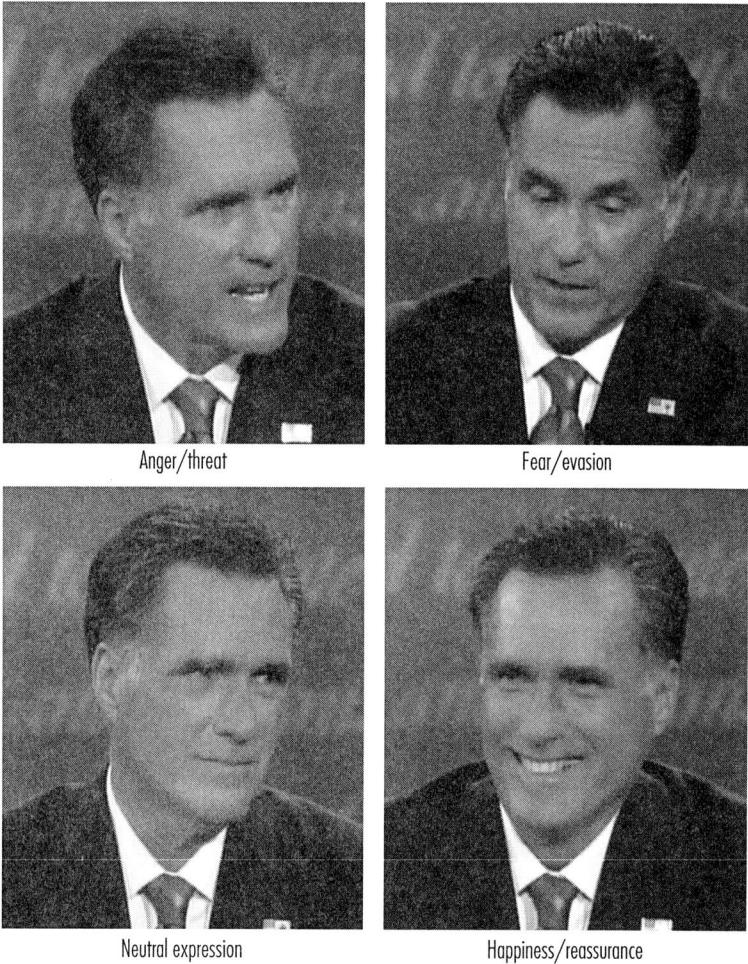

| Anger/threat | Fear/evasion |
| Neutral expression | Happiness/reassurance |

FIGURE 3.2 Romney's expressive variability across prototypical displays, debate 3.

Voice Tone

Voice tone is a paralinguistic cue present in all spoken communication that imparts the emotion of the speaker while modulating the meaning of what's being said. Voice tone also signals social intent, whether to communicate reassurance, as in the case of a friendly tone, or disapproval or even hostility, as in the case of an angry or threatening tone. In any competitive political encounter, a large part of nonverbal influence stems not just from semantic content but also from voice tone and variability (Anderson & Klofstad, 2012; Klofstad, Anderson, & Peters, 2012).

In our analysis of the 2012 debates, we operationalized a voice tone evincing *anger/threat* as statements in which the candidate's vocal quality had a menacing or hostile feel; where the candidate used confrontational verbal tactics to challenge his rival; where the candidate revealed a desire to do political battle, or took exception to and forcefully rebutted a claim by his opponent; or, where the overall tone of a segment could be characterized as enraged, feisty, or aggressive.

A voice tone evincing *happiness/reassurance* was operationalized as statements in which the candidate's vocal quality had an optimistic or cheerful feeling; where the candidate's voice was upbeat and positive and conveyed an affiliative or conciliatory intent; where the candidate offered hopeful predictions about what will happen to the country if elected; or where the tone suggested an attempt at bonding or reinforcing a sense of goodwill with potential supporters.

Similar to the findings for facial displays, longitudinal analysis of presidential election coverage has found that challengers and debate losers tend to be more aggressive in tone than are incumbents and frontrunners (Bucy & Grabe, 2008; Grabe & Bucy, 2009), consistent with their secondary status. Candidates who are behind in the polls or recognized as having lost a debate are more often shown in news reports as angry or delivering statements that are negative in tone than frontrunners and recognized debate winners. This behavioral pattern is consistent with ethological observations that have documented aggression in second-ranking individuals or challengers to power (Masters, 1989).

Having described our main coding categories, we next turn to a discussion of issues that arise during coding, including the need for careful training, techniques to ensure accuracy, and achieving intercoder reliability.

ISSUES IN CODING

In visual content analysis, as with text-based analysis, coding consistency is a vital part of the research process (see Benoit, 2011). Even with precise variable definitions, as presented in the previous section, it takes more than simply generating a list of definitions and having a group of coders accurately document the nonverbal content of a debate. Different viewers may watch the same debate, but without adequate training they may not "see" or recognize the same nonverbal behavior, particularly if two candidates are presented simultaneously. And even small discrepancies in interpretation can lead to sizeable differences in tabulated results, an unacceptable outcome. As is well known in content analysis, achieving a high degree of intercoder reliability is necessary before results can be reported—and even before intensive coding of content should proceed (see Krippendorff, 2012; Neuendorf, 2002).

Thus, training coders to recognize nonverbal behavior during political debates is an important first step in the process. Skilled coding of nonverbal behavior should begin with a systematic understanding of expressive displays from the biobehavioral literature to facilitate careful analysis of cues that are relevant to leadership. Appreciating the social and competitive significance of nonverbal behavior should produce more attentive coding, and with that more accurate data. Starting from the *terra firma* of the research literature also avoids unnecessary (and sometimes haphazard) attempts at inventing new categories of visual variables that have no real conceptual grounding or social meaning, or are so broad as to lack predictive validity. Additionally, some understanding of television production is beneficial to appreciate the visual environment of televised debates to know when production features matter.

Interestingly, our initial coding of anger/threat displays did not produce acceptable intercoder reliability figures, potentially because the candidates' head and body movements were restrained and rarely changed direction during both sound bites (candidate statements) and image bites (reaction shots). Thus, a clear differentiation between a more neutral reaction shot looking at the opponent and a staring gaze indicative of anger/threat could not be made with situational cues from the communication setting alone. To differentiate neutral *looking* from more menacing *staring*, we expanded the definition of anger/threat to include widened eyes and a reduced blinking rate (see Garland-Thomson, 2009). We also defined the generally rigid or tense facial expression indicative of anger/threat in more detail, adding dilated nostrils and vertical lines between the eyebrows (see Knapp, Hall & Hogan, 2013).

To ensure that each candidate's full range of nonverbal behavior is recognized, including small gestures and momentary (or micro) expressions, it is important to *code each candidate individually*, either from the start of the debate to the finish or for each 30-second segment, before moving onto the opponent on the other side of the split screen. This sequential approach allows coders to understand an individual candidate's unique expressive range and tendencies, remain focused on the candidate in question, and not be distracted by the verbal give-and-take of political debate. Focusing on a single candidate at a time also allows coders to become familiar with a candidate's unique nonverbal repertoire (Bucy & Grabe, 2008) or expressive range, which may have a small but important influence on coding decisions where some coder judgment is required. For instance, during the third presidential debate, Mitt Romney, when not speaking, had the tendency to look at President Obama with a slight grimace. Although Romney's rigidity and prolonged gaze might have indicated anger/threat, for Romney it was really a default expression and was more accurately coded as a neutral display.

Another technique for ensuring accurate nonverbal coding is to *turn the sound off*. With the exception of voice tone, which of course must be coded with the sound on, coding with the sound off ensures that coders are responding to the visual channel of televised expressive behavior and not what the candidates are saying. And, indeed, the most accurate coding of visual variables occurs without the distraction of listening to the candidates' verbal utterances, when the audio track is muted. Ekman and Friesen (1975) recognized the utility of this approach early in the development of systematic nonverbal coding techniques.

Finally, to ensure that individual shots or segments are coded accurately within the designated unit of analysis (e.g., the 30-second segment), it is advantageous to *use a digital timer* or auto clicker to precisely start and stop the recording at desired time points and to pause the recording to type numeric codes into a spreadsheet (or handwrite marks on a coding sheet). Auto clickers take the guesswork out of when to code for content and can be used in conjunction with most media players, such as Media Player for Windows or QuickTime for Mac. Analysis of audiovisual content should be approached as a precision endeavor to produce reliable data suitable for use in both descriptive comparisons and predictive modeling.

Because it requires precision, quality coding of nonverbal behavior is necessarily time consuming. To ensure quality and precision when coding a debate, for example, we recommend making *multiple passes* of the same candidate during the same debate for different categories of variables. The first pass of coding may focus on voice tone and inappropriate displays, the second pass on facial displays and evocative gestures, and the third pass on eye blinks. Coding should begin after the moderator completes candidate introductions and turns the floor over to the first candidate for his or her opening statement and continue until the end of the candidates' closing statements at the close of the debate.

Once coding is completed, a sample of the debate should be double-coded by a second trained coder to enable intercoder reliability analysis. Most content analysis textbooks recommend that at least 10 percent of the sample be double-coded for this purpose (Krippendorff, 2012; Neuendorf, 2002). In our coding of the debates, two coders were assigned to perform the coding for all three debates, rotating candidates between debates. To perform reliability analysis, each coder also analyzed 10 percent (roughly eighteen 30-second segments) of the other candidate's nonverbal behavior for each debate. The double-coded segments were then subjected to reliability analysis. In cases in which an alpha coefficient of less than .80 was produced (using Krippendorff's reliability program), the variables in question were recoded by the principal investigator for the entire debate until an acceptable level of agreement was attained.

RESEARCH APPLICATIONS

With reliable data in hand, coding of nonverbal behavior can be used in research for both descriptive comparisons and predictive modeling. Descriptively, nonverbal repertoires or frequency of different display types can be compared between candidates, between different stages of a debate (opening 30 minutes, middle 30, final 30), or across different debates.[2] In general, challengers or rivals to power are expected to act more aggressively than incumbents and exhibit more anger/threat in facial expressions and vocal tone while signaling defiance and rejection of the incumbent's policies, legislative record, and vision for the country. This is particularly true during a president's reelection bid, as with Bob Dole's attacks on Bill Clinton's character during the

1996 presidential debates or John Kerry's aggressive attempt to unseat George W. Bush in 2004 (see Clines, 1996; Nagourney, 2004).

By contrast, in the "happy warriors" tradition of reassuring leadership (Sullivan & Masters, 1988), incumbents should embrace a more confident, empathetic style of communication typical of power holders, evidenced by happiness/reassurance displays, a reassuring tone of voice, and the use of affinity gestures. If sitting presidents are indeed more confident and self-assured than challengers, we would also expect their blinking rate to be lower overall, although blinking may fluctuate considerably across different topics, rhetorical exchanges, and even debate stages. Among recent presidents, perhaps Bill Clinton was the most empathetic of the era, performing feats of projected compassion and understanding that reached viewers on an emotional level through television in a way that few political communicators can (see Bucy & Newhagen, 1999).

Display Repertoires of Obama and Romney, 2012

Using these observations as a point of reference, we next analyze the display repertoires of Obama and Romney on a set of key variables during the first and third presidential debates of 2012. The second debate is not examined because of its unique town hall format, which featured candidates who roved from the podium to engage with the studio audience and a moving camera perspective. The coding issues presented by a moving camera are not insurmountable, but the different format makes direct comparisons more difficult. The first and third debates are highly comparable because they both featured a fixed camera perspective and split-screen presentation format throughout. In the first debate the candidates each stood behind a podium, while in the third debate they sat across from each other at a table.

Nonverbal presentation style has been recognized as an important aspect of political competition since the first televised presidential debates between John F. Kennedy and Richard Nixon in 1960 (see Kraus, 2001). The 2012 debates underscored the importance of effective nonverbal communication in politics, as observers widely criticized President Obama for a lackluster and disengaged nonverbal communication style in the first debate, which the more assertive and assured Mitt Romney was credited with winning. Our

TABLE 3.1 *Nonverbal Display Frequencies, Debates 1 and 3*

	Debate 1		Debate 3	
	Obama	Romney	Obama	Romney
Facial displays				
Anger/threat	23.8% (44)	35.7% (66)	35.9% (65)	32.6% (59)
Happiness/ reassurance	43.2% (80)	40.0% (74)	16% (29)	37% (67)
Fear/evasion	39.5% (73)	17.8% (33)	4.3% (8)	5.4% (10)
Verbal tone				
Anger/threat	32.4% (60)	43.8% (80)	44.2% (80)	49.7% (90)
Happiness/ reassurance	24.9% (46)	21.6% (40)	22.1% (40)	31.5% (57)
Fear/evasion	4.3% (8)	2.7% (5)	1.1% (2)	0% (0)
Gestures				
Affinity	6.5% (12)	16.2% (30)	10.5% (19)	28.2% (51)
Defiance	14.6% (27)	36.8% (68)	37.6% (68)	17.1% (31)

NOTE: Percentages may not add up to 100 because more than one display type may occur in any 30-second segment, or not at all. Frequency counts are shown in parentheses.

data confirm the accuracy of these impressions and show that Obama had changed his approach considerably by the time of the third debate.

As shown in Table 3.1, Obama exhibited some degree of evasion (namely, by looking down or away from Romney while shown in a reaction shot, or image bite) in almost 40 percent of all segments in the first debate. By the third debate he had eliminated this avoidance behavior from his nonverbal repertoire almost entirely, and signs of evasion appeared in just 4.3 percent of segments. Obama's more assertive approach in debate 3 was also evident in a greater percentage of anger/threat displays (in 35.9 percent of segments, compared to 23.8 percent in debate 1) and a more aggressive tone of voice. At the same time, he was more defiant in his use of gestures, using more rigid and emphatic hand movements while speaking. A different picture emerges for Romney, who projected a more upbeat tone and used more affinity gestures in debate 3.

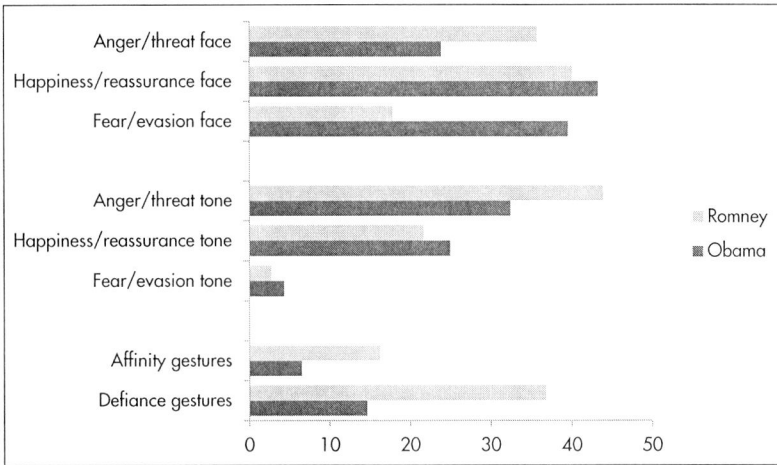

FIGURE 3.3 Nonverbal display frequencies, debate 1.

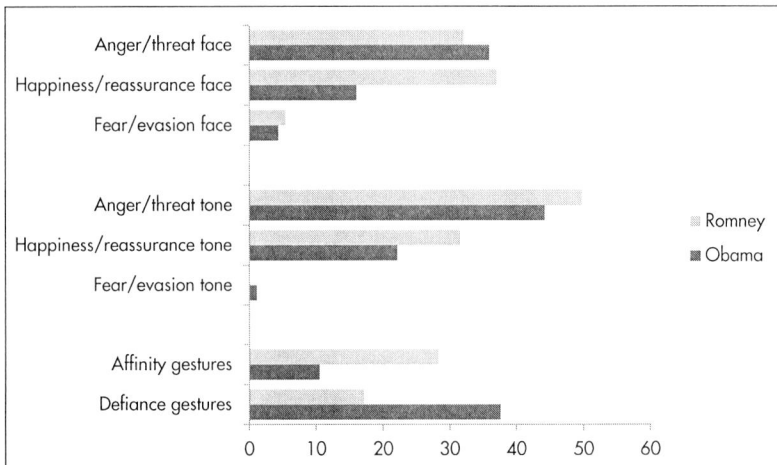

FIGURE 3.4 Nonverbal display frequencies, debate 3.

Figure 3.3 shows the dramatic difference in Obama's fear/evasion displays compared to Romney's in the first debate, and Romney's more aggressive posture as evidenced through anger/threat displays, a critical voice tone, and increased use of defiance gestures. Figure 3.4 illustrates the candidates' nonverbal behaviors in the third debate, showing Obama's increased use of defiance gestures and greatly reduced fear/evasion displays. Figures 3.5 and 3.6 show

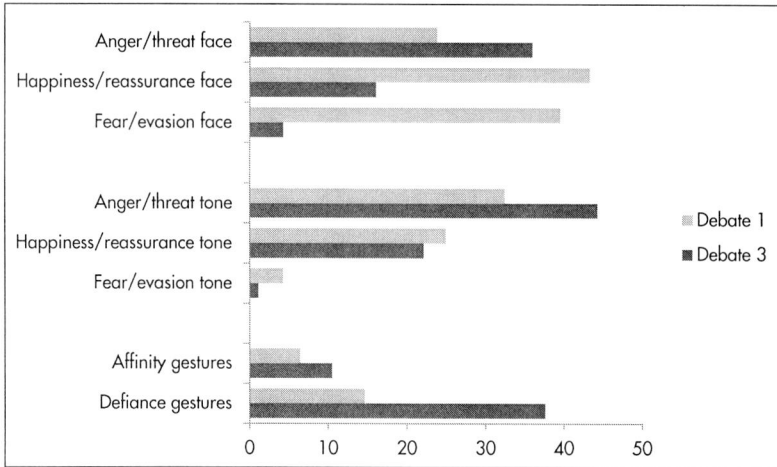

FIGURE 3.5 Obama's nonverbal display repertoire, debates 1 and 3.

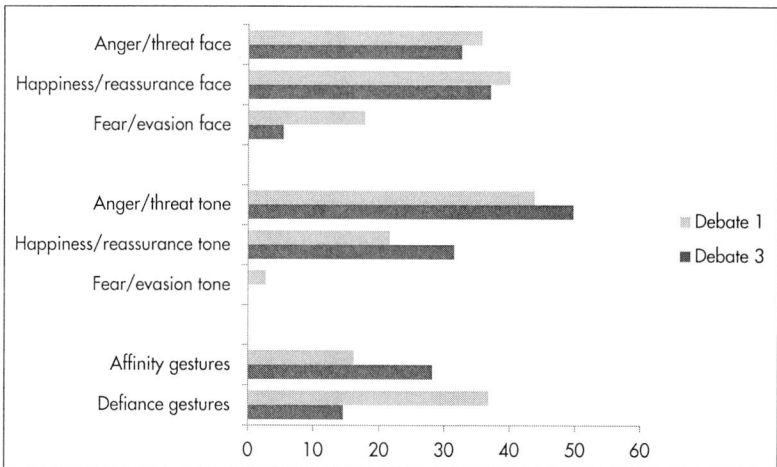

FIGURE 3.6 Romney's nonverbal display repertoire, debates 1 and 3.

within-candidate comparisons across the two debates. Here, the differences between each candidate's communication style between debate 1 and debate 3 become quite obvious. By the third debate, Obama is noticeably more aggressive and defiant and much less concerned about imparting a reassuring, conciliatory tone than he was in the first debate, while Romney remains aggressive but also becomes more reassuring in tone while using more affinity gestures.

Display Appropriateness in the 2012 Debates

In the next phase of research, we convened a series of focus groups and asked participants to assess the appropriateness of President Obama's display behavior during the first and third debates. For this analysis, responses to the two best performing (i.e., most "appropriate" and most "inappropriate") clips from an experimental study (see Gong & Bucy, 2014) were analyzed qualitatively. The two clips, again from C-SPAN's telecast of the debates (archived in the Video Library), both featured Obama and Romney in a split-screen presentation. A 53-second excerpt from debate 1 starting at 33:44 (see C-SPAN, 2012a) represented the inappropriate condition, and a 70-second excerpt from debate 3 starting at 80:16 (see C-SPAN, 2012b) represented the appropriate condition.

Both clips were shown in the context of several other memorable moments from televised politics, so that each group considered a range of different political encounters and was not focused solely on Obama and Romney.[3] In the inappropriate clip from the first debate, Obama was shown glancing downward with a slight smirk while being verbally attacked by Romney in the adjacent split-screen window. In the appropriate clip, from the third debate, Obama is shown much more engaged and visually focused on Romney, interjecting out of turn with short objections, and denying several of Romney's claims. Rather than avoiding or enduring Romney's verbal barrages, Obama in this exchange makes it difficult for Romney to complete his point.

THEMES EMERGING FROM THE DISCOURSE

Overall, focus group participants judged the clip from the third debate, showing an assertive and combative Obama (see C-SPAN, 2012b), to be more presidential and confidence inspiring than the excerpt from the first debate. The clip from the first debate depicted a demur Obama who shied from eye contact and appeared to smirk, while looking downward, in response to some of Romney's comments. Interestingly, some initial interpretations depended on clip order: When Obama's inappropriate clip was shown after an evasive and stone-faced Michael Dukakis from the 1988 presidential debates, for example, Obama was at first rated positively—in comparison to Dukakis. However, in comparison to his own performance in the third debate, Obama's performance in the first debate was judged more critically by focus group participants, and not just for ceding the floor to his opponent by refusing to visually engage Romney. As well, Obama was judged harshly for the way he was perceived as treating Romney. As Douglas, a focus group participant, put it, Obama deserved to experience a dip in the polls following his first debate performance, not because he appeared weak and ineffectual but

> because of his body language and his attitude—it was like, "you don't know what you're talking about and I don't care what you have to say." For me, he did not take what Romney was saying seriously. (Douglas)

> Obama was unprepared. He came across like…he could care less about what Romney had to say. (Leah)

Focus group participants articulated a two-sided view of Obama's inappropriate style from the first debate. First, they acknowledged that he seemed passive and disengaged, as was widely reported in news coverage, a posture that clearly violated nonverbal expectations. But also, and perhaps more interestingly, they criticized his nonverbal demeanor for seeming disinterested, dismissive, and disrespectful toward Romney—to the point of perceiving an element of sarcasm in Obama's expression. The phrases *unprofessional* and *unpresidential* were used in describing Obama's communication. "From a visual standpoint, I … noticed that Obama was kind of smirking," a female participant observed. "That bothered me," added a second female viewer. "He needed an attitude adjustment." The perception of sarcasm in a partial, downcast smile illustrates the sensitivity that viewers have to even small, incomplete expressions.

By contrast, focus group discussion of Obama's clip from the third debate reflected positive assessments of an engaged and assertive leadership style—one that conformed to expectations even while violating norms of polite discussion through interjection and speaking out of turn. Through such positive nonverbal expectancy violations, Obama's communication was uniformly viewed as appropriate and fitting to the rhetorical situation. Even as Romney held the floor and attempted to score points for his economic record and policies toward the auto industry, Obama acted as a nonverbal auditor of Romney's comments and was quick to correct his opponent upon hearing a questionable claim or statement inconsistent with the historical record. Such active auditing and visual accounting of Romney by Obama was described by focus group participants as signaling dominance. "You've got one guy who is on the defense here [Romney] saying stuff. And the other guy who is saying, 'No that's not what your words or the print says.' It's kind of obvious and easy that Obama is winning this," noted Kliff. "I think Obama derailed Romney quite a bit and kind of negated what he said," added Bob.

Discussion about Romney's performance in the clip from the third debate centered on the hurried pace and rehearsed quality of his statements. In Romney's rush to recite facts, viewers discerned an ill-at-ease attempt to command the stage by rotely filling the air with an overstuffed recitation of rehearsed lines. "I think he could have cut out probably 50 percent of what he said and slowed down," observed Bob. Participants characterized Romney's rapid recitation of facts as having a defensive and inauthentic quality. "Romney came across as being very phony and he clearly was just following a script and going through the motions," Donavin commented. "Obama, even with his few words, was able to keep [Romney] in the lane of being a governor versus being a chief commander of a nation," added Sarah. Viewers also noticed Romney's rapid blink rate, a potential sign of stress (or intensive mental activity).

From this we conclude that, when everyday citizens are given the opportunity to reflect on and share impressions of televised political encounters, small visual cues begin to speak loudly.

Linking Biobehavioral and Social Media Approaches to Debate Effects

Thus far we have considered nonverbal communication as a dependent variable or outcome measure to compare the candidates' nonverbal communication styles between debates, and then we used key encounters between Barack Obama and Mitt Romney during the first and third presidential debates of 2012 as stimulus clips to generate focus group discussion about the appropriateness of the candidates' display behavior. These clips were also used experimentally in eye-tracking research to assess the extent to which viewers fixate on inappropriate or unexpected candidate behavior (see Gong & Bucy, 2014).

Another way in which nonverbal coding can be applied in political communication research is *predictively*, as independent variables in a causal model showing debate effects. In an innovative project linking our biobehavioral coding of the first presidential debate to Twitter responses by viewers—perhaps the first study to formally link the content of first and second screens during a political event—Shah and colleagues (2015) compared the ability of non-verbal communication and rhetorical strategies to predict the valence and volume of candidate mentions on the social media platform.

Considerable controversy surrounds the study of presidential debates, particularly efforts to connect their content and impact. Researchers have long debated whether the citizenry reacts to what candidates say, how they say it, or simply how they appear (see Druckman, 2003; Kraus, 1996). Using our detailed coding of the first debate as independent variables in a series of regression models, we examined the relative influence of the candidates' verbal persuasiveness and nonverbal style on viewers' "second-screen" behavior—their use of computers, tablets, and mobile phones to enhance or extend the televised viewing experience. To test these relationships, we merged our coding of the candidates' nonverbal communication, their rhetorical strategies during the debate (coded separately), and corresponding real-time measures, synched and lagged, of the volume and sentiment of Twitter expression about Obama and Romney.

Performing such an analysis requires a "Big Data" approach to parsing the publicly available Twitter postings on the evening of the debate, which numbered in the millions, and ultimately involved a machine learning method for determining the emotional valence, or sentiment, of the Twitter postings.[4] Thus, advanced programming skills are requisite for this kind of large-scale analysis. Once the data are in hand, interesting questions can be asked. In close elections where much is at stake, leader displays and other nonverbal behaviors are likely to take on added significance. And in cases where the incumbent performs particularly poorly or commits a violation of nonverbal expectations (see Burgoon & Hale, 1988), or where the challenger surprises by exceeding expectations, we would expect a higher volume of audience attention and second-screen communication in response to these developments, as well as an outpouring of valenced reactions.

Consistent with evolutionary arguments and the image bites outlook on political communication, our analysis found that the candidates' facial expressions and physical gestures (namely, displays of either affinity or defiance) were more consistent and robust predictors of the volume and valence of Twitter expression than the candidates' persuasive strategies, pithy statements or memes, and voice tone during the debate. Thus, we were able to confirm on a large scale the consequentiality of nonverbal political behavior in driving social media responses during a debate.

Despite their inherent messiness, social media provide political communication researchers with an index of audience behavior that offers unprecedented precision and scope. Like continuous response measures that are typically gathered in small group settings, tweets and other social media posts provide moment-to-moment audience feedback that can be traced down to the second. But unlike continuous response measures, social media responses can have local, national, or international reach depending on how the search parameters are set. Auspiciously, the data they produce (at least publicly available Twitter posts) lend themselves to effects modeling as a promising new form of public reaction to televised political performances. Although Twitter users are not necessarily representative of the population, Shah and colleagues (2015) note that, "they are nonetheless quite diverse, and their voluminous real-time comments allow us to trace, in a highly granular fashion, the connections between the first and second screens that characterize the television viewing experience" (pp. 229–230).

In interpreting the significance of our findings, we posit that second-screen responses to the candidates' nonverbal behaviors indicate greater reliance on *social* rather than *factual* information or rhetorical efforts (see Grabe & Bucy, 2009, pp. 274–276). This interpretation is consistent with evolutionary analyses of political behavior, in which nonverbal communication is regarded as a more reliable predictor of leader traits than are verbal utterances (see Bucy & Grabe, 2008; Masters et al., 1986). If nonverbal cues facilitate inferences about such politically relevant traits as competence and integrity (see Olivola & Todorov, 2010; Rahn, Aldrich, Borgida, & Sullivan, 1990), we may need to rethink our assumptions about the informational cues that voters *actually* use, as opposed to the bases of information that normative theorists would prefer the public to rely on.

FUTURE DIRECTIONS

Though new to debate analysis, the image bites approach to political communication has already been validated as a robust and adaptable methodology for assessing the nonverbal dimension of candidate communication (Bucy & Grabe, 2007, 2008; Grabe & Bucy, 2009, 2011), easily extending to international political contexts (see Esser, 2008). The application of biobehavioral coding to televised presidential debates opens new vistas for investigating this time-honored campaign tradition because it introduces a systematic and easily replicated framework for documenting the nonverbal communication elements that are a continuous feature of competitive candidate encounters. Previous research on the visual dimensions of political debates tended to highlight the role of production techniques, camera angles, and other perceived presentational biases (e.g., Morello, 1988; Tiemens, 1978) rather than the social significance of political display behavior. Moreover, candidate expressions were documented primarily to assess the extent to which they reinforced the verbal message (e.g., Hellweg & Phillips, 1981; Tiemens, Hellweg, Kipper, & Phillips, 1985) rather than the extent to which they wielded persuasive influence on their own. Coding was also highly specific to debates and not generally transferable to other communication contexts.

The categories of analysis reviewed in this chapter overcome these limitations while lending themselves to repurposing in the form of stimulus clips for focus groups and eye-tracking experiments, as well as variables appropriate for use in predictive modeling of public response to campaign events via social media. As research utilizing biobehavioral measures of presidential debates and other political communication progresses, it will be important to enhance coding precision by reducing the standard length of individual coding segments from 30 seconds to as few as, say, 5 seconds to enable finer-grained analysis of communication behavior.[5] A lot of expressive variability can happen in 30 seconds. Thus, in our coding scheme some segments were coded for multiple expressive behaviors—sometimes affiliative and reassuring, at other times defiant and threatening—all occurring in the same segment. Shortening segment lengths would give each segment more distinct meaning and discrete value. Another advance would be to record the durations of expressive displays rather than simply noting whether a given behavior or expression is present or absent, as we were able to do in our original image bites research (see Bucy & Grabe, 2007, 2008; Grabe & Bucy, 2009).

Here, automated coding would represent an enormous leap forward. At present, visual coding of presidential debates and other audiovisual content is a time-consuming and painstaking process. To ensure accuracy, multiple passes of the same content are required, and for every hour of content it takes at least twice that long to perform reliable coding manually. The ability to run a computer program that automatically documents the range of a candidate's expressive behavior would greatly accelerate the coding process while obviating the need for coder training or intercoder reliability checks. Instead of training human coders, the program would simply need to be trained and validated (with human coding) to confirm recognition of the expressive variables of interest. Face-tracking software that locates and tracks facial features in video sequences in real time, such as that offered by Visage Technologies,[6] hold considerable promise for the next wave of image bites research. And debates are a good testing ground for this because they feature an unobstructed, well-lit view of the candidates in relatively fixed positions with an invariant background.

Computer analysis of vocal variables, including voice inflections, tone, pace, and even decibel level, would also bring added precision and leverage to research on nonverbal behavior, in this case bioacoustics. The freely available PRAAT speech analysis software[7] is well suited to this endeavor (see Boersma & van Heuven, 2001). Prior research has shown that presidential debates promote learning about candidate issue positions and influence evaluations of candidate traits (see Benoit, 2013). In both instances, behavioral indicators matter. In terms of the former, candidates can use changes in pitch and decibel level in tandem with evocative gestures to draw attention to an issue. In terms of the latter, candidates can raise and lower the tone of their voice to demonstrate a higher or lower level of emotional engagement. Facial displays of anger/threat combined with defiance gestures, or happiness/reassurance displays combined with affinity gestures, work in concert with voice to convey the communicator's emotional state with added certainty. In either instance, changes in vocal inflection and nonverbal communication can influence how voters perceive presidential candidates.

To date, little research has considered such relationships. The advent and availability of social media archives, however, now makes it possible to model real-time responses to candidate communication on a mass scale. One possibility is to examine whether there is a biobehavioral aspect of agenda-setting influence. When candidates raise their tone of voice, for example, do these verbal punctuation marks act as an attentional cue that predicts Twitter response? Similarly, do vocal factors complement or compete with facial expressions and evocative gestures to enhance perceptions of leadership? Experimental research shows that candidates who speak with a lower pitch tend to receive higher leadership ratings and, consequently, are more likely to garner votes (Klofstad et al., 2012). In these studies vocal pitch is typically measured in isolation. However, pitch often covaries with decibel level (Gramming, Sundberg, Ternström, Leanderson, & Perkins, 1988). A higher vocal pitch combined with a higher decibel level may lead to changes in perceptions of leadership, influencing the evaluation of traits associated with a dominant or lackluster performance.

Ultimately, the ability to perform automated coding of televised nonverbal behavior will continue to present new possibilities for research, allowing reconsideration and much more rigorous testing of long-accepted theories and assumptions—and development of new concepts and insights that were not evident before. As the small data of manual coding gives way to the big data of automated analysis, we should also be able to develop norms for political communication across different settings and contexts, so that a more precise form of discrepancy analysis may be performed on whether candidates are communicating within or outside the average range of typical political behavior, and how these fluctuations affect audience response.

NOTES

We wish to thank Riley Davis for his assistance with coding the 2012 presidential debates.

1. For examples of these candidate displays drawn from presidential election news coverage, see Grabe and Bucy (2009).

2. For an application of this approach to network news coverage of presidential campaigns, see Bucy and Grabe (2008) and Grabe and Bucy (2009).

3. The groups were organized and conducted in the context of a graduate seminar in political communication. No incentive was offered beyond course credit for each moderator. Thus, opinions offered were voluntary and not made in exchange for payment.

4. For details on the method, see Shah et al. (2015).

5. For an even finer-grained approach, see Nagel, Maurer, and Reinemann (2012).

6. www.visagetechnologies.com/products/visagesdk/facetrack

7. www.praat.org

REFERENCES

Alexander, J. C. (2012, October 4). Obama's downcast eyes [Huffington Post Web log post]. Retrieved from http://www.huffingtonpost.com/jeffrey-c-alexander /obama-debate-performance_b_1938755.html

Anderson, R. C., & Klofstad, C. A. (2012). Preference for leaders with masculine voices holds in the case of feminine leadership roles. *PLoS ONE, 7*(12), e51216. http://dx.doi.org/10.1371/journal.pone.0051216

Barnhurst, K. G., & Steele, C. A. (1997). Image-bite news: The visual coverage of elections on U.S. television, 1968–1992. *Harvard International Journal of Press/Politics, 2*(1), 40–58.

Benoit, W. L. (2011). Content analysis in political communication. In E. P. Bucy & R. L. Holbert (Eds.), *Sourcebook for political communication research: Methods, measures, and analytical techniques* (pp. 268–279). New York, NY: Routledge.

Benoit, W. L. (2013). Political election debates: Informing voters about policy and character. Lanham, MD: Lexington Books.

Boersma, P., & van Heuven, V. (2001). Speak and unspeak with Praat. *Glot International, 5*(9/10), 341–347.

Bucy, E. P. (2011). Nonverbal communication, emotion, and political evaluation. In E. Konijn, K. Koveling, & C. von Scheve (Eds.), *Handbook of emotions and mass media* (pp. 195–220). New York, NY: Routledge.

Bucy, E. P., & Ball, J. (2010, August). *Quantifying the claim that Nixon looked bad: Nonverbal analysis of the Kennedy–Nixon debates.* Paper presented at the 20th Biennial Congress of the International Society for Human Ethology, Madison, WI.

Bucy, E. P., & Bradley, S. D. (2004). Presidential expressions and viewer emotion: Counterempathic responses to televised leader displays. *Social Science Information, 43*(1), 59–94. http://dx.doi.org/10.1177/05390184040689

Bucy, E. P., & Grabe, M. E. (2007). Taking television seriously: A sound and image bite analysis of presidential campaign coverage, 1992–2004. *Journal of Communication, 57*(4), 652–675. http://dx.doi.org/10.1111/j.1460-2466.2007.00362.x

Bucy, E. P., & Grabe, M. E. (2008). "Happy warriors" revisited: Hedonic and agonic display repertoires of presidential candidates on the evening news. *Politics and the Life Sciences, 27*(1), 78–98. http://dx.doi.org/10.2990/27_1_78

Bucy, E. P., & Newhagen, J. E. (1999). The micro- and macrodrama of politics on television: Effects of media format on candidate evaluations. *Journal of Broadcasting & Electronic Media, 43*(2), 193–210. http://dx.doi.org/10.1080/08838159909364484

Burgoon, J. K., & Hale, J. L. (1988). Nonverbal expectancy violations: Model elaboration and application to immediacy behaviors. *Communication Monographs, 55*(1), 58–79. http://dx.doi.org/10.1080/03637758809376158

Clines, F. X. (1996, October 17). Dole attacks Clinton's ethics; president parries on economy. *New York Times.* Retrieved from http://www.nytimes.com/1996/10/17/us/dole-attacks-clinton-s-ethics-president-parries-on-economy.html

C-SPAN (Producer). (2012a, October 3). *2012 Presidential candidates debate* [online video]. Available from http://www.c-span.org/video/?308511-1/2012-presidential -candidates-debate

C-SPAN (Producer). (2012b, October 22). *Presidential candidates debate* [online video]. Available from http://www.c-span.org/video/?308547-1/presidential -candidates-debate

Druckman, J. N. (2003). The power of television images: The first Kennedy-Nixon debate revisited. *Journal of Politics, 65*(2), 559–571.

Ekman, P., & Friesen, W. V. (1975). *Unmasking the face: A guide to recognizing emotions from facial expressions.* Englewood Cliffs, NJ: Prentice Hall.

Esser, F. (2008). Dimensions of political news cultures: Sound bite and image bite news in France, Germany, Great Britain, and the United States. *International Journal of Press/Politics, 13*(4), 401–428. http://dx.doi.org/10.1177/1940161208323691

Ferejohn, A., & Kuklinski, J. H. (Eds.). (1990). *Information and democratic processes.* Urbana: University of Illinois Press.

Garland-Thomson, R. (2009). *Staring: How we look.* New York, NY: Oxford University Press.

Gong, Z. H., & Bucy, E. P. (2014, August). *Tracking inappropriate leader displays: A visual analysis of the 2012 presidential debates.* Paper presented at the annual meeting of the Association for Education in Journalism and Mass Communication, Montreal, Canada.

Grabe, M. E., & Bucy, E. P. (2009). *Image bite politics: News and the visual framing of elections.* New York, NY: Oxford University Press.

Grabe, M. E., & Bucy, E. P. (2011). Image bite analysis of political visuals: Understanding the visual framing process in election news. In E. P. Bucy & R. L. Holbert (Eds.), *Sourcebook for political communication research: Methods, measures, and analytical techniques* (pp. 209–237). New York, NY: Routledge.

Gramming, P., Sundberg, J., Ternström, S., Leanderson, R., & Perkins, W. H. (1988). Relationship between changes in voice pitch and loudness. *Journal of Voice, 2*(2), 118–126. http://dx.doi.org/10.1016/S0892-1997(88)80067-5

Hellweg, S. A., & Phillips, S. L. (1981). A verbal and visual analysis of the 1980 Houston Republican presidential primary debate. *Southern Speech Communication Journal, 47*(1), 23–38. http://dx.doi.org/10.1080/10417948109372512

Klofstad, C. A., Anderson, R. C., & Peters, S. (2012). Sounds like a winner: Voice pitch influences perception of leadership capacity in both men and women. *Proceedings of the Royal Society B, 279*(1738). http://dx.doi.org/10.1098/rspb.2012.0311

Knapp, M. L., Hall, J. A., & Hogan T. G. (2013). The effects of the face on human communication. *Nonverbal communication in human interaction* (pp. 258–294). Boston, MA: Cengage Learning.

Kraus, S. (1996). Winners of the first 1960 televised presidential debate between Kennedy and Nixon. *Journal of Communication, 46*(4), 78–96. http://dx.doi .org/10.1111/j.1460-2466.1996.tb01507.x

Kraus, S. (2001). *The great debates: Kennedy vs. Nixon, 1960.* Bloomington: Indiana University Press.

Krippendorff, K. (2012). *Content analysis: An introduction to its methodology* (3rd ed.). Thousand Oaks, CA: Sage.

Lanzetta, J. T., Sullivan, D. G., Masters, R. D., & McHugo, G. J. (1985). Emotional and cognitive responses to televised images of political leaders. In S. Kraus & R. M. Perloff (Eds.), *Mass media and political thought: An information-processing approach* (pp. 85–116). Beverly Hills, CA: Sage.

Masters, R. D. (1981). Linking ethology and political science: Photographs, political attention, and presidential elections. In M. Watts (Ed.), *Biopolitics: Ethological and physiological approaches* (pp. 61–80). San Francisco, CA: Jossey-Bass.

Masters, R. D. (1989). *The nature of politics.* New Haven, CT: Yale University Press.

Masters, R. D. (2001). Cognitive neuroscience, emotion, and leadership. In J. H. Kuklinski (Ed.), *Citizens and politics: Perspectives from political psychology* (pp. 68–102). New York, NY: Cambridge University Press.

Masters, R. D., & Sullivan, D. G. (1993). Nonverbal behavior and leadership: Emotion and cognition in political information processing. In S. Iyengar & W. J. McGuire (Eds.), *Explorations in political psychology* (pp. 150–182). Durham, NC: Duke University Press.

Masters, R. D., Sullivan, D. G., Lanzetta, J. T., McHugo, G. J., & Englis, B. G. (1986). The facial displays of leaders: Toward an ethology of human politics. *Journal of Biological and Social Structures, 9*(4), 319–343. http://dx.doi.org/10.1016/S0140 -1750(86)90190-9

Messaris, P., & Abraham, L. (2001). The role of images in framing news stories. In S. D. Reese Jr., O. H. Gandy, & A. E. Grant (Eds.), *Framing public life: Perspectives on media and our understanding of the social world* (pp. 215–226). Hillsdale, NJ: Erlbaum.

Morello, J. T. (1988). Argument and visual structuring in the 1984 Mondale-Reagan debates: The medium's influence on the perception of clash. *Western Journal of Speech Communication, 52*(4), 277–290. http://dx.doi.org/10.1080/10570318809389642

Nagel, F., Maurer, M., & Reinemann, C. (2012). Is there a visual dominance in political communication? How verbal, visual, and vocal communication shapes viewers' impressions of political candidates. *Journal of Communication, 62*(5), 833–850. http://dx.doi.org/10.1111/j.1460-2466.2012.01670.x

Nagourney, A. (2004, October 1). Bush and Kerry clash over Iraq in debate. *New York Times,* p. A1.

Nagourney, A., Parker, A., Rutenberg, J., & Zeleny, J. (2012, November 8). How a race in the balance went to Obama. *New York Times,* p. A1.

Neuendorf, K. A. (2002). *The content analysis guidebook.* Thousand Oaks, CA: Sage.

Olivola, C. Y., & Todorov, A. (2010). Elected in 100 milliseconds: Appearance-based trait inferences and voting. *Journal of Nonverbal Behavior, 34*(2), 83–110. http://dx.doi.org/10.1007/s10919-009-0082-1

Peters, J. W. (2012, October 9). Networks like split-screens in debates, even if candidates don't. *New York Times,* p. A11.

Prior, M. (2014). Visual political knowledge: A different road to competence? *Journal of Politics, 76*(1), 41–57. http://dx.doi.org/10.1017/S0022381613001096

Rahn, W. M., Aldrich, J. H., Borgida, E., & Sullivan, J. L. (1990). A social-cognitive model of candidate appraisal. In A. Ferejohn & J. H. Kuklinski (Eds.), *Information and democratic processes* (pp. 136–159). Urbana: University of Illinois Press.

Shah, D. V., Hanna, A., Bucy, E. P., Wells, C., & Quevedo, V. (2015). The power of television images in a social media age: Linking biobehavioral and computational approaches via the second screen. *The Annals of the American Academy of Political and Social Science, 659*(1), 225–245. http://dx.doi.org/10.1177/0002716215569220

Stewart, P. A., Salter, F. K., & Mehu, M. (2009). Taking leaders at face value: Ethology and the analysis of televised leader displays. *Politics and the Life Sciences, 29*(1), 48–74. http://dx.doi.org/10.2990/28_1_48

Stewart, P. A., Waller, B. M., & Schubert, J. N. (2009). Presidential speechmaking style: Emotional response to micro-expressions of facial affect. *Motivation and Emotion, 33*(2), 125–135. http://dx.doi.org/10.1007/s11031-009-9129-1

Sullivan, D. G., & Masters, R. D. (1988). "Happy warriors": Leaders' facial displays, viewers' emotions, and political support. *American Journal of Political Science, 32*(2), 345–368. http://dx.doi.org/10.2307/2111127

Tiemens, R. K. (1978). Television's portrayal of the 1976 presidential debates: An analysis of visual content. *Communication Monographs, 45*(4), 362–370. http://dx.doi.org/10.1080/03637757809375981

Tiemens, R. K., Hellweg, S. A., Kipper, P., & Phillips, S. L. (1985). An integrative verbal and visual analysis of the Carter-Reagan debate. *Communication Quarterly, 33*(1), 34–42. http://dx.doi.org/10.1080/01463378509369576

Todorov, A., Mandisodza, A. N., Goren, A., & Hall, C. C. (2005). Inferences of competence from faces predict election outcomes. *Science, 308*(5728), 1623–1626. http://dx.doi.org/10.1126/science.1110589

CHAPTER 4

EXPRESSIVE POLARIZATION IN POLITICAL DISCOURSE

stonegarden grindlife

The idea that America is at its most politically polarized since the Civil War has become a popular sentiment amongst politicians and the media alike. From Jimmy Carter, to James Q. Wilson, to California Governor Jerry Brown, down to the repeated sentiments of fictional news reporter Will McAvoy on the HBO series *The Newsroom,* it is hard to escape the sense that America hasn't been this divided since brother fought brother some 150 years ago. A common focal point of this contention is the behavior of members of Congress and their increasing intransigence in developing policy and working across the aisle. In providing more concrete evidence of such congressional polarization, political scientists rely heavily on voting scores to show a basic divergence in policy positions. Looking at the historical DW-NOMINATE party means in the House on the liberal–conservative economic dimension we see this growing divide (see Figure 4.1).[1]

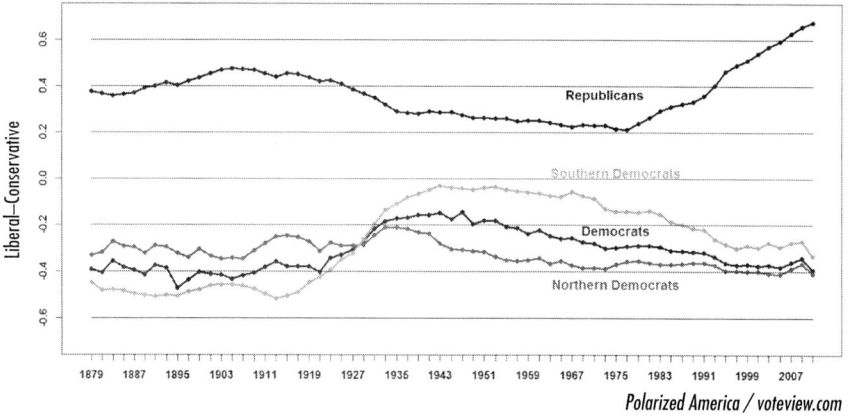

FIGURE 4.1 Party means on NOMINATE liberal–conservative dimension. House (1879–2012). *(Reprinted with permission from Keith T. Poole and Howard Rosenthal, voteview.com.)*

Another means of testing polarization in Congress is found in the lexical analysis of speeches. The field of research on the actual content of speech in legislatures is relatively new but growing. Its primary focus has been on utilizing texts of speeches and legislative proceedings as data to approximate party positions on policy matters (Laver, Benoit, & Garry, 2003; Slapin & Proksch, 2008). Other research has looked at the use of language attacking party rivals on the House and Senate floors, including how such incivility has affected legislative output, and particularly judicial confirmations (Schraufnagel, 2005). There has also been research into incivility as measured in the striking of words from the *Congressional Record* (Jamieson, 2011; Jamieson & Falk, 1999).

While much can be accounted for in an analysis of the *Congressional Record,* these prior textual measurement approaches nonetheless highlight two problems with relying solely on such a data source. The first is that an examination of stricken words reveals that the *Congressional Record* is not a literal transcription of every utterance of members on the House and Senate floors. In fact the striking of words and the even more undesirable rescinding of the privilege to speak that can result from such offending words can bias the data in two ways. On one hand the stricken words are missing data. The other consideration is that the subsequent possible punishment for violating decorum in Congress can itself serve as a bias in what words the legislators choose to speak. As Representative Barney Frank (D-MA) once stated in a section of the *Record* entitled "Do-Nothing Congress":

But I want to come to their [the Republicans'] defense to some extent, Mr. Whip, because there may be some implication that they're not willing to work hard. No, let's be very clear. The reason we have such a dismal record here is not because they are lazy, our Republican colleagues. It's more because of a word that rhymes with "lazy," which the House rules will prohibit me from using. (158 Cong. Rec. H6263, 2012)

Depending solely on the printed word in the *Record* to analyze congressional polarization, either in the use of aggressive and attacking language or incivility, is not a wholly futile venture. It nonetheless has its innate limitations.

Analyzing speaking in Congress follows a basic progression. The first question is "Who speaks?" The second is "What do they talk about?" The third is "How do they speak?" Certainly there are other subsequent and related questions when discussing legislative speech. But for theoretical purposes I focus on these issues. Lexical analysis of speaking and polarization may broach the first topic. However, in addition to the deletion of offending words, there is the more common problem of allowing members to insert speeches that were never delivered. Furthermore, researchers attempting to measure polarization encounter difficulty in disentangling the second and third issues. They can only really infer aggression between members of Congress based on the attendant adjectives and certain key words that may be biased in their absence from the printed word. As much as Barney Frank wants to call the Republicans "crazy," the best he can muster without his words disappearing or his losing the privilege to speak for the rest of the day is to say that the opposite party is "a word that rhymes with 'lazy.'"

In this chapter I provide a complementary analysis that can help disentangle some of the difficulties in relying on the lexical for estimating polarization in congressional speaking. To do this I examined the raw footage of the House and Senate from the C-SPAN Archives' online Video Library for the 109th through 112th Congresses (2005–2012). This video and audio account of the proceedings on the House and Senate floors is immune from at least one of the biases. Spoken language that is subsequently redacted in the *Congressional Record* nonetheless remains intact in the video and audio of the events. This does not directly address the other bias of self-selecting to not engage in as much potentially un-parliamentary speech. That being said, it may still be possible to estimate the level of aggression a legislator is affecting in his speech regardless of whether or not he actually calls members of the other party "crazy," impugns the general intelligence of his fellow legislators, or speaks ill of a particular other-party member's mother during floor proceedings.

I focus in this chapter on the prosodic elements of volume and speaking pace that can serve as indicators of aggression and anger. Largely ignoring the potentially sanitized actual words spoken, I attempt to measure the revealed, perhaps even subconscious, anger and frustration that members of Congress feel in their mere utterances. Such potential expressive fluctuations are examined in the context of two types of debate. The first encompasses debate surrounding *Congressional Quarterly (CQ)* key votes in both the House and Senate.[2] For contrast I also look at debate on legislation considered under suspension of the rules in the House.[3] Reviewing trends in the possible revealed expression of anger over time, I test to determine whether there is evidence of an increased expressive polarization during my period of analysis. Finally, I take into account general political factors as well as those at the individual level that might contribute to fluctuations in prosodic evidence of anger and aggression.

PREVIOUS RESEARCH

The literature suggesting what motivates legislators to speak in the first place is somewhat sparse. What exists on legislators' vocal patterns is even more lacking. As such, this chapter relies on tangentially related literature in the fields of linguistics and psychology to begin the construction of a bridge between the analysis of written and spoken records of congressional proceedings. A major difficulty in approaching this subject is that there is little readily apparent direct literature addressing strategies of speaking in legislative bodies as such. This is not to say that there is no literature that involves using the legislative proceedings as data. Maltzman and Sigelman (1996) as well as Morris (2001) look at the politics of talk by analyzing 1-minute, 5-minute, and Special Order speeches in the House. People who speak in Congress are generally in leadership positions, either in their party or on a committee relevant to legislation on the floor. Otherwise they tend to be first-dimension

NOMINATE score outliers (Morris, 2001). Furthermore, they tend to be minority party outliers. This makes sense, especially considering they are examining a House where there can be a party filter of the Rules Committee and a germaneness rule interfering with speaking in the context of debate. This narrow analysis in the C-SPAN era suggests that speaking tends not to be motivated by reelection concerns but by policy formation. Furthermore, these ideological outliers tended to speak in a divisive and partisan manner.

The strength or weakness of the parties, both within Congress (Aldrich & Rohde, 2000) and as electoral parties, can feed into a legislator's desire to cultivate a personal vote (Cain, Ferejohn, & Fiorina, 1987). This may discourage speaking in Congress as a personal vote can be built with solid constituency service and pressing of flesh in a state or district. It could also encourage aggressively uncivil and polarizing speaking on a chamber floor as the personal vote can be built in running as a maverick or outsider against one's own party. This should be more likely if the party is too weak to either punish a legislator in Congress or depose the legislator in the primary process. However, if the majority party is ideologically diverse enough it may reduce expressed anger and aggression overall as the majority party should be more open to working across the aisle and granting more policy concessions to those in the minority.

An Annenberg study on civility in Congress from 1935 to 2011 suggests that such inflammatory speech is not, in fact, the norm (Jamieson & Falk, 2011). Operationalizing incivility in the frequency of words taken down or withdrawn from the *Congressional Record,* the study finds that generally there is civility in discourse. What spikes there were in incivility were tied to turnover after an extended period of control by one party, and tended to be isolated to the House. The most common types of incivility across all time frames were found in accusations of lying and abusing basic prejudices to acquire votes. Blatant impugning of a legislator's intelligence has fallen off since the early 1940s.

Measures of incivility and polarization in Congress can sometimes rely on secondhand reports of proceedings in the House and Senate. In Schraufnagel's (2005) review of partisanship, incivility, and a general lack of comity in Congress, he develops newspaper and *CQ Almanac* indices to account for changes in conflict in the 1977–2000 period. While there is a divergence in the *CQ* and newspaper scores prior to the late 1980s, with *CQ* reporting lower levels of incivility, he finds a convergent increase in the apparent incivility based on his two indices thereafter. As Schraufnagel mentions, using newspapers as a source can involve its own limitations, though for him this is a concern about a constant onslaught of actual incivility in Congress leading to burnout by the media and a reduced likelihood of covering it. His own data collection suggests that such a growing insensitivity to incivility is not the case. In fact the media reports more and more on conflicts. While it is not impossible that incivility and expressive polarization in Congress is on the rise, relying on secondhand reports of conflict and aggression in Congress can present us with another bias. Legislators may be less likely to express their most uncivil sentiments on their chamber floor for fear of having them stricken, having to withdraw them, and possibly being censored for the remainder of the legislative day. A counter-bias may be present in news reporting. Conflict can lead to more coverage. With the rise of the explicitly partisan era in the United States, such a pro-conflict biasing can be amplified in a feedback loop.

This possible overstatement of conflict can be the observationally equivalent outcome of either high liberal or conservative partisan biasing in the media. This should especially be the case in media outlets such as Fox News and a post-2005 MSNBC. These outlets benefit economically from conflict, so in attempting to either foment or sustain outrage they can overstate incivility in Congress. Either parallel to partisan news sources or in response to these outlets' accusations of bias to the left or right in their reporting, less explicitly partisan news sources can also contribute to the overstatement of conflict.

In a less nefarious way the mainstream (center-right/center-left) media can engage in what Sellers (2010) refers to as "balancing" in their reporting of politics. Here the media attempt to find counter-arguments within Congress, which may not in fact be representative of the proportion of statements actually emanating from The Hill. So, for example, no matter how few Democrats speak on partial-birth abortion, the media will attempt to display something approximating a 1-to-1 ratio of statements for and against the policy. In doing so they can pick up on more ideologically extreme Democratic outliers who are more than willing to speak in an aggressive and angered manner. Sellers argues that this balancing seems to occur the farther along in the legislative process a bill progresses. There is more of this forced balancing once a bill crosses chambers than there is if it is being discussed in an originating House or Senate subcommittee. Regardless of the way the reporting of conflict may be biased in the media, it can feed back onto itself. As Forgette and Morris

(2006) suggest, such emphasis on conflict-laden reporting can reduce trust in the political system and reduce evaluations of Congress generally. Whether, of course, this translates into a person's estimation of his or her own legislator is another question (Hibbing & Theiss-Morse, 1995).

When the average person thinks of polarization and conflict in Congress, it is unlikely that multidimensional voting spaces and ideological scoring distances come to mind. The average person is more likely to bring to his or her consciousness images of partisans yelling at each other and framing those across the aisle as somehow either fundamentally evil or stupid—sometimes even both. If such expressions in debate on the House and Senate floors may be naturally biased to understate aggressive tones and the media may have a natural bias to overstate conflict, then might there be a third option? In this chapter I present analyses of aggression and anger in Congress as revealed in the sounds legislators utter in the course of their debate. To frame this properly I must venture briefly into some linguistic and psychological literatures.

As is the common experience of conversing with our fellow humans in daily life, what we say is not merely a series of words devoid of detail such as tone, volume, and pace. We are not computers. We do not send and receive information in discourse as a string of ones and zeroes. The speed with which we acquire and disseminate our words matters. The words "I hate you" or "I love you" are still merely these words to a computer, whether it takes 5 milliseconds or 5000 milliseconds to process them. Dissociation of tone from these phrases can in fact relate the opposite sentiment from the lexical content of these utterances (Mehrabian, 1968). Similarly, this information is transmitted and received in intensity scalings varying wildly from a 0 to 1 level. Through these cues and the context in which they are spoken—occasionally including a historical knowledge of the speaker and whether that person is prone to express him- or herself at a particular volume and pace—we receive not only the words but the spirit with which those words were spoken. Linguists and psychologists have enumerated some consistent speaking patterns over time. Charismatic speaking is associated with pitch fluctuations that can denote expressiveness (Hirschberg & Rosenberg, 2005). People speaking in monotone are generally not thought of as passionate in their speech. There's a reason that Ben Stein was the one writing speeches for Presidents Nixon and Ford and not the one delivering them.[4] People who are sad tend to speak more slowly (Nwe, Foo, & De Silva, 2003). Pauses in arguments between two people are associated with shifts in the emotional tone of the interaction (Cowie et al., 2000). Of interest are the prosodic indicators of anger and aggression. Psychologists and linguists readily admit that it can be hard to distinguish between fear and anger, especially across languages, and particularly when those languages seem especially harsh to nonnative speakers, such as German (Polzehl, Schmitt, & Metze, 2010). The difficulties in disentangling fear and anger may be due to the fact that the former can lead to the latter.

Both fear and anger are associated with increases in the speed and volume of speaking (Chuenwattanapranithi, Xu, Thipakorn, & Maneewongvatana, 2007; Siegman, Anderson, & Berger, 1990). However, the two can often be distinguished when taking into account vowel stress. Statements of fear involve consistently loud and fast utterances, while anger usually involves the use of vowel stress accompanying this elevated pacing and volume.

C-SPAN provides us with a fairly consistent linguistic universe to pull from. There are occasional outliers, such as Representative Adam Schiff (D-CA) delivering an emotional speech in Armenian on the House floor in support of a resolution commemorating victims of the Armenian Genocide (159 Cong. Rec. H2251). Such linguistic deviations are rare and tend to be limited to 1-minute, 5-minute, and Special Order speeches. However, even in cross-cultural analysis it is common for speakers to associate speaking extremes "with emotionally charged text, regardless of what system of intonation that language might have developed" (Wennerstrom, 2001, p. 62).

HYPOTHESES

Drawing from the literature and practical considerations, I look at speaking volume and pace within the debates at the level of individual legislators. If the contention that Congress has become a more hostile place in the past 20-plus years is in fact more than an overstatement by the media, I expect that over the time range of my sample there should be a similar increase in these prosodic indicators of anger and aggression. I further anticipate that debate conducted in the House would involve more positive anger indicators than in the Senate.

House members tend to represent less ideologically diverse constituencies than their Senate counterparts. Likewise there are more of them fighting in a restricted speaking time frame due to both the sheer number of them and the involvement of a Rules Committee.[5] I expect that a weaker majority party, as measured by higher ideological standard deviation within the majority party, should encourage speaking aggression in majority party speakers. However this may be balanced out by a decrease in minority party aggression due to more ideological overlap amongst legislators and more policy concessions by the majority. Electoral and institutional effects such as divided government should increase aggressiveness.[6]

At the speaker-specific level I expect the ideological extremity of the speaker to positively correlate with speaker volume and pace. Legislators who speak longer should show less aggressive tendencies. I expect that minority party members will speak more aggressively. Finally, I anticipate that older legislators, who have been around long enough to fully understand and experience the difference between sincere and strategic voting to potentially translate it into sincere and strategic speaking, will speak more moderately.

DESIGN AND METHODOLOGY

To select the speeches for my analysis, I first collected key votes for the 109th to 112th Congresses from the *CQ Press Congress Collection*. These votes are chosen by the *CQ* staff for their controversy and larger impact on Americans, among other factors. This resulted in 194 votes. Because of current gaps in the C-SPAN transcripts I had to drop 14 of these cases. This left me with 180 cases covering 159 distinct days of debate. Looking solely at the House cases I then located the first day preceding a key vote that the House engaged in debate on legislation under suspension of the rules. This provided me with data for 78 extra days in the House. These served as my control for noncontroversial debate. In total I ended up isolating 306 suspension debates over 75 distinct days.

I collected the transcripts from the each of these days' video pages from the C-SPAN Archives' online Video Library and extracted the names of the speakers as well as the time code of their speeches for segmenting the streams. I omitted instances where legislators spoke as the presiding officer. For the *CQ* key votes I only looked at the debate on the day of the vote between when the consideration began, up to the actual vote. If the key vote was on an amendment, I attempted to isolate the debate to only the amendment of interest.

Finding the cut points for suspension debate was fairly straightforward in scanning the *Congressional Record* for the phrase "I move to suspend the rules" and locating the in and out points for the days in my sample.

With these edit points I then used the software program ffmpeg to extract WAV files and ran them through server-side audio analyses. To get the volume measures I used the program SoX to get the root mean square (RMS) amplitude of a speech segment.[7] I then converted these amplitude outputs to their respective volumes (in decibels relative to the maximum volume processing capacity of the software—generally referred to as dBFS or decibel relative to full scale) for over 10,000 speeches. To get the pace of speech I used PRAAT, a standard linguistics analysis program, and an off-the-shelf script for estimating the syllables uttered per second. This script allows for a distinction between *speech rate* and *articulation rate* of the speaker. The important distinction here is that the speech rate estimates pace while including pauses in speech for the calculation. The articulation rate only counts syllables when it is clear that the speaker is actually speaking. For the purposes of this paper I relied on speech rate as a potentially more accurate measure of pace as a proxy for anger and aggression in the context of congressional discourse. Ignoring the gaps of silence in using the articulation rate could inflate the measurement of feigned aggression. With the speech rate metric, pauses for page turns and the speaker recollecting where he or she was during a speech would be included and temper the pacing measure of aggression.

Variables

With my response variables established, I constructed a series of binary explanatory variables, including the following:

- Speaker was a Republican
- Speaker was in the minority
- Speech was occurring in the House
- Republicans control the chamber
- Midterm election year
- Presidential election year
- Divided government (when the presidency and at least one of the chambers of Congress are controlled by different parties)

I included a time series variable of the year the debate occurred to account for any general upward trend in my indicators of anger. To measure conditional party activation interactions with aggression, I calculated the NOMINATE median distance between the majority and minority party in each chamber, as well as the standard deviation of the majority party. I also included the raw NOMINATE score for an individual speaker as well as his or her ideological extremity. I calculated this extremity as the absolute value of the distance between the speaker's NOMINATE score and the median score of his or her chamber.

FINDINGS

At the individual-speaker level of analysis I found statistically and substantively significant relationships between speaking trends and my explanatory variables. However, it is important to separate the more substantively significant variables from those that are merely statistically significant.

In line with expectations, the key votes model shown in Table 4.1 indicated that the louder debate in the House, the lower the ideological spread of the majority party, and across time. While increased ideological spread in the majority party leading to less intense speech was also anticipated, the signs on presidential and midterm years as well as divided government periods were not as expected. Examining the explanatory variables for relevant ranges of the data, we get a sense of some of these relationships. For example, there was a 23 dB increase in volume when the Republicans were in charge of a chamber. In this case the 23 dB difference in volume can be understood as a little over a 1300 percent greater speaking loudness under Republican majorities.[8]

Debate on key votes in the House was 22 percent louder than in the Senate. The volume increased 43 percent per year. From 2005 to 2012 this increase was 1100 percent. Speaking loudness was 21 percent lower in presidential years and 31 percent lower in midterm years. Primary effects, the competitiveness of these primaries, the need for the Congress to appear more hard right or left, and then the need to correct back to the middle almost certainly are at play whenever an election occurs. Leaving this to future research, we would also expect that moderating effects from the primary to the general election should be stronger in the Senate than in the House.

TABLE 4.1 *Legislator Speaking Volume in Key Votes Debate*

	Raw Model		By CQ Bill Subject	
Chamber Variable				
House	1.692 ***	(0.099)	1.60 ***	(0.096)
Republican Majority	22.67 ***	(1.38)	23.56 ***	(1.47)
Majority–Minority Ideological Distance	−113.3 ***	(9.2)	−101 ***	(9.49)
Majority Party Ideological Spread	−395 ***	(22)	−409 ***	(23.17)
Timing Variable				
Divided Government	−3.64 ***	(0.37)	−4.63 ***	(0.38)
Presidential Year	−2.01 ***	(0.20)	−1.9 ***	(0.21)
Midterm Year	−3.21 ***	(0.21)	−2.91 ***	(0.223)
Year	3.08 ***	(0.20)	2.98 ***	(0.205)
Speaker-Specific Variable				
Republican	0.526 **	(0.182)	0.447 *	(0.177)
Ideology	−0.483 **	(0.175)	−0.406 *	(0.17)
Ideological Extremity	−0.082	(0.164)	0.039	(0.156)
Minority Party Member	0.108	(0.099)	0.041	(0.096)
Male	−0.103	(0.073)	−0.103	(0.071)
Age	0	(0)	0	(0)
Length of Speech	−0.0005 ***	(0.0001)	−0.0005 ***	(0.0001)
CQ Bill Subject				
National Security	—		2.14 ***	(0.14)
Law and Justice	—		−0.45 *	(0.18)
Health	—		0.36 .	(0.20)
International	—		0.418 **	(0.135)
Business and Banking	—		0.699 *	(0.337)
Budget	—		0.864 **	(0.275)
Taxes	—		−0.503	(0.312)
Military	—		−2.57 ***	(0.298)
Constant	*−6066 ****	*(381)*	*−5869 ****	*(401)*
N	*6740*		*6740*	
R-Square	*0.4144*		*0.4499*	

NOTE: Standard errors for coefficients are shown in parentheses.
Signif. codes: 0 '***'; 0.001 '**'; 0.01 '*'; 0.05 '.'; 0.1 ' ' 1.

TABLE 4.2 *Legislator Speaking Volume in Suspension Debate*

Chamber Variable		
Republican Majority	-16.33***	(1.162)
Majority Party Ideological Spread	384.2***	(28.9)
Timing Variable		
Presidential Year	1.62***	(0.156)
Midterm Year	-0.656***	(0.083)
Year	-0.778***	(0.088)
Speaker-Specific Variable		
Republican	-0.391	(0.253)
Ideology	0.441.	(0.237)
Ideological Extremity	-0.709**	(0.246)
Minority Party Member	0.424**	(0.158)
Male	-0.315***	(0.087)
Age	0.00002	(0.00001)
Length of Speech	0.00017	(0.00031)
Constant	*1472* ***	*(172.7)*
N		*3326*
R-Square		*0.274*

NOTE: Standard errors for coefficients are shown in parentheses.
Signif. codes: 0 ' ***'; 0.001 '**'; 0.01 '*'; 0.05 '.'; 0.1 ' ' 1.

Whereas Republicans tended to be 6 percent louder than their Democratic counterparts, more conservative legislators were quieter. As anticipated, longer speeches were delivered in more dulcet tones. A 10-minute difference in speech length translated to a 3 percent drop in loudness. An hour difference meant an 18 percent quieter delivery.

Looking solely at the suspension votes in the House, I had to modify my model slightly (Table 4.2). With my suspension cases there was a strong correlation between the year of debate and the ideological distance between the two major parties not seen in the key votes. There was also a similar correlation between divided government and the ideological spread of the majority party. Due to the correlation between these two explanatory variables, I had to remove the divided government and NOMINATE distance variables. In the House, where suspension debate occurs, the sign of many variables switched.

An increase in majority party ideological spread relates to an increase in loudness. Each 0.01 increase in standard deviation translated to a 56 percent increase in volume. In later years there was a slight downward trend in speaking volume for suspension debate, while speaker volume tended to be driven by the ideological center rather than the extremes. Of note is a discrepancy between the two parties when they were in the minority. Democrats were less expressive in their speech compared to the minority Republicans. Minority Republicans spoke 555 percent louder than the Democrats when they were in the minority. An intriguing observation is that during suspension debate, female legislators were 6 percent louder than their male counterparts. This effect was fairly minimal compared to other controls.

In Table 4.3 I translated the key votes model for dBFs to account for the speech rate of a legislator. While the response variable is measured in syllables per second, this measure is itself again not intuitively understandable. As such I will express the changes in speaking pace in percentages of increase or decrease. Speaking in the House was roughly 7 percent faster than in the Senate. To prevent confusion of loudness versus pace findings, it is important to understand that a 7 percent increase in speaking pace is much more readily apparent to a listener than a 7 percent increase in loudness.

The speaking pace was some 5 percent faster during presidential election years. While more conservative legislators spoke at a more laconic pace, ideologically extreme members (both left and right) spoke at an increased pace. As with loudness, we see a similar legislator effect where women spoke 3 percent faster than men.

As shown in Table 4.4, Republican majorities led to 28 percent faster speaking pace during suspension debate. In line with expectations, the more ideologically spread out the majority party was, the more relaxed the speaking pace was. With each year that passed there was a 2 percent bump in speaking pace. From 2005 to 2012 this translated to a 13 percent increase in pace. While Republicans spoke more slowly, more conservative legislators did not. Being older and having more time to speak both resulted in more relaxed speaking. Speech length made a difference, with a 10-minute increase in speech length resulting in an 8 percent reduction in pace, while an hour difference meant a 49 percent reduction in pace. As with some of the other models, the gender of the legislator had some effect. Males spoke 5 percent more slowly than their female counterparts.

TABLE 4.3 *Legislator Speaking Pace in Key Votes Debate*

	Raw Model		By CQ Bill Subject	
Chamber Variable				
House	0.235 ***	(0.020)	0.23 ***	(0.02)
Republican Majority	−0.217	(0.286)	−0.091	(0.313)
Majority–Minority Ideological Distance	2.896	(1.91)	2.15	(2.03)
Majority Party Ideological Spread	5	(4.5)	2.94	(4.95)
Timing Variable				
Divided Government	−0.096	(0.077)	−0.113	(0.082)
Presidential Year	0.164 ***	(0.041)	0.147 ***	(0.045)
Midterm Year	0.008	(0.044)	−0.011	(0.048)
Year	−0.073 .	(0.041)	−0.055	(0.0439)
Speaker-Specific Variable				
Republican	0.174 ***	(0.038)	0.185 ***	(0.038)
Ideology	−0.138 ***	(0.036)	−0.148 ***	(0.037)
Ideological Extremity	0.186 ***	(0.034)	0.183 ***	(0.034)
Minority Party Member	−0.094 ***	(0.021)	−0.093 ***	(0.021)
Male	−0.12 ***	(0.02)	−0.121 ***	(0.015)
Age	−0.000024 ***	(0.000002)	−0.000024 ***	(0.000002)
Length of Speech	−0.00031 ***	(0.00002)	−0.0003 ***	(0.00002)
CQ Bill Subject				
National Security	—		0.009	(0.03)
Law and Justice	—		−0.108 **	(0.039)
Health	—		0.0079	(0.044)
International	—		0.056 .	(0.029)
Business and Banking	—		0.223 **	(0.072)
Budget	—		0.023	(0.059)
Taxes	—		−0.07	(0.07)
Military	—		0.065	(0.064)
Constant	146.9 .	(78.97)	112.2	(85.54)
N	6740		6740	
R-Square	0.2077		0.212	

NOTE: Standard errors for coefficients are shown in parentheses.
Signif. codes: 0 '***'; 0.001 '**'; 0.01 '*'; 0.05 '.'; 0.1 ' ' 1.

TABLE 4.4 *Legislator Speaking Pace in Suspension Debate*

Chamber Variable		
Republican Majority	0.95 ***	(0.22)
Majority Party Ideological Spread	−22.3 ***	(5.6)
Timing Variable		
Presidential Year	0.023	(0.0299)
Midterm Year	0.0058	(0.016)
Year	0.063 ***	(0.017)
Speaker-Specific Variable		
Republican	−0.108 *	(0.049)
Ideology	0.173 ***	(0.045)
Ideological Extremity	−0.089 .	(0.047)
Minority Party Member	0.048	(0.03)
Male	−0.192 ***	(0.017)
Age	−0.00003 ***	(0.000002)
Length of Speech	−0.0005 ***	(0.00006)
Constant	*−118****	*(33.2)*
N		*3326*
R-Square		*0.162*

NOTE: Standard errors for coefficients are shown in parentheses.
Signif. codes: 0 '***'; 0.001 '**'; 0.01 '*'; 0.05 '.'; 0.1 ' ' 1.

REVIEW AND DISCUSSION

During this study I tested for variation in basic prosodic elements of speech indicative of anger and aggression in congressional speeches. In particular I looked at the loudness and pace with which legislators spoke. The psychology and linguistics literatures suggest that certain emotions such as anger are heavily associated with these factors. Taking into account the expectation that certain historically divisive social issues may be more likely to elicit anger in their discussion, in society at large and in Congress in particular, I assembled a sample of debate drawn from *CQ* key votes for the 109th through the 112th Congresses to reflect a range of topics. As a contrast I also included debate on less controversial legislation considered under suspension of the rules in the

House. Relying on an extensive data set of video from the C-SPAN Archives, I isolated these key vote and suspension debate speeches and ran the resultant segments through server-side audio analysis programs. After extracting the loudness of speech (in decibels) and speaking pace (in syllables per second) for individual speeches of legislators, I looked at these potential indicators of anger at the key votes and suspension subsets of my data.

I found multiple statistical and substantively strong correlates for speaking volume and pace across all levels of analysis. Among the results of interest across my models was a trend of legislators speaking louder and faster as time progressed. Increased majority party ideological spreads were related to decreases in indicators of aggression. When I looked at both key vote and suspension debates together for the House, indicators of potential aggression were higher for key votes.

I have not yet coded for length of tenure in Congress or a specific chamber of Congress, but I suspect that the influx of relatively rigid and uncompromising Tea Party Republicans who are concerned with reducing government intrusion in the day-to-day lives of citizens may be contributing to louder and possibly angrier speaking among Republicans. The apparent increase of ideological spread contributing to increases in speaker loudness during suspension debate may be evidence of such a situation. The libertarian bent of these Tea Partiers further suggests that they would be more likely to speak aggressively about national security policies regarding surveillance, the rise of a national health care system, and issues of international involvement.

As with any findings there are caveats that can and should be expressed. While the psychology and linguistics literature on talking loud and fast suggests that it could indicate either fear or anger, I suspect a closer review of vowel emphasis and tone variation, which I did not address in this study, will reinforce that what I am observing is in fact evidence of anger. Loudness and pace of speech are not the only possible prosodic indicators available to us when measuring fluctuations in anger or aggression among legislators. The literature on speaking suggests, among other things, that including speaker pitch would aid in my analysis.[9]

Looking beyond these technical matters, while I suspect I am capturing aggression in legislative speech, there are certain nuances that can and will be addressed. Aggression usually has a target. It can be an extension of generalized fear and frustration. But displaying aggression in speaking is not necessarily the same as displaying aggression *toward* a particular group or individual. It could involve aggression *about* general processes, such as holds in the Senate. This will likely involve complementing prosodic analysis with lexical analysis. The wrinkle to this is that, as is evident to anyone who compares the text of the *Congressional Record* to the video in the C-SPAN Archives, the *Record* is not a literal transcription of the proceedings on The Hill.

In my project I looked at speech within the context of debate. While this may not be as much of an issue in the Senate, the role of a Rules Committee in the House limits the range of legislators who can contribute to debate. Outside of debate there is a panoply of interesting cases that can exist in more open speaking during 1-minute, 5-minute, and Special Order speeches. Such speeches are going to display more marked indicators of aggression than those in the context of a proper legislative debate, such as the one I examined here. In my analysis, factors like the length of a speech demonstrably tempered such expressions of aggression. There is some indication in research on morning hour 1-minute speeches in the House that they can have spillover effects into the tone of debate throughout the rest of the day. A Congressional Research Service (CRS) report mentions attempts by legislators to move 1-minute speeches to later in the day after the completion of all legislative business. This was out of a concern by some that "partisan and poisonous 1-minute speeches unfavorably set the tone for our legislative business" (Schneider, 2015, p. 5). If there are in fact priming effects of negative aggressive speaking affecting legislating throughout the day, what might they be? The most immediate outcome that comes to mind is that it could contribute to gridlock. If this is the case there might be a certain logic in minority party leaders' not only encouraging but strategically deploying speakers in the use of 1-minutes.

Finally, there is another practical reality of examining legislators and their speaking patterns. As individual humans, we are all naturally calibrated by our own experiences, backgrounds, and occasionally physical realities such as illness and health. Such variations can inform and influence the way that we speak; both in our words and in the literal sounds which escape our heads when we form these words. One person's natural speaking pace and loudness can be drastically different from another's. Former Senator Joe Lieberman's expression of a range of emotions is not going to be the same as that of a Paul Ryan (R-WI). To an uninformed observer, Joe Lieberman's version of frothy-mouthed rage may appear indistinguishable from a naturally louder and faster speaking Paul Ryan's version of casually telling a person the time of day. It may be wise to develop legislator-specific baselines of speaking. As part of my larger research agenda, and with the aid of the transcripts for the C-SPAN Archives, I am developing these controls. I am further employing coders and machine learning workflows to aid in developing consistent cut points for categorizing emotional states beyond anger and aggression. With these improvements to the process of analyzing prosodic cues, we can determine not only whether legislators are expressing a specific emotional state, but also whether it is out of line with their regular state of affairs. In doing so we can more effectively pick up on not only expressions such as anger, but also joy, sarcasm, and even uncertainty as revealed by micro-fluctuations that would be invisible in the broader context of the Congress and speakers more generally.

In the course of this piece I have provided complementary analyses to the vote-scoring and text-focused measures of polarization in Congress. I've found that the presence of indicators of anger and aggression are not merely random. They are related in consistent ways with the mechanics of a chamber, the level of controversy associated with the debate topic, and party strength. They are also immune to the assorted biases of relying on either direct statements of aggression from the *Record* or secondhand reports of incivility in the media. Finally, they tie closely to a broader sense of polarization as the waning of comity between political actors. Relying on the perhaps unconscious vocal reflexes of speakers in the ways they deliver their speeches taps into polarization and intransigence in policy formation in a way that the average voter can understand. With this in mind, future research can begin to address other causes of such prosodic cues. How much can a majority party rein in debate on prized legislation before there is not only incivility from across the aisle but within the majority party's own ranks? How can such in-party incivility further harm the reputation of the majority and alter their electoral prospects? The news value of such infighting is high and can present the minority party with opportunities to claim that the majority is untrustworthy, as it can't even be counted on to keep its own house in order (Groeling, 2010, pp. 47–58). What role can issues of constituencies and the redrawing of districts have on the shifting of vocal patterns for legislators? Can a more historically aggressive speaker in the House suddenly modulating her speech signal her intention to cross chambers to a more diverse audience of voters? When party control changes occur, might the tendency of a legislator to speak in an alienating manner serve in the future majority party's decisions on committee chair placements?

On the other side of things, such prosodic measures of emotional states can be helpful in accounting for policy outcomes, both directly and downstream. Are legislators who speak angrily more or less likely to be legislatively successful compared to those taking a more moderated approach? Are those who will speak with passion and make at least a good show of effort in fighting the good fight more or less likely to have their proposed amendments cleared for debate by the Rules Committee? At the electoral stage of the game, might regional speaking proclivities work for or against candidates as they seek higher and higher office? While a more strident tone may work well for a northeastern legislator in a fairly homogenous district, does it translate effectively once he seeks the Executive Office at the State level? How well would his penchant for vociferous speaking play out in front of a presidential caucus audience in Iowa or a South Carolina primary? In looking at the expressiveness of the speech of political actors, we should be able to take into account the role of assorted revealed and projected emotional states in the way policy is formed, as well as who is chosen to be the face, and the voice, of policy.

NOTES

1. See "Jimmy Carter Says US More Polarized Than During Civil War (1861–64 Secession)" at http://www.youtube.com/watch?v=ugZxfGsYAkY. See James Q. Wilson, "How Divided Are We?" at http://www.commentarymagazine.com/article/how-divided-are-we/. See "Jerry Brown: California, Country Facing 'Regime Crisis' Similar to the Civil War" at http://losangeles.cbslocal.com/2011/04/10/jerry-brown-gop-stalling-budget-reform/. For an explanation of DW-NOMINATE scores and polarization, consult http://www.slate.com/articles/life/do_the_math/2001/12/growing_apart.html.

2. *CQ* key votes have historically been used as a measure of how important a vote is based on criteria such as controversy, shifts in presidential or political power, and the general importance of the vote for citizens at large.

3. Legislation considered under suspension of the rules is fairly noncontroversial. Such items require a two-thirds majority to succeed, cannot be amended, and are only allotted 40 minutes of debate time. Suspension legislation often addresses issues such as naming post offices.

4. I am referring to the caricature of Ben Stein that he has portrayed, for example, in the movie *Ferris Bueller's Day Off,* not necessarily Ben Stein speaking as himself.

5. The House Rules Committee can limit the time of debate as well as the number and type of amendments available for consideration of a bill on the House floor in ways not present on the Senate floor.

6. Electoral effects can vary. With everyone up for reelection every two years in the House, such effects should be more pronounced for that chamber. Higher competitiveness in the primaries and general elections should further increase speaking aggression.

7. I used RMS amplitude, as the mean amplitude could be potentially negative. Since converting amplitudes to decibels involves a logarithmic calculation, such negative raw amplitudes were not helpful.

8. Discussion of raw decibels can be somewhat confusing. So to facilitate the understanding of my findings, I converted the reported dB differences into relative percentage volume differences. This is done with a simple calculation of:

$$Volume\ Percent\ Change = \left(100 * 10\left(\tfrac{decibel\ change}{20}\right)\right) - 100$$

9. See, for example, the work of Bryce Dietrich (2014) in "You Wouldn't Like Me When I Am Angry: Anger, Audio, and Legislative Effectiveness in the 111th and 112th U.S. House of Representatives."

REFERENCES

158 Cong. Rec. H6263 (daily ed. Sep. 21, 2012) (statement of Rep. Frank).

159 Cong. Rec. H2251 (daily ed. Apr. 24, 2013) (statement of Rep. Schiff).

Aldrich, J., & Rohde, D. (2000). The Republican revolution and the House Appropriations Committee. *Journal of Politics, 62*(1), 1–33.

Cain, B., Ferejohn, J., & Fiorina, M. (1987). *The personal vote: Constituency service and electoral independence.* Cambridge, MA: Harvard University Press.

Chuenwattanapranithi, S., Xu, Y., Thipakorn, B., & Maneewongvatana, S. (2007). The roles of pitch contour in differentiating anger and joy in speech. *International Journal of Signal Processing, 3,* 129–134.

Cowie, R., Douglas-Cowie, E., Savvidou, S., McMahon, E., Sawey, M., & Schröder, M. (2000). Feeltrace: An instrument for recording perceived emotion in real time. In *Proceedings of the ISCA Workshop on Speech and Emotion: A conceptual framework for research* (pp. 9–24). Winona, MN: International Society for Computers and Their Applications.

Dietrich, B. (2014, April). *You wouldn't like me when I am angry: Anger, audio, and legislative effectiveness in the 111th and 112th U.S. House of Representatives.* Paper presented at the Annual Meeting of the Midwest Political Science Association, Chicago, IL.

Forgette, R., & Morris, J. (2006). High-conflict television news and public opinion. *Political Research Quarterly, 59*(3), 447–456.

Groeling, T. (2010). *When politicians attack: Party cohesion in the media.* Cambridge: Cambridge University Press.

Hibbing, J., & Theiss-Morse, E. (1995). *Congress as public enemy: Public attitudes toward American political institutions.* Cambridge: Cambridge University Press.

Hirschberg, J., & Rosenberg, A. (2005). Acoustic/prosodic and lexical correlates of charismatic speech. In *Proceedings of Interspeech—Eurospeech, 9th European Conference on Speech Communication and Technology* (pp. 513–516). Retrieved from http://www1.cs.columbia.edu/~amaxwell/pubs/charisma-euro05-final.pdf

Jamieson, K. (2011, September 28). *Civility in Congress (1935–2011) as reflected in the taking down process* (Annenberg Public Policy Center Report No. 2011-1). Retrieved from http://www.annenbergpublicpolicycenter.org/Downloads /Civility/Civility_9-27-2011_Final.pdf

Jamieson, K., & Falk, E. (1999, March). *Civility in the House of Representatives: The 105th Congress* (Annenberg Public Policy Center Report Series, No. 26). Retrieved from http://cdn.annenbergpublicpolicycenter.org/wp-content /uploads/REP261.pdf

Laver, M., Benoit, K., & Garry, J. (2003). Extracting policy positions from political texts using words as data. *American Political Science Review, 97*(2), 311–331.

Maltzman, F., & Sigelman, L. (1996). The politics of talk: Unconstrained floor time in the U.S. House of Representatives. *Journal of Politics, 58*(3), 819–830.

Mehrabian, A. (1968). Communication without words. *Psychology Today, 2*(9), 52–55.

Morris, J. (2001). Reexamining the politics of talk: Partisan rhetoric in the 104th House. *Legislative Studies Quarterly, 26,* 101–121.

Nwe, T. L., Foo, S. W., & De Silva, L. C. (2003). Speech emotion recognition using hidden Markov models. *Speech Communication, 41*(4), 603–623. http://dx.doi .org/10.1016/S0167-6393(03)00099-2

Polzehl, T., Schmitt, A., & Metze, F. (2010). *Approaching multilingual emotion recognition from speech—On language dependency of acoustic/prosodic features for anger detection.* Retrieved from http://speechprosody2010.illinois.edu /papers/100442.pdf

Schneider, J. (2015, March 16). *One-minute speeches: Current House practices* (CRS Report No. RL30135). Retrieved from Congressional Research Service website: https://www.fas.org/sgp/crs/misc/RL30135.pdf

Schraufnagel, S. (2005). Testing the implications of incivility in the United States Congress, 1977–2000: The case of judicial confirmation delay. *Journal of Legislative Studies, 11,* 216–234.

Sellers, P. (2010). *Cycles of spin: Strategic communication in the U.S. Congress.* Cambridge: Cambridge University Press.

Siegman, A., Anderson, R., & Berger, T. (1990). The angry voice: Its effects on the experience of anger and cardiovascular reactivity. *Psychosomatic Medicine, 52,* 631–643.

Slapin, J., & Proksch, S. (2008). A scaling model for estimating time-series party positions from texts. *American Journal of Political Science, 52*(3), 705–722.

Wennerstrom, A. (2001). *The music of everyday speech: Prosody and discourse analysis.* Oxford: Oxford University Press.

APPENDIX
Adjusting the Levels

Before proceeding with building and running my assorted models, I had to correct for an intervening variable I discovered in C-SPAN video related to the estimated loudness of speech. This is more readily observed by regressing the estimated decibels of a speech on the year it occurred.

As we can see in Table 4.A.1 below, this simple model yields a rather large R^2 value of 0.7973. Upon a closer inspection it became clear that the innate volume of C-SPAN video had been slowly ratcheted up over time. While some of this could be the microphones themselves, it was similarly apparent that it was the general feed volume that had been incremented up for my 2005–2012 time frame. A discount factor to correct the estimated decibel levels was necessary.

To calibrate down the decibel estimates I needed to rely on what I refer to as anchor speakers. These would be speakers who would have no motive to fluctuate the volume of their speech and would deliver their words in as consistent a manner as possible whenever they speak.[1] Even more ideally, they would essentially be reciting a text that is so rote to them that its delivery would be on par with an unconscious reflex. At first glance, sampling the speaking patterns of the reading clerks in each chamber would have been a fairly ideal situation. However, locating and isolating them proved too

TABLE 4.A.1 *Legislator Speaking Volume by Year*

Timing Variable	
Year	2.5^{***} (0.012)
Constant	-5051^{***} (25.09)
N	10178
R-Square	0.7973

NOTE: Standard errors for coefficients are shown in parentheses.
Signif. codes: 0 '***'; 0.001 '**'; 0.01 '*'; 0.05 '.'; 0.1 ' ' 1.

cumbersome. Instead I relied on the hosts of C-SPAN's *Washington Journal* program. More specifically I focused on open call-in segments and the hosts' recitations of the phone numbers for audience members to call into the show. I took a 5 percent sample of the days on which an open call-in segment was mentioned in a query of the C-SPAN Video Library website. I further isolated the first 10 minutes of an open call-in session. With the aid of the data on the Web pages for these segments, I was able to identify 12 distinct hosts. In the course of coding the in and out points I also made note of whether there was any music playing when the phone numbers were being displayed and recited. Running these phrases through the prior decibel estimation process, I was able to capture 177 data points.

With the aid of the names and years of the speakers, I had to map volumes down relative to one speaker in a specific year. Prior to deciding on my baseline year-speaker for comparison, I first estimated how much of a discount would be necessary to account for the presence of music. This was calculated as the median difference in my sample of speakers compared to themselves in a given year when I had segments with and without music. For example, if I had a clip of a host in 2005 where she was speaking over music and one where she wasn't, I accounted for this difference and calculated a similar difference for another host in 2007. Taking the median of these differences resulted in a musical discount factor of 0.193 dBFS. I eventually settled on one host in 2005 as my baseline of comparison and performed a similar mapping of relative volumes of speakers to this host by year, taking account of each speaker's median difference in volume and applying that discount as necessary.[2] After completing these mappings I took the median difference between other speakers and the C-SPAN host by year and compared it to the median of the selected host in 2005. While it was not perfectly linear, I was nonetheless able to determine that there was a distinct upward trend in volume and applied these dBFS discounts at the yearly level.[3]

Reviewing the regression of these adjusted decibel levels by year shown in Table 4.A.2 (p. 102), we see that the intervening volume bumps in the C-SPAN footage appear to have been accounted for as the R^2 was been reduced to 0.1034.[4]

TABLE 4.A.2 *Adjusted Legislator Speaking Volume by Year*

Timing Variable	
Year	0.392^{***} (0.0114)
Constant	-823.18^{***} (22.95)
N	10178
R-Square	0.1034

NOTE: Standard errors for coefficients are shown in parentheses.
Signif. codes: 0 '***'; 0.001 '**'; 0.01 '*'; 0.05 '.'; 0.1 ' ' 1.

Notes

1. As a matter of practicality, these anchor speakers should (and generally do) speak their words with a consistent pace and pitch as well.

2. The presence of a speaker throughout the whole of the time frame was unnecessary. As long as there is some overlap for speakers across this span it is possible to reliably map the volume levels down relative to a specific speaker in a specific year. As a practical matter, my 2005 anchor speaker was present in each year of the sample.

3. Using 2005 as the base of comparison the dBFS discount factors were as follows: 2006, −2.3922; 2007, −2.02865; 2008, −1.3834; 2009, −7.60687; 2010, −11.241; 2011, −13.073; 2012, −11.7719.

4. There was no need to rerun the PRAAT pacing script with these adjusted levels in place. The script is agnostic as to the base range of loudness for a sound clip. It counts syllables and gaps in sound based on fluctuations in decibel levels. To PRAAT, a 10 dB spike is a 10 dB spike, whether it occurred in a move from −30 dBFS to −20 dBFS or in a shift from −50 dBFS to −40 dBFS. This was confirmed as more than a mere programmatic assumption. Speech segments were sampled and their decibel levels were bumped and lowered 10 dBFS in each direction relative to their levels before the anchor speaker mapping of decibels. Each time the resultant speech rate and articulation rate estimates remained unchanged.

CHAPTER 5

C-SPAN, MOOCS, AND THE POST-DIGITAL AGE

David A. Caputo

I still remember when I was department chair and Robert Browning called and asked me to join him and Brian Lamb in a meeting to discuss the concept of the C-SPAN Archives. I have heard a lot of great ideas in my time, but few surpass what Brian wanted us to do and what Robert thought could be done. Now it is up to all of us who conduct research in public policy, issue analysis, communication theory, and the countless other disciplines that use the Archives for their research to use that research to better inform the public.

From the beginning I thought that C-SPAN would be a great success and that it would increase our understanding of American democracy. This is brought home to me every time I watch a debate, committee hearing, call-in session, or one of the many interviews. C-SPAN informs, provides relevant information, and most importantly educates.

Let me provide an example. I was teaching a course titled Congressional Elections 2014. Part of our work included watching the Senate candidate debates in the various campaigns. We watched portions of debates in Colorado, New Hampshire, and North Carolina, and at one point a student interested in politics as a career noted that each Republican candidate cited the same business organization to point out that each Democratic incumbent had a very poor record on votes to help small businesses. The student did some quick research and realized that the organization had been put together in late summer and had carefully selected its votes so as to cast the incumbents, all Democrats, as opposed to small businesses. This was a "eureka" moment for my student when she realized that there was such a thing as a national playbook and that it could be very partisan. This is just one of many teaching moments C-SPAN has provided me over the years.

C-SPAN is an elixir that energizes the spirit and recharges the mind. In short, American democracy and its leaders and citizens are better and more resolute because C-SPAN is there recording these leaders' decisions and the decision-making processes. Perhaps another anecdote will prove my point.

I always enjoy telling the story about being in a Washington taxicab and the driver, intently listening to coverage on the C-SPAN radio network, asking me three or four times what address I wanted. When he finally listened to me and not the radio and I gave him the C-SPAN address, he almost stopped the cab as he asked me whether I was going to C-SPAN then told me that, if so, I needed to tell them what a great job they were doing. So on behalf of the taxicab driver and the numerous others who have shared their opinions with me, thank you, C-SPAN.

CHALLENGES C-SPAN FACES

While C-SPAN and the Archives have worked tirelessly to provide outstanding service and to develop a unique brand, their greatest challenges are ahead. In fact, if these challenges are not met, C-SPAN and the Archives eventually may not be the beacons they are today. I want to discuss several of these challenges.

First, C-SPAN, and indeed the entire telecommunication industry, faces new and interesting challenges. One such challenge is determining the best way to deliver the product—for example, through Internet streaming, as video on demand, or in the more traditional cable and satellite format. Another is identifying potential challengers (e.g., social media) that could offer the same service in a different format and thus threaten C-SPAN. The same is true for the Archives. To anticipate and meet these possible challenges, C-SPAN and the Archives must continue to adapt to change, as well as continue to be true to their core mission.

In his comments included in the 2014 book about the first C-SPAN Archives research conference, *The C-SPAN Archives: An Interdisciplinary Resource for Discovery, Learning, and Engagement,* Brian Lamb recognizes this problem with his comment that "we [C-SPAN] can't have our heads in the sand about the future" (Lamb, 2014, p. 26).

Second, C-SPAN needs to continue to be innovative while at the same time being the video diary of Congress as well as expanding its coverage. Brian Lamb (2014) summarizes how much effort has been directed toward getting the Supreme Court to permit C-SPAN to record the approximately 75 hours of oral arguments the Court hears per term. He reports no progress here, and I hope at some point the justices realize that the American public is entitled to an unfiltered view of how that Court functions. This is an example of where C-SPAN must continue to press for change.

The third area of concern has to do with the various models of presenting information. We all know of the decrease in viewership of the nightly news of the major broadcast and cable news networks. Today's anchors do not have the impact of their predecessors, and the news is often quite different. I often scratch my head in wonder when any of the national broadcast news programs opens its evening news with a story about the polar vortex or some other weather event that has limited impact on the general public—in essence a weather forecast! Is this the hard news we need in order to understand what is happening in an increasingly complex and interconnected world?

One of the major implications in the loss of viewership is that network news departments have lost revenue, which means fewer reporters and foreign offices and limits on the ability to get network reporters into the field. C-SPAN has to ensure that it has the resources it needs to provide the coverage it does and that this coverage can be expanded when new opportunities arise.

Fourth, C-SPAN has to adapt, but it also needs to do so in a cautious way. What may seem as a game-changing innovation may not turn out to be and

C-SPAN would be well served to be slightly behind the curve than attempting to always being on the cutting edge. Perhaps a little perspective from my experience with a reputed cutting edge innovation would be helpful here.

THE EXPECTATIONS OF MOOCS

For the past three years I have been doing research attempting to better understand a new pedagogical model that many have claimed will make brick and mortar colleges and universities nearly obsolete. Let me explain.

Between 2006 and 2012, MOOCs (Friedman, 2013) burst onto the higher education scene. The Massive Open Online Course, according to its advocates (Kolowich, 2013a) and some early supporters in the mass media, would do these things:

1.   provide quality instruction by the intellectual and academic leaders in a particular field (initially, engineering and science);
2.   deliver this instruction to large numbers of students via the Internet;
3.   accomplish both 1 and 2 with low unit costs; and
4.   in doing so, would broaden the base of higher education and improve educational levels globally.

During this period, a few MOOCs (mainly covering artificial intelligence and other engineering topics) began with enrollments of 20,000 plus. Many argued that degrees would cost tens of thousands of dollars less because MOOCs would lower instructional costs. It was often argued that only the elite undergraduate residential colleges and universities would be able to survive as knowledge became readily available and at a much lower cost or even no cost (Meisenhelder, 2013). Colleges and universities were told to adapt or perish. Boards and presidents were excited because MOOCs presented the best of two worlds: lower unit costs and a possible geometrical expansion of knowledge.

When I reviewed the 200-plus scholarly and large summary articles on MOOCs, I found that most talk about their promise and their far-reaching implications, and few talk about whether MOOCs will actually work or what their potential shortcomings might be. Even MIT and Harvard and the newly formed companies (Coursera is a good example) that are developing MOOCs have stressed only the potential, and with little empirical evidence to support their claims (Caputo, 2014).

THE REALITY OF MOOCS

By 2012 the reality of what MOOCs could and could not accomplish had begun to cloud their future (Caputo, 2014). These were the actual and perceived major shortcomings:

1. It was discovered that for many of the MOOCs in the sciences and engineering, the audience was largely those with a degree who were interested in learning more and updating their knowledge base.

2. Many MOOCs had completion rates of less than 2 percent, and more than half of the students often dropped out of the MOOC by the second or third lecture.

3. Even the successful MOOCs, often defined as having a greater than 3 to 4 percent completion rate, could not show the value added for the student. Learning outcome measurements were seldom used during this period and so it was difficult to know if the MOOC was achieving the same result as the more traditional pedagogical approaches.

4. Well-executed MOOCs also generated significant costs to the institutions, which were not being offset by revenue in the form of tuition or fees. Thus instructional unit costs increased and MOOCs lost some or all of their competitive financial advantage.

5. Not surprisingly, faculty began to oppose the development of MOOCs, seeing them as a threat to the traditional classroom and the values (e.g., interaction, face-to-face conversation, debate) that the traditional classroom is said to impart (Kolowich, 2013b). Heated discussions concerning MOOCs took place at Harvard, San Jose State, and other higher education institutions as faculty questioned if resources should be allocated to MOOCs.

6. Education accrediting agencies had a difficult time evaluating the MOOCs, and in some cases MOOC providers decided to go with certificates or other programs as a way to avoid the delays and often negative decisions reached by accrediting agencies. This remains a

major impediment to the growth of MOOCs and if resolved could help to foster a renaissance for MOOCs.

I won't bore you with all that has happened as MOOCs went from the revolutionizing idea that was going to change higher education forever to an idea where there is now little media attention and claims have yet to be proven (Marks, 2012). Even the for-profit companies, such as Coursera, have lowered their expectations, and other MOOC providers such as edX continue their work but in a more research-driven way and with a financing model that charges for some courses and does not charge for others.

MY EXPERIENCE WITH MOOCS

For the past two semesters I have developed and taught a MOOC on the 2014 congressional elections, and I am in the process of developing a MOOC for the 2016 presidential elections (Caputo, 2014). The original research was funded by the Verizon Foundation through a grant to Pace University's Thinkfinity project.[1]

My experience with developing and teaching a MOOC leads me to conclude the following:

1. MOOCs are difficult to plan and deliver for a variety of reasons. One is that you are dependent on others for the actual production of the MOOC, and this can cause a variety of problems.
2. There are many hidden costs associated with MOOCs.
3. Developing learning outcomes and then testing to see if the outcomes are reached involves considerable effort and care.
4. Devising how you are going to grant credit and deciding what to charge, if anything, for the MOOC are often complicated, and we know educational institutions often have difficulty with complexity.

I was able to use C-SPAN material in my MOOC in a variety of ways, from interviews with Brian Lamb and Robert Browning to the coverage of the Florida 13th Congressional District race in the spring of 2014, which was in many ways a harbinger of the fall election to the various candidate debates held around the country. The ability to use the C-SPAN video material enhanced the MOOC.

THE FUTURE OF MOOCS

Based on my research and experience to date, I think MOOCs will have an increasing role to play in the delivery of knowledge, but they will not be the "killer application" that changes higher education as we know it. Perhaps the following quote best summarizes this killer application thinking:

> MOOCs started in 2008; and, as often happens with disruptive technologies they have so far failed to live up to their promise. … MOOCs will disrupt universities in different ways. … Were the market for higher education to perform in [the] future as that for newspapers has done over the past decade or two, universities' revenues would fall by more than half, employment in the industry would drop by nearly 30 percent and more than 700 institutions would shut their doors. The rest would need to reinvent themselves to survive. (A Cost Crisis, 2014)

After attempting to convince you that MOOCs are not going to dominate higher education, I now want to convince you that there is a potentially major role for a different type of MOOC. This is the advocacy MOOC. I will be spending the next year to 18 months developing one in the energy area and then turning my presidential elections course into an advocacy MOOC.

An advocacy MOOC provides basic information on a specific issue or issues and then attempts to motivate students and other citizens to get involved in influencing the decisions by various political and social agencies. Advocacy MOOCs can be used by many different organizations and I think offer a potential way to increase participation in democracies.

This is done by educating and then mobilizing and acting for a desired outcome. An advocacy MOOC does not define the desired outcome—it instead provides an overview and a strategy for the individual interested in influencing public policy and public policymakers. In this regard it should be informative and instructive, but the instructor should be nonpartisan.

Advocacy MOOCs also need to provide specific information on candidate and party issue positions. Here the Archives and ongoing C-SPAN coverage will often provide the needed material. A student can follow candidates or parties as they develop their positions on various issues and know when key variations were developed or a position actually changes.

What the MOOC revolution has taught us is that new technology does not always immediately overwhelm other technology, especially in areas such as higher education where tradition and routine often make change difficult or slow to happen.

I think the lessons of the MOOC experience for C-SPAN and the Archives are clear: explore, keep abreast of developments, but remember your core business and adapt to protect and strengthen that core. To use a business analogy, be sure you have a wide and deep moat between what you do and what others do.

REFLECTING ON C-SPAN AND DEMOCRACY

I want to close this chapter by going back to an earlier point. C-SPAN and the Archives play an important role in our understanding of policy and policy decision making. In his insightful keynote address at the first Archives research conference, Professor Roderick Hart (2014) indicated that he was concerned about the impact of the Internet on democracy because the Internet may be causing younger Americans to abandon their activism. He argued that democracy requires face-to-face interaction and that without it accountability is lessened and incivility is likely to increase.

Professor Hart raises an important set of points; much like Robert Putnam (2000) did over a decade ago with his book, *Bowling Alone: The Collapse and Revival of American Community*.[2] Putnam's analysis raised concerns about the decline of civic engagement and social capital leading to a potential decline in democracy.

Professor Hart's arguments, since they address the impact of the Internet after such rapid change in the past 15 years since Putnam's analysis, are important to our understanding of democracy in an increasingly technological era. While I am sympathetic to Professor Hart's arguments, I do not share his pessimism for two reasons.

First, it is very unlikely that the new technology will be eliminated or ignored, so the task of teachers is to convince students of the liberating aspect of the Internet and how it can be used to educate and broaden horizons regardless of personal views.

In political science courses, this means building in exercises that require students to sample a variety of websites—from conservative to liberal, from radical to reactionary—and to evaluate how the sponsors of these sites view issues and what they recommend as an appropriate response. As students learn from and experience the great wealth of information and diversity of opinion on the Internet, they will hopefully be more apt to understand valid arguments and reasonable proposals while at the same time realizing the importance of their own individual participation.

C-SPAN and the Archives are critical as a source of information without a partisan bias. We know that partisanship, whether on the floor of our legislative bodies or in the mass media, has increased and that for many what is reported with partisan bias often becomes the objective truth. C-SPAN can help mute this increasing partisanship by permitting the average citizen to obtain more objective information.

Second, while there are those who will use the Internet only to reinforce their views, there are others who have found and will find Internet-based knowledge that challenges their perspective and views. The task of teachers is to sponsor that debate and provide ways for students and all citizens to participate and to have a sense of civic community in the digital age and beyond.

In a democracy, individual citizens are responsible not only for understanding the issues but for voting for the candidates they believe will most likely advance their position. Accurate and timely information is the key to a robust and vibrant democratic system. The Internet may be a powerful resource in providing that information.

This is why I titled this chapter as I did: "C-SPAN, MOOCs and the Post-Digital Age." Clearly C-SPAN and the Archives have a continuing and crucial role to play in our knowledge-based economy and in our political process. Even if the information is imperfect at times, the viewer will ultimately be able to discern its reliability and its truthfulness.

As the post-digital age evolves, it will be interesting to see the impact on American democracy. Unlike many, I think there is the possibility that C-SPAN, the Archives, and the other institutions committed to providing basic information will help individuals reach responsible decisions, reinforcing democratic norms not in all but in most cases.

What more can we ask for going forward? As has been true throughout American history and in other democracies, we are dependent on individuals making the appropriate decisions that reinforce democracy and provide a path forward. These decisions will often be imperfect, but even imperfect decisions based on unbiased information will help us progress. I am confident that, with the help of C-SPAN and the Archives, that will continue to be the case and that the promise of American democracy will continue to be realized.

NOTES

These comments are based on work I began in 2011 and the paper I presented at the American Political Science Association's Teaching and Learning Conference in 2014 (Caputo, 2014) and the American Political Science Association's national meeting in 2014. I would like to acknowledge Enxhi Brahja's research assistance during her Pace University undergraduate research fellowship, as well as during the research phase of the Verizon Thinkfinity research grant. She provided outstanding bibliographical research assistance and was helpful in reviewing the various papers that resulted from this work. I will be continuing this work while on sabbatical in the fall of 2015. My work during this time will be to develop an advocacy-based MOOC which can be used for both the 2016 presidential nominating process and the 2016 presidential general election process. Access to the material on C-SPAN and the material available through the C-SPAN Archives' online Video Library will be a central part of the MOOC.

1. Here is an interesting side story: My student assistants and I were working on the 2014 course when we wondered if the domain name Presidentialelection2016.com was available. It was so I purchased it and also the Congressionalelections2018.com domain name. Look for websites using these in 2015 and 2017, respectively.

2. See especially Putnam's discussion of social capital and its importance in a democracy on pp. 148–180 and 402–413.

REFERENCES

A cost crisis, changing labour markets and new technology will turn an old institution on its head. (2014, June 28). *The Economist,* 11. Retrieved from http://www

.economist.com/news/leaders/21605906-cost-crisis-changing-labour-markets
-and-new-technology-will-turn-old-institution-its

Caputo, D. (2014, February). *MOOCs and political science: Questions and tentative (very) answers.* Paper presented at the American Political Science Association Teaching and Learning Conference, Philadelphia, PA.

Friedman, T. (2013, January 26). Revolution hits the universities. *New York Times,* p. 9.

Hart, R. P. (2014). Partisanship without alternatives: keynote reflections on C-SPAN and my mother. In R. X. Browning (Ed.), *The C-SPAN Archives: An interdisciplinary resource for discovery, learning, and engagement* (pp. 155–167). West Lafayette, IN: Purdue University Press.

Kolowich, S. (2013a, March 18). The professors behind the MOOC hype. *Chronicle of Higher Education,* pp. A2, A4.

Kolowich, S. (2013b, November 18). With open reform, Stanford seeks to reclaim MOOC brand. *Chronicle of Higher Education,* pp. A2, A4.

Lamb, B. (2014). C-SPAN's origins and place in history: Personal commentary. In R. X. Browning (Ed.), *The C-SPAN Archives: An interdisciplinary resource for discovery, learning, and engagement* (pp. 15–26). West Lafayette, IN: Purdue University Press.

Marks, J. (2012, October 5). Who's afraid of the big bad disruption. *Inside Higher Education,* p. 28.

Meisenhelder, S. (2013). MOOC mania. *Thought and Action, 29,* 7–26.

Putnam, R. D. (2000). *Bowling alone: The collapse and revival of American community.* New York: Simon and Schuster.

CHAPTER 6

USING THE C-SPAN ARCHIVES: EVIDENCE IN POLICYMAKERS' DISCOURSE ON SCIENCE

Mary L. Nucci

Much effort has been focused on understanding the public perceptions of science, as attitudes toward science can drive the acceptance and support of scientific research and development (Munoz, Morena, & Lujon, 2012). Researchers have examined the public's perceptions of a wide range of science issues, including food irradiation (Fox, Hayes & Shogren, 2002), nanotechnology (Cobb & Cobb, 2004; Cook & Fairweather, 2007; Currall, King, Lane, Madera, & Turner, 2006; Macoubrie, 2005, 2006; Siegrist, Cousin, Kastenholz & Wiek, 2007; Siegrist, Stampfli & Kastenholz, 2009), genetic engineering (Frewer, Howard, & Shepherd, 1997; Gaskell et al., 2003; Gaskell et al., 2010; Hallman, Adelaja, Schilling, & Lang 2002), stem cells (Goldston, 2009; Ho, Brossard & Scheufele, 2008; Nisbet, 2005), functional foods (Lahteenmaki, Lyly & Urala, 2007) and cloning (Einseidel, 2000, 2005; European Commission, 2008).

Promoting the acceptance of new science has long been predicated on the knowledge deficit model (Einsiedel, 2000; Hansen, Holm, Frewer, Robinson, & Sandøe, 2003; Irwin & Wynne, 1996), which suggests that providing more information will lead to greater acceptance and support for science. The idea that knowing more about the science behind a specific technology will lead to greater approval of that technology has been a staple of the educational and communication communities for many years. However, although some studies have found a positive relationship between increased knowledge and approval of the application of science (Evans & Durant, 1995; Hayes & Tariq, 2000; Sturgis & Allum, 2004, other studies have failed to find any relationship between knowledge and acceptance (Pfister, Böhm, & Jungermann, 2000) or found only a partial relationship between the two variables (Jallinoja & Aro, 1999; Peters, 2000).

It appears that for science in general, and controversial science in particular, where only minimal amounts of new information are assimilated to inform or reinforce a viewpoint (Nisbet, 2005), the knowledge deficit model is incomplete. It has been suggested that because most people do not have an extensive background in a scientific discipline, the influence of scientific knowledge on attitudes may be directly related to the extent to which scientific information is seen as consistent with personal experience (Jasanoff, 2000) or the specific worldview, core beliefs, or values held by individuals (Slovic & Peters, 1998). The impacts of scientific information may also be moderated or contextualized by other types of knowledge that may include an understanding of how scientific expertise is developed and how science is organized, financed, and controlled. Each can affect whether or not the public places trust in the "truths" developed by science (Wynne, 1992).

Most science communicators and disseminators today recognize that the preferred approach to promoting an understanding of science lies in placing it in context. This alternative contextualist approach to the public understanding of science looks to the interaction between the social values, social identity, and alternative forms of knowledge of the public and the actions of experts (Nisbet & Goidel, 2007). This approach points out that in decisions about science, knowledge may not be relevant to the issues, as the public may only understand a debate in moral or political terms (Michael, 1996). When no value consensus exists between science and the public, the risk attached to the science arises from social or cultural "knowledges" rather than from the science itself (Legge & Durant, 2010), which has been quite prominent in public advocacy regarding scientific developments in food and agriculture (genetic engineering), environment (climate change), engineering (nanotechnology, robotics) and medicine (synthetic biology, nanotechnology, genetic engineering, stem cells).

As Humphreys and Piot (2012) note, scientific evidence is valuable for informing a range of science policy decisions, with the caveat that democratic or human rights considerations must be part of the decision equation. The question remains, though: What do policymakers draw upon for their policy decisions—scientific studies or cultural knowledge? Echoing Sutherland et al. (2012), "we need to ask not just how science can best inform policy, but also how policy and political processes affect what counts as authoritative evidence in the first place." To address this question of evidence in science decision making, as well as its potential value as a research tool, the C-SPAN Archives' online Video Library collection of statements by members of Congress, and testimony by the public and other elected officials who speak about science and technology topics in their debates, was examined. Based on the research discussed here, the C-SPAN Archives offers a high potential for researchers interested in evidence use in decision making and should play a key role in furthering the research agenda on evidence-based science policy.

SCIENCE IN POLICYMAKING

Education, or expert opinion, has been found to be limited in promoting the public acceptance of science (Gauchat, 2012; Kahan et al., 2012). For new developments to be understood, science must fit with and be embedded in daily public discourse (Ronteltap, van Trijp, Renes & Frewer, 2007). As key voices in the public discourse on science, policymakers in the U.S. federal government occupy a unique position in science decision making: their knowledge and beliefs about science are based in their own culture, but their decisions should be based on evidence, not personal values. Unfortunately, science has become one of the most polarizing topics in American politics (Scheufele, 2014), particularly with regard to new developments where long-term studies are not available to clearly present risks and benefits (Spruijt et al., 2014). New scientific developments (Ho, Brossard, & Scheufele, 2008) are contested in local and federal campaigns, while issues supported by scientific evidence are challenged by federal officials.

Regardless, for science policy, evidence-influenced decision making, where evidence is defined as "data, information, concepts, research findings, and theories that are generally accepted by the relevant scientific discipline" (Prewitt, Schwandt, & Straf, 2012, p. 8), has become the desired norm (Sutherland et al., 2012), and scientific expertise has been integrated into policymaking across the branches of the U.S. federal government. Trust in science remains high among all groups except conservatives, and science and scientists still retain credibility due to cultural perceptions of their neutrality and objectivity (Gauchat, 2012). In May 2012, the Office of Management and Budget circulated a memo that called for agencies to "demonstrate the use of evidence throughout their Fiscal Year (FY) 2014 budget submissions. Budget submissions also should include a separate section on agencies' most innovative uses of evidence and evaluation" (Office of Management and Budget, 2012, p. 1).

Programs such as the Climate Science Rapid Response Team, founded in 2010,[1] aim to improve policymakers' knowledge and understanding of the science behind controversial issues. In the executive branch, the President's Council of Advisors on Science and Technology (PCAST),[2] consisting of leading scientists and engineers, provides recommendations to the president and the executive office. In Congress, the House Committee on Science, Space, and Technology (n.d.) "review[s] and stud[ies] on a continuing basis, all laws, programs and Government activities relating to non-military research and development." In the Senate, the Committee on Commerce, Science, and Transportation (2014) "stud[ies] and review[s], on a comprehensive basis, all matters relating to science and technology, oceans policy, transportation, communications, and consumer affairs, and report thereon from time to time."

As a force in science policy, the use of evidence can range from instrumental or direct effects on policy to political effects, where evidence is used in debates against an opponent (Weible, 2008). Instrumental use is based on problem solving and may require outcomes that conflict with beliefs. Political uses of evidence, on the other hand, may include a distortion or misuse of evidence to support mobilization or counter-arguments or to affect policy images.

It is clear from recent controversies that the relationship between congressional policymakers and evidence-based science is challenged by issues related

TABLE 6.1   *Federal Agencies and Departments That Are Involved in Science Policy*

Departments and Agencies	Information Centers
Department of Agriculture (USDA)	Defense Technical Information Center
Department of Energy	National Agricultural Library
Department of Homeland Security	National Library of Medicine
Research	National Technical Information
Environmental Protection Agency	Service
Federal Communications Commission	Office of Scientific and Technical
National Aeronautics and Space	Information (DOE)
Administration (NASA)	Federal Research Policy
National Institute of Standards and	National Science and Technology
Technology	Council
National Institutes of Health	National Science Board
National Oceanic and Atmospheric	Office of Science and Technology
Administration	Policy (White House)
National Science Foundation	
Patent and Trademark Office	
U.S. Geological Survey	

to culture and expertise (see Tables 6.1 and 6.2). Recent examples include the proposed Flake Amendment to end National Science Foundation (NSF) funding for political science research (Uscinski & Klofstad, 2013) and the ongoing debate over scientific understandings of climate change (Hulme, 2009), where Lamar Smith (R-TX), the chair of the House Committee on Science, Space, and Technology accused the White House through its National Climate Assessment Report[3] of misstating the truth about climate change, saying:

> This is a political document intended to frighten Americans into believing that any abnormal weather we experience is the direct result of human CO_2 emissions. In reality, there is little science to support any connection between climate change and more frequent or extreme storms. It's disappointing that the Obama administration feels compelled to stretch the truth in order to drum up support for more costly and unnecessary regulations and subsidies. (Committee on Science, Space, and Technology, 2014)

Paul Broun (R-GA), also a member of the House Committee on Science, Space, and Technology, expressed disbelief in evidence-influenced science

TABLE 6.2 *Members of the 113th Congress House Committee on Space, Science and Technology and the Senate Committee on Commerce, Science and Transportation*

Republicans	Democrats
113th Congress: House Committee on Space, Science and Technology	
Lamar Smith, Texas (Chair)	Eddie Bernice Johnson, Texas
Dana Rohrabacher, California	Zoe Lofgren, California
Ralph M. Hall, Texas	Daniel Lipinski, Illinois
F. James Sensenbrenner, Wisconsin	Donna Edwards, Maryland
Frank D. Lucas, Oklahoma	Frederica Wilson, Florida
Randy Neugebauer, Texas	Suzanne Bonamici, Oregon
Michael T. McCaul, Texas	Eric Swalwell, California
Paul Broun, Georgia	Dan Maffei, New York
Steven Palazzo, Mississippi	Alan Grayson, Florida
Mo Brooks, Alabama	Joe Kennedy, Massachusetts
Randy Hultgren, Illinois	Scott Peters, California
Larry Bucshon, Indiana	Derek Kilmer, Washington
Steve Stockman, Texas	Ami Bera, California
Bill Posey, Florida	Elizabeth Esty, Connecticut
Cynthia Lummis, Wyoming	Marc Veasey, Texas
David Schweikert, Arizona	Julia Brownley, California
Thomas Massie, Kentucky	Robin Kelly, Illinois
Kevin Cramer, North Dakota	Katherine Clark, Massachusetts
Jim Bridenstine, Oklahoma	
Randy Weber, Texas	
Chris Collins, New York	
Bill Johnson, Ohio	
113th Congress: Senate Committee on Commerce, Science and Transportation	
John Thune, South Dakota	John D. Rockefeller IV, West Virginia
Roger Wicker, Mississippi	(Chair)
Roy Blunt, Missouri	Barbara Boxer, California
Marco Rubio, Florida	Bill Nelson, Florida
Kelly Ayotte, New Hampshire	Maria Cantwell, Washington
Dean Heller, Nevada	Mark Pryor, Arkansas
Dan Coats, Indiana	Claire McCaskill, Missouri
Tim Scott, South Carolina	Amy Klobuchar, Minnesota
Ted Cruz, Texas	Mark Begich, Alaska
Deb Fischer, Nebraska	Richard Blumenthal, Connecticut
Ron Johnson, Wisconsin	Brian Schatz, Hawaii
	Ed Markey, Massachusetts
	Cory Booker, New Jersey
	John Walsh, Montana

theories, saying "All that stuff I was taught about evolution and embryology and the Big Bang Theory, all that is lies straight from the pit of Hell" (Rayfield, 2014). Within the same committee, there is an ongoing multiyear attempt by Chair Lamar Smith (R-TX) on the "much admired" 60-plus-year NSF grant review process. He seeks to collect evidence that the $7 billion research agency is wasting taxpayer dollars on frivolous social science projects (Mervis, 2014).

Although some would like to argue that cultural versus evidence-influenced decision making is a function solely of ideology, the political parties differ in what science they support or decry: Some Republicans are against evolution, global warming, and stem cell use, while some Democrats question vaccines, nuclear power, and biotechnology (Bailey, 2011; Berezow & Campbell, 2012; Fisher, 2013). At issue behind these battles between science and legislators in Congress is the question of what constitutes evidence, and where evidence arises. The selective use of evidence (Goldberg 2012; Pielke, 2007) in discussions about climate change, vaccines, and biotechnology has become a major concern in science debate, not only in terms of what decisions are made, but also because exposure to politicized science affects support for scientific evidence (Bolsen, Druckman, & Cook, 2014; Brittle & Muthuswamy, 2009).

The assumption that science policymaking must be decided by scientific evidence and not by social or cultural knowledge begs the research question, "How can we identify what evidence policymakers use in public discourse and eventual decision making about science?"

To explore this question, I investigated the potential for using the C-SPAN Video Library as a source for conducting research on the use of evidence in the federal government. The C-SPAN Archives contain all C-SPAN programming from 1987 to the present, totaling more than 210,000 hours of video. The C-SPAN Video Library website notes that

> the Archives records all three C-SPAN networks seven days a week, twenty-four hours a day. Programs are extensively indexed making the database of C-SPAN programming an unparalleled chronological resource. Programs are indexed by subject, speaker names, titles, affiliations, sponsors, committees, categories, formats, policy groups, keywords, and location. The congressional sessions and committee

hearings are indexed by person with full-text. The video collection can be searched through the online Video Library. All C-SPAN programs since 1987 are digital and can be viewed online for free. (C-SPAN, n.d., para. 2–3)

Building upon previous research that has examined the movement, use, and understanding of scientific evidence in the public domain (Hallman, Cuite, Dellava, Nucci & Condry, 2009; Hallman & Nucci, 2015; McInerney, Bird, & Nucci, 2004; Nucci, Cuite, & Hallman, 2009; Nucci & Hallman, 2012a, 2012b, 2015; Nucci & Kubey, 2007, 2010), I used the following questions to guide my evaluation of the C-SPAN Video Library:

- What science topics are discussed (i.e., considered important) at the federal level?
- What party affiliations are represented in these debates? Is their discourse positive or negative as it relates to science in general, and the science topic in specifics?
- Who is granted expertise through inclusion in the discussions about science (and conversely, who is not included)?
- What is provided as expert information (e.g., what content is promoted as evidence)?
- How is expertise granted (e.g., institutional affiliation, academic degrees)?

C-SPAN ARCHIVES: RESEARCHING EVIDENCE IN SCIENCE POLICY

The C-SPAN Video Library is easy to retrieve and navigate. Our research team was able to quickly search for and locate videos (data sets), then create and save clips to a personal account for analysis. The Video Library provides embed codes so that users may include clips in PowerPoint or other presentation programs.

Initial searches focused on the following questions:

- What science issues are being discussed during the bill process (see Table 6.3)?

- Who is sponsoring science-based bills in Congress (see Table 6.4)?
- What science issues were being promoted during policy discussions (see Table 6.4)?
- What level of professional is granted authority by virtue of being present to speak about science issues (see Table 6.5)?
- What institutions are granted authority in science discussions (see Table 6.6)?
- What individuals are granted authority by being involved in talking about science (see Table 6.7)?

A follow-up analysis looked at specific science topics to understand what issues are considered important (see Table 6.8).

It was apparent that science is a point of discussion at the federal level, although there were no analyses performed on non-science topics (e.g., housing) to compare where science ranked in inclusion as a debate topic. Broadly though, by searching the Video Library the team found that of the more than 118,176 bills referred to committee during the time period searched,[4] science-based bills constituted 14 percent (16,948; see Table 6.3[5]). Two percent (931) of these were enacted into law. Using the same data set, the team drilled down to examine science bill sponsorship (Table 6.4), which enabled them to focus on specific individuals in Congress to examine their focus and efforts in science-related issues. Though not discussed here, the Video Library can also be used to identify specific bills by status (e.g., pending, withdrawn, referred to committee, enacted into law), cosponsor, specific session of Congress, or other search terms.

The team was able to determine the level of expertise of science policy discussants by conducting a search of people with professional titles that included the term *science* in the title or affiliation using the PEOPLE tab under BROWSE (see, for example, Figure 6.1). As shown in Table 6.5, the most common professional title was that of *professor,* indicating that evidential discussions do rely on participants with academic expertise. Indeed, the 738 professor titles far outstrip the second most common title, *director,* which appeared only 178 times. *Associate professor* appeared 129 times, and *assistant professor* 77 times, indicating that seniority in academics is tied to expertise. The value of academic expertise was further demonstrated in a search that yielded the institutions aligned with science discussions on C-SPAN (see Table 6.6). Of

TABLE 6.3 *Science Bill Topics in the C-SPAN Archives*

Number of Bills	Topic	Number of Bills	Topic
16,400	Science, technology, communications	3,450	Armed forces and national security
12,974	Government operations and politics	3,382	International affairs
8,867	Economics and public finance	3,043	Foreign trade and international finance
8,226	Congress	3,007	Civil rights and liberties, minority issues
7,660	Commerce	2,966	Data banks
7,595	Law	2,897	Federal advisory bodies
7,407	Congressional reporting requirements	2,777	Executive reorganization
6,130	Health	2,588	Taxation
5,875	Government paperwork	2,578	Elementary and secondary education
5,218	Labor and employment	2,557	Fines (Penalties)
5,119	Education	2,492	Public lands and natural resources
4,881	Crime and law enforcement	2,470	Agriculture and food
4,556	Administrative procedure	2,427	Minorities
4,395	Social welfare	2,365	Emergency management
4,139	Higher education	2,358	Licenses
4,094	Finance and financial sector	2,289	Housing and community development
4,036	Environmental protection	2,214	Energy
3,743	Families	2,198	Authorization
3,690	Government publicity	2,189	Internet
3,480	Transportation and public works		

the 14 institutions that appeared 15 or more times, 9 represented higher education. To conduct this search, the team also used the PEOPLE tab, then reviewed the organization names in which the term *science* appeared. Three of these institutions were local to Washington, DC, which may indicate some bias in selection, or that there is a greater effort toward science advocacy at institutions close to the capitol.

The research results also demonstrated the relationship between specific individuals and their involvement in science discussions (see Table 6.7).

TABLE 6.4 *Sponsors of 100 or More Science-Based Bills in the C-SPAN Archives*

Number of Bills	Bill Sponsor
182	John S. McCain III (Senator)
160	Olympia J. Snowe (Senator)
147	Jeff Bingaman (Senator)
146	Orrin Hatch (Senator)
138	Edward "Ted" M. Kennedy (Senator)
130	Dianne Feinstein (Senator)
130	Hillary Rodham Clinton (Senator)
120	John F. Kerry (Senator)
117	Jay D. Rockefeller IV (Senator)
117	Charles E. Schumer (Representative)
115	Patrick J. Leahy (Senator)
115	Edward J. Markey (Senator)
111	Christopher "Chris" J. Dodd (Senator)
100	Barbara Boxer (Senator)
100	Russell "Russ" Feingold (Senator)

TABLE 6.5 *Professional Affiliations of Science Discussants in the C-SPAN Archives*

Number of Mentions	Title	Number of Mentions	Title
738	Professor	14	Official
178	Director	13	Adjunct Professor
129	Associate Professor	13	Assistant Secretary
101	Correspondent	13	Distinguished Professor
77	Assistant Professor	12	Chief
52	President	12	Founding Director
48	Dean	12	Scientist
37	Chair	11	Visiting Professor
32	Professor Emeritus	10	Graduate Student
29	Senior Fellow	10	President and CEO
25	Chairman	10	Student
25	Executive Director	10	Undersecretary
24	Deputy Director	9	Associate Administrator
24	Member	9	Physician
21	Vice President	8	Instructor
18	Associate Director	8	Manager
18	Member of Congress	8	Senior Scientist
15	Author	8	Teacher
15	Editor	7	Adviser
14	Fellow	7	Analyst

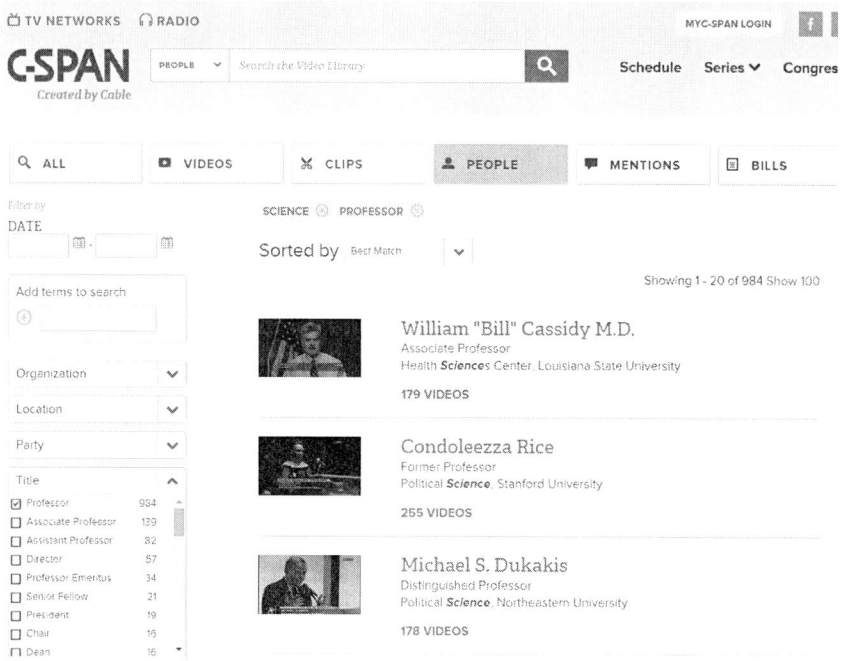

FIGURE 6.1 Screenshot example of a C-SPAN Archives Video Library search.

TABLE 6.6 *Institutions Participating in Science Discussions in the C-SPAN Archives*

Number of Mentions	Organization
38	George Washington University
33	Massachusetts Institute of Technology
31	National Science Foundation
30	Harvard University
30	NASA
26	National Academy of Sciences
24	Stanford University
20	White House
19	Columbia University
19	University of Maryland, College Park
18	London School of Economics and Political Science
18	George Washington University Political Science Department
16	University of California, Los Angeles
15	White House Office of Science and Technology

TABLE 6.7 *Individuals Who Are Mentioned in 100 or More Scientific Discussions in the C-SPAN Archives*

Number of Mentions	Name
652	Barack Obama (President)
200	Sheila Jackson Lee (Congressman)
198	Edward "Ted" M. Kennedy (Senator)
196	Gina Kolata (Science writer)
167	Barbara Hinckley (Professor)
156	Sheldon Whitehouse (Senator)
156	Kathleen M. Dalton (Teacher)
155	Robert Scigliano (Professor)
151	George W. Bush (President)
146	Barbara A. Mikulski (Senator)
146	Barbara Boxer (Senator)
136	Kiron K. Skinner (Professor)
133	Henry Waxman (Congressman)
132	James M. Inhofe (Senator)
129	Vernon J. Ehlers (Congressman)
123	Harry Reid (Senator)
120	Dick J. Durbin (Senator)
116	Jean Edward Smith (Professor)
116	Ralph M. Hall (Congressman)
107	Dan Vergano (Science writer)
105	Peter Skerry (Professor)
105	Lamar Alexander (Senator)
104	John F. Kerry (Senator)
104	Robert "Bob" S. Walker (Congressman)
102	William "Bill" Frist (Senator)
101	Byron L. Dorgan (Senator)

Using the MENTION tab and the search term *science,* the researchers were able to determine the number of times the word *science* was mentioned by specific individuals and indexed in the database. Although no conclusions can be drawn regarding the stance a particular individual took on the issue being discussed, this data does indicate a direction for future research on that individual's positions.

The Video Library is also useful for evaluating authority in science policy: the use of celebrities, such as Seth Rogen speaking before the Senate

TABLE 6.8 *Number of Times Specific Science Topics Were Found in the C-SPAN Archives*

Topic	Number of Videos	Number of Mentions	Number of Bills
Biodiversity	13	142	24
Climate change	912	6,234	1,144
Ebola	161	1,047	2
Evolution	384	1,750	4
Fracking	34	439	0
Genetically modified	14	83	3
Global warming	353	3,083	52
Infectious disease	27	717	44
Nanotechnology	4	228	43
Nuclear energy	121	1,309	330
Nuclear power	273	3,256	454
Sea level rise	2	284	5
Space aliens	0	6	0
Synthetic biology	2	26	0
Vaccines	83	1,888	348

NOTE: Videos = videos on these topics. Mentions = indexed text references to the topics. Bills = bills that reference these topics.

Committee on Appropriations about the lack of funding for Alzheimer's research (Figure 6.2; see C-SPAN, 2014b); lack of clear expertise, such as Lord Monckton speaking on climate change (Figure 6.3; see C-SPAN, 2010); failure in expertise, as illustrated when Dr. Mehmet Oz was chastised for his recommendation of untested weight loss supplements (Figure 6.4; see C-SPAN, 2014a); and personal agenda, such as the comments of Representative Bill Posey (R-FL) on the link between vaccines and rising autism rates (Figure 6.5; see C-SPAN, 2012).

In her 2014 paper, Helga Nowotny writes that science/technology/society (STS) scholars, in their focus on public engagement with science, have failed to recognize that policymakers and politicians are part of the public sphere.

There can be no doubt that their ideas [policymakers and politicians] of how science worked and towards which ends it could be made to work, had far greater influence on the directions of research and its funding than any degree of acceptance or resistance from the public. (Nowotny, 2014, p. 17)

FIGURE 6.2 Seth Rogen testifying before a congressional committee.

The ability to easily access and quantify the range of science discourse at the federal level is key to including policymakers and politicians in the public sphere of science, beginning with the question that drove the research agenda in this study: How can we identify what evidence policymakers use in public discourse and eventual decision making about science?

It is clear from these results that the C-SPAN Video Library is valuable for examining policy discourse on science. The results indicate that the Video Library could be used to:

- Generate a baseline of the range of science issues discussed at the federal level to consider such questions as change over time in volume and focus on science concerns.
- Define expertise in science discussions to answer the questions of who is considered expert, what these experts represent, what information is presented as evidence, and who is or is not included in discussions.
- Correlate possible connections between party affiliation and use of evidence in science discussions to address the role of ideology in these discussions.
- Generate data that would be useful for future research on the role and use of evidence in science debate by House and Senate science

FIGURE 6.3 Christopher Monckton testifying before a congressional committee.

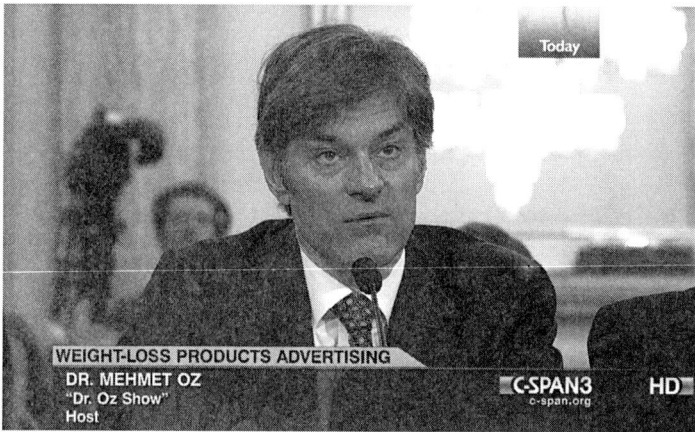

FIGURE 6.4 Dr. Mehmet Oz testifying before a congressional committee.

committee members, asking such questions as whether House or Senate committee members are more informed about science in debates, and what is used as evidence in science debates.

To explore these issues further, the research team considered specificity in science policy discussions. What topics were considered key or framed as important to be included in discourse at the federal level? A search of key

FIGURE 6.5 Representative Posey questioning a witness on vaccines.

issues in public debate pointed to additional questions for a research agenda on evidence in science (see Table 6.8). It should consider the role of rhetoric (global warming versus climate change; nuclear power versus nuclear energy) in policymaking, the relationship between media coverage and legislative action (e.g., fracking), and whether the media drive federal discourse or federal discourse drives the media. This would include a consideration on such issues as the role of novelty or controversy in the media (e.g., synthetic biology, Ebola) on federal discourse. Finally, research should examine the reach and impact of pseudoscience (e.g., space aliens) in policy discourse.

Ultimately, the C-SPAN Video Library is a readily accessible source for research on evidence-influenced science policy discourse, and it offers the researcher in policy, government, science discourse, or a similar field a source for data that can be used to advance a research agenda to further understand the role and use of evidence in science policy. Using the C-SPAN Video Library, researchers could study the relationship between party affiliation and science stance, changes over time in science discourse, and the effectiveness of key players in the development of enacted legislation. As I have shown in this chapter, the C-SPAN Video Library serves as a readily accessible starting point for research that examines how evidence and expertise are used in science policy.

NOTES

1. For information about the Climate Science Rapid Response Team, see http://www.climaterapidresponse.org/.

2. For more information on PCAST, see http://www.whitehouse.gov/administration/eop/ostp/pcast.

3. Report available at http://nca2014.globalchange.gov/report.

4. All numbers are based on the timeline of the research and will have changed with ongoing Congressional activities.

5. Using the bill search feature and the bill topics assigned to the bills, we limited the bills to science, technology, and communications over the 101st to 113th Congresses (1989–2014). The table is limited to classifications of these science bills.

REFERENCES

Bailey, R. (2011, October 4). Are Republicans or Democrats more anti-science? Comparing the scientific ignorance of our mainstream parties. *Reason.* Retrieved from http://reason.com/archives/2011/10/04/more-anti-science-democrats-or

Berezow, A. B., & Campbell, H. (2012). *Science left behind: Feel-good fallacies and the rise of the anti-scientific left.* New York, NY: PublicAffairs.

Bolsen, T., Druckman, J. N., & Cook, F. L. (2014). How frames can undermine support for scientific adaptations: Politicization and the status-quo bias. *Public Opinion Quarterly, 78*(1), 1–26. http://dx.doi.org/10.1093/poq/nft044

Brittle, C., & Muthuswamy, N. (2009). Scientific elites and concern for global warming: The impact of disagreement, evidence strength, partisan cues, and exposure to news content on concern for climate. *International Journal of Sustainability Communication, 4,* 23–44.

Cobb, M.D., & Macoubrie, J. (2004). Public perceptions about nanotechnology: Risks, benefits and trust. *Journal of Nanoparticle Research, 6*(4), 395–405. http://dx.doi.org/10.1007/s11051-004-3394-4

Committee on Commerce, Science, and Transportation. (n.d.). Jurisdiction. Retrieved from http://www.commerce.senate.gov/public/index.cfm?p=Jurisdiction

Committee on Science, Space, and Technology. (n.d.). A brief history of the committee. Retrieved from http://science.house.gov/history

Committee on Science, Space, and Technology. (2014, May 6). *Smith: White House climate report stretches truth.* Retrieved from http://science.house.gov/press -release/smith-white-house-climate-report-stretches-truth

Cook, A. J., & Fairweather, J. R. (2007). Intentions of New Zealanders to purchase lamb or beef made using nanotechnology. *British Food Journal, 109*(9), 675–688. http://dx.doi.org/10.1108/00070700710780670

C-SPAN. (n.d.). About C-SPAN video library: Our mission. Retrieved from http:// c-spanvideo.org/about

C-SPAN (Producer). (2010, May 6). *Foundation for climate science* [online video]. Available from http://www.c-span.org/video/?293366-1/foundation-climate -science

C-SPAN (Producer). (2012, November 29). *Federal response to rise in autism rates* [online video]. http://www.c-span.org/video/?309672-1/federal-response-rise -autism-rates

C-SPAN (Producer). (2014a, June 17). *Weight-loss product advertising* [online video]. Available from http://www.c-span.org/video/?320015-1/weightloss-product -advertising

C-SPAN (Producer). (2014b, December 25). *Celebrity activists* [online video]. Available from http://www.c-span.org/video/?323507-1/celebrity-activists

Currall, S. C., King, E. B., Lane, N., Madera, J., & Turner, S. (2006). What drives public acceptance of nanotechnology? *Nature Nanotechnology, 1,* 153–155. http:// dx.doi.org/10.1038/nnano.2006.155

Einsiedel, E. F. (2000). Cloning and its discontents—A Canadian perspective. *Nature Biotechnology, 18,* 943–944. http://dx.doi.org/10.1038/79419

Einsiedel, E. F. (2005). Public perceptions of transgenic animals. *Revue Scientifique et Technique (Office International des Epizooties), 24*(1), 149–157.

European Commission. (2008). *Europeans' attitudes towards animal cloning: Analytical report.* Retrieved from http://ec.europa.eu/food/food/resources/docs/euroba rometer_cloning_en.pdf

Evans, G., & Durant, J. (1995). The relationship between knowledge and attitudes in the public understanding of science in Britain. *Public Understanding of Science, 4*(1), 57–74. http://dx.doi.org/10.1088/0963-6625/4/1/004

Fisher, M. (2013, November 11). The Republican Party isn't really the anti-science party. *The Atlantic.* Retrieved from http://www.theatlantic.com/politics/ar chive/2013/11/the-republican-party-isnt-really-the-anti-science-party/281219/

Fox, J. A., Hayes, D. J., & Shogren, J. F. (2002). Consumer preferences for food irradiation: How favorable and unfavorable descriptions affect preferences for irradiated pork in experimental auctions. *The Journal of Risk and Uncertainty, 24*(1), 75–95. http://dx.doi.org/10.1023/A:1013229427237

Frewer, L. J., Howard, C., & Shepherd, R. (1997). Public concerns in the United Kingdom about general and specific applications of genetic engineering: Risk, benefit, and ethics. *Science, Technology & Human Values, 22*(1), 98–124. http://dx.doi.org/10.1177/016224399702200105

Gaskell, G., Allum, N., Bauer, M. W., Jackson, J., Howard, S., & Lindsey, N. (2003). *Ambivalent GM nation? Public attitudes to biotechnology in the UK, 1991–2002.* London, UK: London School of Economics and Political Science. Retrieved from https://ec.europa.eu/research/biosociety/pdf/ambivalent_gm_nation_uk.pdf

Gaskell, G., Stares, S. Allansdottir, A., Allum, N., Castro, P., Esmer, Y … &. Wagner, W. (2010). *Europeans and biotechnology in 2010: Winds of change?* Retrieved from https://ec.europa.eu/research/swafs/pdf/pub_archive/europeans-biotechnology-in-2010_en.pdf

Gauchat, G. (2012). Politicization of science in the public sphere: A study of public trust in the United States, 1974 to 2010. *American Sociological Review, 77*(2), 167–187. http://dx.doi.org/10.1177/0003122412438225

Goldberg, D. S. (2012). Against the very idea of the politicization of public health policy. *American Journal of Public Health, 102*(1), 44–49. http://dx.doi.org/10.2105/AJPH.2011.300325

Goldston, D. (2009). Science, policy, and the U.S. Congress. *Cell, 139*(4), 647–648. http://dx.doi.org/10.1016/j.cell.2009.10.044

Hallman, W., Adelaja, A., Schilling, B., & Lang, J. T. (2002). *Consumer beliefs, attitudes and preferences regarding agricultural biotechnology* (Food Policy Institute Report). New Brunswick, NJ: Rutgers University.

Hallman, W. K., Cuite, C. L., Dellava, J. E., Nucci, M. L., & Condry, S. C. (2009). Public response to the 2006 recall of contaminated spinach. In X. Fan, B. A. Niemira, C. J. Doona, F. E. Feeherry, & R. B. Gravani (Eds.), *Microbial safety of fresh produce* (pp. 351–368). Ames, IA: Blackwell Publishing.

Hallman, W. K., & Nucci, M. L. (2015). Consumer perceptions of nanomaterials in functional foods. In C. M. Sabliov, H. Chen, & R. Yada (Eds.). *Nanotechnology and functional foods: Effective delivery of bioactive ingredient.* New York, NY: John Wiley & Sons.

Hansen, J., Holm, L., Frewer, L., Robinson, P., & Sandøe, P. (2003). Beyond the knowledge deficit: Recent research into lay and expert attitudes to food risks. *Appetite, 41*(2), 111–121. http://dx.doi.org/10.1016/S0195-6663(03)00079-5

Hayes, B. C., & Tariq, V. N. (2000). Gender differences in scientific knowledge and attitudes toward science: A comparative study of four Anglo-American nations. *Public Understanding of Science, 9*(4), 433–447. http://dx.doi.org/10.1088/0963-6625/9/4/306

Ho, S. S., Brossard, D., & Scheufele, D. A. (2008). Effects of value predispositions, mass media use, and knowledge on public attitudes toward embryonic stem cell research. *International Journal of Public Opinion Research, 20*(2), 171–192. http://dx.doi.org/10.1093/ijpor/edn017

Hulme, M. (2009). *Why we disagree about climate change: Understanding controversy, inaction and opportunity.* Cambridge: Cambridge University Press.

Humphreys, K., & Piot, P. (2012). Scientific evidence alone is not sufficient basis for health policy. *BMJ, 344*(e1316), 1–9. http://dx.doi.org/10.1136/bmj.e1316

Irwin, A., & Wynne, B. (Eds.). (1996). *Misunderstanding science? The public reconstruction of science and technology.* Cambridge: Cambridge University Press.

Jallinoja, P., & Aro, A. R. (2000). Does knowledge make a difference? The association between knowledge about genes and attitude toward gene tests. *Journal of Health Communication, 5,* 29–39.

Jasanoff, S. (2000). The "science wars" and American politics. In M. Dierkes & C. Von Grote (Eds.), *Between understanding and trust: The public, science and technology* (pp. 27–40), Amsterdam, The Netherlands: Harwood Academic Publishers.

Kahan, D. M., Peters, E., Wittlin, M., Slovic, P., Ouellette, L. L., Braman, D., & Mandel, G. (2012). The polarizing impact of science literacy and numeracy on perceived climate change risks. *Nature Climate Change, 2*(10), 732–735. http://dx.doi.org/10.1038/nclimate1547

Lähteenmaki, L. Lyly, M, & Urala, N. (2007). Consumer attitudes towards functional foods. In L. Frewer & H. Van Trijp (Eds.), *Understanding consumers of food products* (pp. 412–427). Cambridge, UK: Woodhead Publishing.

Legge, J. S., Jr., & Durant, R. F. (2010). Public opinion, risk assessment, and biotechnology: Lessons from attitudes toward genetically modified foods in the European Union. *Review of Policy Research, 27*(1), 5976.

Macoubrie, J. (2005). *Informed public perceptions of nanotechnology and trust in government.* Washington, DC: Woodrow Wilson International Center Project on Emerging Nanotechnologies.

Macoubrie, J. (2006). Nanotechnology: Public concerns, reasoning and trust in

government. *Public Understanding of Science, 15*(2), 221–241. http://dx.doi
.org/10.1177/0963662506056993

McInerney, C., Bird, N., & Nucci, M. (2004). The flow of scientific knowledge from lab
to the lay public: The case of genetically modified food. *Science Communication,
26*(1), 44–74. http://dx.doi.org/10.1177/1075547004267024

Mervis, J. (2014). Congress, NSF spar on access to grant files. *Science, 346*(6206),
152–153. http://dx.doi.org/10.1126/science.346.6206.152

Michael, M. (1996). Ignoring science: Discourses of ignorance in the public under-
standing of science. In A. Irwin & B. Wynne (Eds.), *Misunderstanding science?
The public reconstruction of science and technology* (pp. 107–125). Cambridge:
Cambridge University Press.

Munoz, A., Moreno, C. & Lujan, J. L. (2012). Who is willing to pay for science? On
the relationship between public perception of science and the attitude to public
funding of science. *Public Understanding of Science, 21*(2), 242–253. http://dx
.doi.org/10.1177/0963662510373813

Nisbet, M. C. (2005). The competition for worldviews: Values, information, and public
support for stem cell research. *International Journal of Public Opinion Research,
17*(1), 90–112. http://dx.doi.org/10.1093/ijpor/edh058

Nisbet, M. C., & Goidel, R. K. (2007). Understanding citizen perceptions of science controversy: Bridging the ethnographic–survey research divide. *Public Understanding
of Science, 16*(4), 421–440. http://dx.doi.org/10.1177/0963662506065558

Nowotny, H. (2014). Engaging with the political imaginaries of science: Near misses
and future targets. *Public Understanding of Science, 23*(1), 16–20. http://dx.doi
.org/10.1177/0963662513476220

Nucci, M. L., Cuite, C. L., & Hallman, W. K. (2009). When good food goes bad:
Television network news and the spinach recall of 2006. *Science Communication,
31*(2), 238–265. http://dx.doi.org/10.1177/1075547009340337

Nucci, M. L., & Hallman, W. K. (2012a). Food and scientific illiteracy. *Museums &
Social Issues, 7*(1), 59–70. http://dx.doi.org/10.1179/msi.2012.7.1.59

Nucci, M. L., & Hallman, W. K. (2012b). Mork and Mindy, canola oil and mustard
gas: The dilemma of scientific illiteracy in decisions about food and health. In
J. Goodwin (Ed.), *Between scientists and citizens: Proceedings of a conference at
Iowa State University, June 1–2, 2012.* Ames: Iowa State University.

Nucci, M. L., & Hallman, W. K. (2015). The role of public (mis)perceptions in the
acceptance of new food technologies: Implications for food nanotechnology

applications. In D. Wright, E. A. Malone, & J. V. Stone (Eds.), *Communication practices in engineering, manufacturing, and research for food, drug, and water.* Manuscript submitted for publication.

Nucci, M. L., & Kubey, R. (2007). "We begin tonight with fruits and vegetables": Genetically modified food on the evening news 1980–2003. *Science Communication, 29*(2), 147–176. http://dx.doi.org/10.1177/1075547007308173

Nucci, M. L., & Kubey, R. (2010). Television and science: How the media shapes the public's understanding of crucial new developments. *Television Quarterly.* Retrieved from http://www.tvquarterly.net/tvq_39_1/05_television_and_science.html

Office of Management and Budget. (2012, May 18). Memorandum to the heads of executive departments and agencies. Retrieved from http://www.whitehouse.gov/sites/default/files/omb/memoranda/2012/m-12-14.pdf

Peters, H. P. (2000). From information to attitudes? Thoughts on the relationship between knowledge about science and technology and attitudes toward technologies. In M. Dierkes & C. Von Grote (Eds.), *Between understanding and trust: The public, science and technology* (pp. 265–286). New York, NY: Routledge.

Pfister, H. R., Böhm, G., & Jungermann, H. (2000). The cognitive representation of genetic engineering: Knowledge and evaluations. *New Genetics and Society, 19*(3), 295–316. http://dx.doi.org/10.1080/713687603

Pielke, R. A. (2007). *The honest broker: Making sense of science in policy and politics.* Cambridge: Cambridge University Press.

Prewitt, K., Schwandt, T. A., & Straf, M. L. (Eds.). (2012). *Using science as evidence in public policy.* Washington, DC: National Academies Press.

Rayfield, J. (2014, October 8). Least scientific members of the House Science Committee. Retrieved from Salon Web site: http://www.salon.com/2012/10/08/least_scientific_members_of_the_house_science_committee/

Ronteltap, A., van Trijp, J. C. M., Renes, R. J., & Frewer, L. (2007). Consumer acceptance of technology-based food innovations: Lessons for the future of nutrigenomics. *Appetite, 49*(1), 1–17. http://dx.doi.org/10.1016/j.appet.2007.02.002

Scheufele, D. A. (2014). Science communication as political communication. *Proceedings of the National Academy of Sciences, 111*(Suppl. 4), 13585–13592.

Siegrist, M., Cousin, M.-E., Kastenholz, H., & Wiek, A. (2007). Public acceptance of nanotechnology foods and food packaging: The influence of affect and trust. *Appetite, 49*(2), 459–466. http://dx.doi.org/10.1016/j.appet.2007.03.002

Siegrist, M., Stampfli, N., & Kastenholz, H. (2009). Acceptance of nanotechnology foods: A conjoint study examining consumers' willingness to buy. *British Food Journal, 111*(7), 660–668. http://dx.doi.org/10.1108/00070700910972350

Slovic, P., & Peters, E. (1998). The importance of worldviews in risk perception. *Journal of Risk Decision and Policy, 3*(2), 165–170.

Spruijt, P., Knol, A. B., Vasileiadou, E., Devilee, J., Lebret, E., & Petersen, A. C. (2014). Roles of scientists as policy advisers on complex issues: A literature review. *Environmental Science & Policy, 40,* 16–25. http://dx.doi.org/10.1016/j.envsci.2014.03.002

Sturgis, P., & Allum, N. (2004). Science in society: Re-evaluating the deficit model of public attitudes. *Public Understanding of Science, 13*(1), 55–74.

Sutherland, W. J., Bellingan, L., Bellingham, J. R., Blackstock, J. J., Bloomfield, R. M., Bravo, M. ..., & Tyler, C. P. (2012). A collaboratively-derived science-policy research agenda. *PloS one, 7*(3), e31824. http://dx.doi.org/10.1371/journal.pone.0031824

Uscinski, J. E., & Klofstad, C. A. (2013). Determinants of representatives' votes on the Flake Amendment to end National Science Foundation funding of political science research. *PS: Political Science & Politics, 46*(03), 557–561. http://dx.doi.org/10.1017/S1049096513000504

Weible, C. M. (2008). Expert-based information and policy subsystems: A review and synthesis. *Policy Studies Journal, 36*(4), 615–635.

Wynne, B. (1992). Public understanding of science research: New horizons or hall of mirrors? *Public Understanding of Science, 1,* 37–43. http://dx.doi.org/10.1088/0963-6625/1/1/008

CHAPTER 7

PERSONAL NARRATIVES AND REPRESENTATION STRATEGIES: USING C-SPAN ORAL HISTORIES TO EXAMINE KEY CONCEPTS IN MINORITY REPRESENTATION

Nadia E. Brown
Michael D. Minta
Valeria Sinclair-Chapman

Over the past two decades, political representation scholars have examined whether legislators' conceptions of race and gender influence their behavior. These studies find that racial or ethnic background is significant in determining why Black legislators are more likely than White legislators to provide better substantive representation to Black constituents. As a result of this rich literature, we know when race matters; however, why it matters with regard to African American legislators' decisions about how to represent their constituents is not settled. Rarely do existing studies examine the diversity in representational styles within the Congressional Black Caucus (CBC) or how members' racial group experiences interact with other personal background factors to shape specific kinds of political advocacy. How does a legislator's formative experience influence political behavior? How does local party politics in the district from which a candidate emerges affect his or her representational style once elected? Do legislators voluntarily raise concepts such as linked fate, racial/ethnic, or gender group consciousness?

Many scholars have argued that the life experiences of legislators such as their religion, place of birth, health scares, previous employment, and encounters with racial and gender discrimination contribute to their descriptive representation, which, in turn, affects their substantive representation (Bowen & Clark, 2014; Broockman, 2013; Brown, 2014; Burden, 2007; Canon, 1999; Fenno, 2003; Mansbridge, 1999; Minta, 2011; Preuhs, 2006; Tate, 2003; Wallace, 2014; Whitby, 1997). Political representation is a complex phenomenon that is shaped by many factors, including constituency demands, partisanship, committee systems, party leadership, lobbyists, and interest groups. Typically, legislative studies use roll call voting patterns, committee assignments, agenda setting, and legislators' behavior to draw conclusions about the influence of race or gender on legislators' policy preferences (Bratton & Haynie, 1999; Bratton, Haynie, & Reingold, 2006; Casellas, 2009; Haynie, 2001; Hero & Tolbert, 1995; Hutchings, McClerking & Charles, 2004; Reingold, 2000; Swers, 2002; Tate, 2003). As informative as these approaches are, they do not allow for rich or detailed portrayals of how legislators' experiences and identities influence their actions. In this way, much existing scholarship fails to capture the nuance and dynamism of legislators' personal roots.

Here, we use C-SPAN's archived oral histories from African American members of Congress (MCs) to examine the degree to which legislators' self-described experiences shape individual representational styles and perceptions of the role that the CBC plays in helping to achieve their political objectives.[1] Additionally, we examine how the CBC helps legislators achieve their strategic and personal goals. Connecting who legislators are to what they do in Congress speaks to the larger role of identity in political representation. Analysis of the oral histories of African American MCs enables scholars to present a broader examination of these legislators, how they came to be who they are, and the representational strategies they adopt. With the exception of Charles Rangel, the five MCs in this study were the first African Americans to be elected from their districts. Our project considers the fit between minority representation scholarship and legislators' perceptions of who they are and what they do. As such, the C-SPAN oral histories, many collected as part of the Congressional Black Caucus Oral History Project, illuminate how a legislator's experiences may shape identity and, in turn, political behavior.

Because these oral histories are told by legislators in their own words, they provide valuable insight into what legislators think, their values, and their self-representation. Oral histories are partial and subjective evaluations of events. Legislators' stories reflect the processes by which individuals have constructed events and their personal histories to fit into their own conceptions of "self" (Mishler, 1999). Any narrative is a set of choices leading to a particular self-presentation, and subjects may seek to alter how they are perceived by revising history or framing personal stories in a more flattering light. Oral histories do not provide unbiased facts in the way that an impartial observer might but rather present potentially biased portrayals and reconstructions (Ochs & Capps, 2001). In this way, oral histories are instructive for understanding how an individual makes sense of his or her own life (Brown, 2014). With these caveats in mind, legislators' narratives, built on personal memory, are the foundation for this study.

DATA AND METHODOLOGY

We use the C-SPAN Archives' online Video Library to analyze the oral histories of five African American members of Congress.[2] The legislators were elected between 1965 and 1973 and were either founding members or in the second cohort of the CBC. The importance of examining intragroup diversity within a single case study is guided by shortcomings in the extant literature on minority representation. The concept of linked fate—the recognition that one's individual life chances are intimately tied to the race as a whole (Dawson, 1994)—is largely used to explain Blacks' disposition toward group politics. However, centering the narratives of Black MCs allows us to uncover diversity among Black political elites, which demonstrates the complexity of intragroup identity politics. Careful attention to legislators' own words presents a broader view of Black political representation and reveals a nuanced understanding of racial and gender politics at the national level. Specifically, the oral histories allow us to move beyond cross-group differences between White and Black members of Congress to consider differences within Black legislators as a group.

TABLE 7.1 *Racial and Ethnic Minority Members of Congress in C-SPAN Archives Oral Histories*

Representative	Years of Service	Race	Gender	Date Interview Recorded
Yvonne Brathwaite Burke (D-CA)	1973–1979	Black	Female	6/22/2010
John Conyers Jr. (D-MI)	1965–Present	Black	Male	7/18/2007
Walter Fauntroy (D-Washington, DC)*	1971–1991	Black	Male	6/14/2007
Elizabeth Holtzman (D-NY)	1973–1981	White	Female	4/5/2007
Daniel Inouye (D-HI)	1959–2013	Asian	Male	3/3/2008
Doris Matsui (D-CA)	2005–Present	Asian	Female	4/2/2008
Charles Rangel (D-NY)	1971–Present	Black	Male	7/21/2007
Louis Stokes (D-OH)	1969–1999	Black	Male	6/13/2007

NOTE: Data compiled by authors.

*Nonvoting delegate.

Out of more than 400 oral histories in the C-SPAN Video Library, only eight non-White-male MCs were interviewed. As shown in Table 7.1, accounting for individuals who represent more than one demographic category, there are five African American, two Asian American, and three female (one Black, one White, and one Asian) legislators: Yvonne Brathwaite Burke, John Conyers, Walter Fauntroy, Elizabeth Holtzman, Daniel Inouye, Doris Matsui, Charles Rangel, and Louis Stokes. In what follows, we analyze the oral histories of the five African American legislators to examine whether and how their self-perceptions map onto key concepts in minority representation. This small sample, while not representative, is sufficient to our objectives and will allow for disaggregated analysis of how Blackness impacts political representation. We analyze representational narratives to better understand how legislators make meaning from their lives and represent the interests of marginalized groups in Congress.

The oral history interviews appear to have taken place in the caucus members' legislative office, church, or home. Most of the interviews with Black legislators were conducted during June and July of 2007, with the exception of Braithwaite Burke's, which was conducted in June of 2010. Burke's interview is also the shortest at 26 minutes, while the longest is Walter Fauntroy's at 84 minutes.

IDENTITY FORMATION AND GROUP POLITICS IN CONGRESS

Extant literature has documented the breadth and depth of common political beliefs, attitudes, predilections, and behaviors among African Americans as a group (Allen, Dawson, & Brown, 1989; Dawson, 1994; Harris-Lacewell, 2004; Price, 2009; Walton, 1985). The mechanisms underlying Black communal politics are multifaceted and wide ranging (Dawson, 1994; Gay, 2004; Gurin, Hatchett, & Jackson, 1989; Shelby, 2005). Blackness, when understood as a political identity, requires that group members articulate common unifying experiences and draw connections with other group members (Walters, 2007, pp. 22–24). Tommie Shelby (2005) contends that Black group identification is based on collective experiences with, and an obligation to ending, anti-Black racism. The communal nature of Black politics and Black political identity are introduced and strengthened in Black institutions, media, and social contexts (Dawson, 1994; Harris-Perry, 2011; Spence, 2011). Historically rooted, group-based race politics position African Americans' political preferences within the belief that "individual life chances are linked to the fate of the race" (Dawson, 1994, p. 45).

Examining group formation offers a deeper understanding of group cohesion than one based solely on shared characteristics. Social psychologists understand social identity as part of an individual's self-concept beginning with her knowledge of her membership in a social group (or groups). Social identity is saturated with the value and emotional importance that is attached to group membership (Tajfel, 1981). An individual group member acknowledges that she or he is a unique social entity comprising socially relevant characteristics that, in turn, produce self-awareness. Essential for our purposes is the premise in social identity theory that identity can be "switched on" or primed in particular situations that prompt individuals to "act as a group" (Turner, Hogg, Oakes, Reicher, & Wetherell, 1987, p. 42). Turner and colleagues' self-categorization theory is beneficial in explaining how individuals shift their self-perception from personal to social identity. It makes room for scholars to study how a Black representative acts as an individual whose cognitive connection to a group of other Blacks is based on a sense of linked fate. In this section, we examine the effect of racial identity on Black legislators' decisions to either form or join the CBC, the nation's first race-based congressional caucus.

Delegate Walter Fauntroy (D-Washington, DC) was first elected as a nonvoting delegate representing Washington, DC, in 1971. A founding member of the CBC, Fauntroy served two decades in the House of Representatives. According to his oral history in the C-SPAN Archives, Fauntroy's racial identity was deeply influenced during his youth when he learned that Blacks in Washington did not enjoy the same political rights as Blacks in some northern states. Growing up in Washington, DC, "in the heart of American democracy," Fauntroy articulated that his formative years, "defined all that [he] did later in the civil rights movement and in the Congress of the United States." Although a young Fauntroy had career aspirations of being a preacher, he was enamored with the auspices of government he saw in DC from his earliest years:

> I tell people I was not born on a farm, so I don't know very much about chickens and ducks. And, I wasn't born in Detroit; I don't know how to make cars. I wasn't born in West Virginia, so I don't know anything about mining. I was born in Washington, D.C. where my curiosity was about a building downtown called the White House and another one across town called the Capitol, and a bunch of block-filling buildings downtown called the Department of this and the Department of that … usually lines or something are cited from the transcript. (C-SPAN, 2009a)

Fauntroy's narrative uncovers his love for the political system and a strong desire for African Americans to have full political inclusion. He speaks admiringly of the courage of Emmett Till's mother, Mammie Till Mobley, to show the lynched body of her son so that the "world [could see what] you did to him" (C-SPAN, 2009a), and connects her decision with Black political rights. Fauntroy notes that Mammie Till Mobley and Blacks around the country were "vindicated when, at least 100,000 people around the country, Black and White, Red and Brown, and Yellow together said we know a nonviolent way to get the country to change policy. We're going to say to those who want our votes, unless you do that, we're not going to vote for you" (C-SPAN, 2009a).

As a young leader, Fauntroy's racial identity served as the mobilizing factor for his involvement in grassroots activism within the civil rights movement. He traveled the country urging Blacks to register to vote and explaining the importance of casting one's vote for candidates who would support Black civil rights. Reflecting upon his journey, Fauntroy draws connections between the movement and his own electoral fortunes, noting, "I was the first person from the movement elected to the Congress. We had come through hell that year" (C-SPAN, 2009a). Following a short discussion of his role in advocating and organizing for civil rights, Fauntroy begins to contextualize these experiences as influencing not only his legislative work, but also his inclination to organize a Black caucus in Congress. Fauntroy notes that "the achievements of the 60s and the fruit of it at that time, 13 members of the Congressional Black Caucus [was] sufficient, we thought, to form a caucus of Black members who had become the conscience of the nation. So it was a joy to be a part of that group" (C-SPAN, 2009a).

While Fauntroy remembers how his time as a civil rights activist led to his efforts to establish the CBC, Representative Charles Rangel's (D-NY) experience in the New York state legislature and his racial identity influenced heavily his support for organizing the Congressional Black Caucus. Rangel also credits Representative Charles Diggs (D-MI), the first chairman of the CBC (1971–1972), as a great mentor and friend who helped introduce him to the concept of mobilizing in the legislature for racial progress:

> So when the four of us came in, it was then that we started thinking about formally forming the Congressional Black Caucus. Diggs had talked to them. I think they called themselves a "study group" but, it was not formal. And because I had this great experience with the [New York State Legislative] Black Caucus that Percy Sutton had formed at Albany, and having to struggle getting Black people to admit that they are Black, or becoming trouble makers—shaking the structure and seeing that it worked and people respected you for it rather than thinking that you're not working with them—I was able to work with Charlie Diggs when we formed the Congressional Black Caucus. Charlie Diggs was a great man. … And, really, he advised every new member as to the committee assignments so he was a big mentor of mine.

Representative Rangel (D-NY) parses out groups of African Americans that see themselves as politically Black and those that do not. Ron Walters contends that "political Blackness" is "an issue of political trust" and an "appropriate evaluative tool in political behavior" (2007, 12–13). Claiming that one must have a strong racial identity and connection to Blackness in order to make demands on the political structure to demand inclusion and political rights for Blacks, Rangel notes that he learned the value of organizing with other Blacks in the state legislature and that his non-Black colleagues learned to respect rather than be suspect of their efforts. Like Fauntroy's, Rangel's racial identity and experiences with the civil rights movement influenced his decisions about group membership. For him, the march from Selma to Montgomery was a catalyst that "more than anything else created the Congressional Black Caucus we are today" (C-SPAN, 2009d). Indeed, Rangel credits "the power of the civil rights movement and the power of Dr. King" (C-SPAN, 2009d) as forces that helped to launch a consciousness among Blacks to use politics to demand government protection from anti-Black racism.

Representative John Conyers (D-MI) links his involvement with racial group politics in Congress to a historical understanding of the position of African Americans. Conyers believes that understanding the historical trajectory is important to understanding why the CBC is a necessary component of the national legislature. He sees it as his responsibility to ensure that Blacks are being treated fairly and equally. For Conyers, the "hugely structural discrimination that has marked the history of the struggle of Black people in America" (C-SPAN, 2009c) is the impetus for the work he does in Congress and a rationale for organizing a race-based caucus in the House. He offers a sweeping historical timeline connecting Black struggles for citizenship and inclusion during Reconstruction to the establishment and growing size of the CBC at the start of the 21st century:

> So this enhances this great struggle from enslavement to the 13th, 14th and 15th Amendments, which said that we were Americans, but there was segregation, particularly after the Reconstruction Era in which those few African Americans that were elected to the Senate and the Congress were literally chased out of office, driven out of office. The Klan rose up and other violent hate groups, and so we gradually moved back into the first African Americans coming into the Congress and the Senate at the turn of the 20th Century, and our numbers have gradually grown till we are larger now than ever before. We have 43 members of the Congressional Black Caucus. I

was the seventh member[. W]hen we finally got to about a dozen, we decided to organize and that number has been steadily growing. Another phenomenon that occurred that I think is very telling is that all of us—not all of us, most of us, many of us[—]represent many people other than African Americans[. M]any represent a few Haitians. Some of us represent Hispanic Americans. Others of us represent Americans that are not people of color at all, and so, in that sense we have grown. (C-SPAN, 2009c)

Elsewhere in the oral history, Conyers discusses the need to "pass [legislation] to create a society that we can point to rather than empty rhetoric of a couple of hundred years ago" (C-SPAN, 2009c). In this manner, Conyers seeks to pass legislation that reduces the "structural discrimination and the great disparity ... of an economic, employment, education, and housing in America that has created, in effect, two Americas" (C-SPAN, 2009c). Racial identity, for Representative Conyers, is directly linked to past racial injustices that continue to impede the political, social, and economic progress of African Americans.

Representative Louis Stokes's (D-OH) formative experiences growing up in Cleveland and serving in the United States Army inform his commitment to Black organizing in the House. Upon reaching the draft-eligible age of 18, Stokes was drafted into a segregated U.S. Army. As he recounts: "I had to wear the uniform of this country, but I had to do so under segregated circumstances. I was put in an all-Black unit and [was] not permitted to have any contact with White soldiers" (C-SPAN, 2009b). These formative experiences with racism helped to shape how both Stokes and his brother Carl, who would later become the first Black mayor of Cleveland, Ohio, would engage the U.S. political system. In 1969, Louis Stokes, Bill Clay, and Shirley Chisholm were elected to Congress—the largest number of Black members to serve in Congress at the same time. Stokes recalls:

Now you have to understand this was recognized all over the nation as being a historic day because this was the first time that nine Blacks had ever sat in the Congress at one time. The earlier period when they had the largest number was 1875, 1877 when we had six in the House and one in the Senate. Then between 1875 and 1900 there were a total of twenty-two … but by 1900 by virtue of enactment of the Black laws and the intimidation by the Ku Klux Klan and other racial means of getting Blacks out of office all of them had been defeated. (C-SPAN, 2009b)

Like Conyers, Stokes discusses the historical legacy of Blacks in the national legislature to illustrate the trials and tribulations that Blacks faced in order to descriptively represent African American constituents. Specifically, Stokes recalls the final speech Representative George White (R-NC), the last Reconstruction Era Black legislator to serve in Congress, delivered in 1900, foreshadowing the moment when more African Americans would be elected to Congress:

Just before he left the Congress he made a brilliant and historic speech. In his speech he said "This Mr. Speaker is perhaps the Negro's temporary farewell to the United States Congress, but Phoenix-like we will rise up and come another day." George White was right, we would rise up and come another day. But it took 28 years with no Blacks sitting in the U.S. Congress from 1900 to 1928, before another Black would come to the U.S. Congress. In 1928 Arthur Mitchell from Chicago came in and then between 1928 and 1968 Bill, Shirley and I were elected[. T]here was a total of six Blacks elected to and serving in the U.S. Congress and so this was a historic day. (C-SPAN, 2009b)

Like Fauntroy and Rangel, Stokes contends that it was the momentum from their activities in the civil rights movement that capitulated additional Black candidates into electoral success. The election of Chisholm, Clay, and Stokes meant "the three of us immediately [started] working together and we were getting a lot of press. We came to Congress to change things. We raised a lot of sand" (C-SPAN, 2009b). However, as the second chairman of the CBC from 1972 to 1976, Representative Stokes realized that the CBC could not be "all things to all Black people in America" and instead sought to focus attention on enacting legislation "that betters the condition of Black people and minorities all over this country" (C-SPAN, 2009b).

The oral histories also provided some insight into an individual representative's multiple identities and the ways that racial–gender identity influenced decisions about group politics. While Representative Yvonne Brathwaite Burke also got her start as a civil rights leader, her shared racial identity was made more complex by her gendered identity as a Black woman. Indeed, she was one of the few Black congresswomen during a time when men—both Black and White—dominated Congress. Unlike her male counterparts, Brathwaite Burke underscores the importance of coming together with allies and supportive individuals to advance the "issues that affected *women* and affected African Americans" (C-SPAN, 2011). Along with other Black female representatives Barbara Jordan and Shirley Chisholm, Brathwaite Burke used her platform as a legislator to speak out against issues that highlighted the intersection of race, gender, and vulnerability that characterized the experiences of many Black women. It seems that certain issues activated not only a racial identity, but also what Brown (2014, p. 5) calls "racial and gender identities." When the Black women in the CBC organized to speak out against the involuntary sterilization of southern Black women, Brathwaite Burke reports that their male colleagues were somewhat put out:

> There was an issue that came up as far as women in the south, and some of the states that were having sterilization rules. So, we decided we would have our own press conference on that, and boy, the Caucus said, *"Now, we got a Black women's caucus."* So, you know that was the only thing of where there was ever any kind of contention, that there was a little sensitivity that we would come forward and have our own issues. But the Women's Caucus grew out of the Black Caucus. They formed and many of us were involved in the formation of the Women's Caucus and also the foundation concept for the women's caucus came about as a result of some of us being involved on women's issues. (C-SPAN, 2011)

In contrast to the male members of Congress in our sample, Brathwaite Burke explicitly discusses how her gendered identity impacted her involvement with the CBC. As the first woman chair of the CBC, Brathwaite Burke used her racial/gendered identity as a Black woman to draw attention to issues that disproportionately affected African American women. Baxter and Lansing (1983) suggest that the twofold discrimination of racism and sexism experienced by Black women for generations has produced an intensified political awareness in this group that enables recognition of gender- *or* race-specific issues as well as those issues that are both gender *and* race specific. Hence, it comes as little surprise that Black women were instrumental in forming both the CBC and the Women's Caucus.

In a fashion not previously detailed in existing research, the oral histories demonstrate the ways that identity- and race-specific experiences influenced the decisions of individual members to pursue group-based politics in the halls of Congress. The next section considers the ways in which local party politics influence amenity to group politics and decisions about representational connections for African American legislators.

BLACK REPRESENTATION, INDEPENDENCE, AND THE URBAN MACHINE

Historically, examinations of Black representation and Black legislators have focused on the factors that united Black elected officials in their representation of the Black community. Myriad books and articles analyzing whether and how race matters in representation have approached these questions primarily by addressing the degree to which Black representatives differ in their behavior from White representatives. This work has led to a rich and engaging literature demonstrating both the strong connections of Black MCs to the Democratic Party, as well as the potential for generational, and even geographical, differences in representation (Canon, 1999; Grose, 2011; Minta, 2011; Tate, 2003). Our examination of the oral histories of CBC founders reveals another interesting and important difference that merits further scholarly attention: the influence of local politics, particularly urban machines, on the emergence of Black political candidates and their representational styles.

Urban political machines dominated politics in American cities for nearly a century beginning in the mid-1800s. Party machines and "bosses" in major cities such as Chicago and New York organized politics from the local precinct or ward level all the way to the governor's office, sometimes influencing the fortunes of presidential politics. For Blacks exercising newfound political muscle during this era, the machine was either a demanding ally or a formidable opponent in their efforts toward self-determination and responsive politics (Erie, 1990; Grimshaw, 1992). A look at the politics of three founding CBC members, Cardiss Collins (D-IL)[3], Louis Stokes (D-OH), and Charles Rangel

(D-NY), provides a rare view of the different ways Black politicians aligned themselves for or against, within and without, the Democratic Party machine.

New York is infamous for the Tammany Hall political machine and strong party bosses from the mid-19th century through the 1930s. No New York boss is more notorious than William M. "Boss" Tweed, who used patronage and favors to gain personal wealth and help cronies for more than two decades beginning in 1858. Progressive reforms and the election of an independent Mayor LaGuardia in 1934 began the downfall of the Tammany machine, and by the mid-1960s, machine politics in New York had been all but swept away. Representative Adam Clayton Powell, elected in 1944 and the first Black representative from the state of New York, operated in a connected, but independent, fashion with the waning machine (Hamilton, 1991). In many ways (and especially near the end of his political career), Powell was a thorn in the side of New York City's Democratic Party leadership (Capeci, 1977). Although the Democratic Party continued to be a tight-knit and insular group in New York City politics, requiring assent from party leaders to credibly run for office, by the time that Charles Rangel ran for and won Powell's seat, the strict control of party bosses was a relic of the past.

Party leadership could not, however, be avoided or easily challenged. Rangel learned an early lesson about the power of New York's Democratic leadership when, because of his actions, he cost his grandfather a much needed work extension to avoid retirement. As Rangel tells it, he had signed a petition supporting the candidacy of an establishment opponent and word got back to party leaders. When his grandfather went down to request an extension, it was denied because of young Rangel's actions. Rangel was directed to meet with the leader of the state Democratic Party, Carmine DeSapio, and make amends. He later ran for state assembly with the machine's blessings. It was also with the machine's blessings that Rangel challenged and beat Powell in the Democratic primary in New York's 18th Congressional District in 1970. It is apparent that Rangel's political career was deeply tied to connections in New York's political machine, connections that Powell had never depended on and had ultimately shunned. As Rangel recalls:

> Governor Rockefeller authorized me to go to Bimini to [talk] to Congressman Powell to share with him that if he would come back home they would remove the criminal sanctions and things would

work out. But, Adam would have none of it. I went to Bimini. I spent the day there by myself waiting to see him. And, he made it abundantly clear to me that he wasn't thinking much about coming home and I had to make a decision *because I knew Adam Powell politically was vulnerable and there were six people running against him, and also running against me.* And so I decided to become a candidate and I succeeded in the primary. (C-SPAN, 2009d)

Like those of Black representatives in New York, the political fortunes of Black MCs from Chicago were also deeply tied to the urban machine. Representative William "Boss" Dawson (D-IL), the second Black legislator sent to Congress by the state of Illinois, was a direct product and protégé of Chicago's Daley machine. Representative George Collins (D-IL) also rose through the ranks in the Daley machine. When Collins died in a plane crash shortly after reelection to his second term, his wife, Cardiss, was encouraged to run by Boss (Mayor Richard) Daley himself. In an oral history recorded by the National Visionary Leadership Project (n.d.), Cardiss Collins recalls that the day after her husband's funeral, "the mayor, Richard J. Daley, called my house and he said that he wanted to talk to me in about a week's time" about completing the remainder of her husband's unexpired congressional term. Black members of the Chicago machine and the ministerial alliance in the Black church urged her to run as well. She won the special election and went on to win 10 more elections, serving more than two decades in the House. Cardiss Collins was an unabashed member of the Daley machine. When she decided to retire in the early 1990s, one of her first calls was to Mayor Richard M. Daley, the son of the man who first encouraged her to enter public affairs. She complied when he asked her to stay on one more term while he "got somebody ready" (National Visionary Leadership Project, n.d.) to compete for her seat.

Like Rangel and Collins and in contrast to Fauntroy, Representative Louis Stokes (D-OH) did not have long political ambitions and claims to have "sort of backed into politics" (C-SPAN, 2009b) when he first won office in 1968. His connection to politics was mostly to ensure that his brother, Carl Stokes, was successful in the political arena:

I loved being a criminal trial lawyer. My practice was such that I was in some case or some courtroom trying a case every day and I loved it. I could have tried lawsuits for the rest of my life and been perfectly content. I didn't have any political ambition, I'm not even sure I liked politicians. I had no interest what so ever in politics. My only interest in politics was my brother and helping him do what he wanted to do in politics. (C-SPAN, 2009b)

Stokes's emergence onto the national political stage had very different roots in Cleveland. His beginnings were more akin to Powell's than to those of Rangel or Cardiss Collins. Stokes spent little time in his oral history discussing the origins of his political career. He did, however, discuss his role in drawing the Black-majority district that would eventually elect him the first Black congressman from Ohio:

Ohio had never had a Black in the U.S. Congress and there were people who intended that would not occur, so they gerrymandered the 21st congressional district in such a way that they completely diluted the Black population and … there was not basic strength in that congressional district. Carl came home from Columbus, OH and went to the NAACP and asked them [to] file a lawsuit against the legislature. … I was the NAACP's Legal Redress Committee Chairman so … they gave me the case for me and my committee to handle. … [W]e filed a lawsuit on his behalf and it took three years for the case to come up in court. … We lost the case in the lower court, but because we had a three judge panel … we could take the case directly into the U.S. Supreme Court. So, we took the case to the U.S. Supreme Court and the Supreme Court held in our favor … and ordered the local District Court to redistrict along constitutional lines and … when they did the district came out 65% Black, 35% White, which meant for the first time in our state's history, we could elect a Black.

In the late 1960s, Stokes and his brother Carl ran insurgent campaigns built on the support of newly empowered Black voters to win historic congressional and mayoral offices in Ohio. During his second term as mayor of Cleveland, Carl Stokes organized the Twenty-first District Democratic Caucus as a Black power base in local Democratic Party politics (Nelson, 1987, p. 176). When the Democratic Party refused to acknowledge the Twenty-first District

Caucus's recommendations of new candidates and policy reforms, the Caucus withdrew from the Democratic Party to begin pursuing a non-partisan, Black-focused, political agenda. The Twenty-first District Caucus, under Stokes's chairmanship, consolidated power among local Black leaders and Black voters. Despite the proclamation of a Stokes staffer that they were creating a Black "[political] machine like Tammany Hall or like Daley did in Chicago," by 1976, the Twenty-first District Caucus had evolved into Representative Stokes's own personal party organization and was an indispensable source of support for his electoral campaigns (Fenno, 2003, pp. 38–41). For all the value of having an independent electoral base, Stokes also recognized that independence could be costly. He vividly recalls that, "Adam Clayton Powell the day we had been sworn in was stripped of his chairmanship and other attributes of office." [4] These young legislators were deeply aware of the high price Powell had paid for going it alone and independently challenging the norms and mores of the House. For Stokes, one lesson from Powell's troubles was a commitment to beat the system while working within it (see Fenno, 2003, p. 22).

An examination of the personal recollections of Black representatives' relationships with the local Democratic Party and their Black constituents may shed light on previously unrecognized, but important, differences between legislators who emerged within or outside of local party machines. Our analysis of oral histories suggests that local politics, and particularly the politics of White-dominated urban machines, influence candidate emergence and may influence the nature of Black representation. As we shall see in the next section, legislators' early personal and political experiences likely also shaped their decision making about pursuing group-based political strategies in Congress.

THE GENESIS OF THE CONGRESSIONAL BLACK CAUCUS

Legislators are motivated by a variety of factors, such as a desire to make good public policy, power-seeking, and ideology, but ultimately reelection motivations are the primary organizing principle of legislators' behavior (Arnold, 1990; Fenno, 1978; Mayhew, 1974). Political representation scholars have challenged the assumption that strategic reelection goals are the main drivers of legislators' actions. They have found minority legislators' connection to their racial/ethnic group is a strong factor that motivates and constrains their representational activities in Congress (Fenno, 2003; Gamble, 2007; Grose, 2011; King-Meadows, 2011; Minta 2011; Minta & Brown, 2014; Minta & Sinclair-Chapman, 2013; Swain, 1993; Tillery, 2011; Whitby, 1997). This is not to say that minority legislators are not motivated by the same concerns as White legislators, but rather that minority legislators are additionally expected to collectively uplift their racial group (Minta, 2011; Swain, 1993; Tate 2014; Whitby, 1997). Although there is strong empirical evidence to suggest that racial group consciousness exists among Black legislators, there is no systematic survey or attitudinal data to test directly for the existence of this concept. Scholars usually infer the presence of racial group consciousness from the greater time and resources that Black legislators devote to the advocacy of racial and social welfare issues in committees, bill sponsorships, floor speeches, and roll call voting. Not only are Black legislators strong advocates for minority interests, they pioneered an organization, the Congressional Black Caucus, with the express purpose of advocating for the interests of Blacks nationally and internationally. Similar to Aldrich's question, "Why parties?," we ask the question, "Why the Congressional Black Caucus?" Why isn't membership in the Democratic Party enough? The idea that Black legislators would naturally organize into a CBC is a common assumption of political scientists; however, we argue that the evolution of such an institution is not preordained. Why did Black legislators agree to form a group that did not necessarily advance their reelection goals? How do Black legislators balance demands to meet the needs of their district constituents and yet fulfill the demands of the CBC?

Oral histories provide insight into how race and a legislator's own personal background motivate the political enterprise. The U.S. House had three Black members from 1930 to 1969, but these members usually did not work together and did not organize. In fact, the most prominent member in the 1960s, Representative Adam Clayton Powell Jr. (D-NY), even questioned the need for a Black caucus (Tillery, 2011). Powell claimed that he could, and did, represent the interests of Blacks without an organization on Capitol Hill. Representative William Dawson (D-IL), and later Arthur Mitchell (D-IL), saw fit to work mainly through the Chicago political machine. The oral histories in our sample reveal differing views of how to represent Black constituents and varying explanations for why, in 1971, 13 members decided to organize and form a caucus dedicated to fulfilling the interests of Blacks while at the same time satisfying their reelection goals. The formation of the CBC was indeed a significant step in the evolution of Black interests on the federal level, but it also provides insights into how members viewed themselves and their relationships to local and national constituencies. The previous literature on minority political representation assumes that racial or ethnic group consciousness is motivating the actions of these legislators, but the oral histories provide an insider's view on how these legislators see their roles as representatives. The oral histories demonstrate that legislators experienced a demand for group representation that sometimes surprised them. These accounts also reveal that organizing themselves into a group-based legislative organization was not purely the outgrowth of psychological forces such as consciousness or sociopolitical forces such as the civil rights movement; instead, individual legislators carefully weighed the costs and benefits organizing a race-based caucus that would ultimately set them apart, within both the House of Representatives and the Democratic Party.

Increased attention to minority interests is not based solely on whether Democrats control the chambers or other familiar features of congressional institutions, such as the median ideology of legislators and divided government. Rather, the decision of small numbers of minority legislators to dedicate scarce resources to the creation, maintenance, and expansion of a diversity infrastructure reflects the creation of an "extraparty" system to allow for advocacy, agency, and a departure from routine behavior in the party (Minta & Sinclair-Chapman, 2013). For a period of time minority legislators pursued their legislative goals primarily within the boundaries of the major political parties. Beginning in the 1970s and 1980s, legislators determined that neither the Democratic Party nor the Republican Party was adequately addressing the issues that were most salient to Blacks and Latinos. In response, minority legislators began constructing infrastructures to facilitate information gathering and coordination on issues important to the larger national constituencies they represented. Unlike members of other caucuses, members of racial or ethnic caucuses were mostly Democrats and motivated by a commitment to uplift the interests of all minorities, including those minority constituents who do not live in their districts (Clay, 1993):

> We realized that Black people all over America as well as other minorities all over America needed and wanted us to represent them as

well as the congressional districts from which we were elected. What do I mean by that, what I mean is there were no Black congress persons in Mississippi, Georgia, Alabama, Arkansas and those other states and so Black people in those states expected Lou Stokes, Shirley Chisholm and Bill Clay to represent them also. Many times we appointed Mississippi youth to West Point and to the Naval Academy and things of that sort because they couldn't get appointed by their own White congressman in their congressional districts. That's when we realized that we had to represent Black people not only in our own districts but we had to try to get representation throughout America. (C-SPAN, 2009b)

Although Black legislators were committed to representing all Blacks, these elected officials also recognized that they were not civil rights workers. The task was to pass legislation. As a result, Black legislators formally organized the CBC in 1971 to help them fulfill their individual district legislative goals as well as to sustain advocacy for Black interests nationally and internationally (Minta & Sinclair-Chapman, 2013). The Caucus allowed for the sharing of resources across legislative offices, enhanced communication and information sharing, and provided for the coordination of agendas and messages. John Conyers stated that Black legislators decided to form the Caucus because "we wanted to inform each other of what was going on in the committees" (C-SPAN, 2009c).

Minority legislators were intentional and strategic about expanding their ability to influence the congressional agenda, particularly as their numbers began to grow. As recounted by Charles Rangel, "We believed that organizing as a caucus would give us significant voting power in the House. We wanted [to] cultivate leaders and not compete with each other. The civil rights leaders would work on the outside and other people would work on the inside" (C-SPAN, 2009d). Minority legislators expanded information task forces within the caucuses to develop positions on a variety of issues, including the economy, social welfare, and civil rights (Bositis, 1994). Rangel states that "the CBC can get more done today with 42 members" (C-SPAN, 2009d) than when it had only 13 members. As conservative Democrats' power has decreased, minority members have become more prominent. Over time, the number of racial and ethnic minority committee chairs and leaders has grown in the House. As a result, minority legislators are able to influence not only legislation but also federal agencies that are enforcing existing federal civil rights laws and other regulations that are salient to minorities (Minta, 2009, 2011; Walton, 1988). Currently, the CBC continues to advocate for minority interests and sponsor legislation to promote the betterment of marginalized peoples. For example, each year the CBC releases an alternative budget that focuses on how to be both morally and fiscally responsible to America's most economically vulnerable communities. In addition, the CBC has had an active presence in social justice issues that has led to congressional hearings and often legislation such as the anti-apartheid movement, stopping the genocide in Darfur, and #BlackLivesMatter.

CONCLUSION

Oral histories are a rich source of data, and the C-SPAN Video Library is an important resource. As the CBC nears its 50th anniversary, it is unfortunate that oral histories of only five Black MCs are cataloged at C-SPAN. Additional oral histories would allow for extended analysis of the role of race in political representation and likely raise new questions.

The narratives of the members of Congress in this study show that racial identity is a consistent factor in explaining why legislators from across the country were inclined to form a cohesive racial bloc in the national legislature. Their social identity as Blacks gave these legislators a rationale for reaching out to each other, as well as a generally shared perspective on the role they would serve for Blacks nationwide. In a fashion not previously detailed in existing research, the oral histories in this study demonstrate the ways that identity and race-specific experiences have influenced the decisions of individual members to pursue group-based politics within the halls of Congress.

In this chapter we discussed what scholars can learn when we allow representatives to tell us why they do what they do. Our analysis of oral histories demonstrates that legislators' self-representations confirm, challenge, and expand our understandings of Black representation. Our work shows that Black legislators' formative experiences affect their perspectives on Black group politics. Several MCs in our sample referenced youthful experiences with racism and activism in the civil rights movement as an explanation for their support of creating the CBC. The civil rights movement was an important factor in establishing the CBC, but the oral histories reveal that Black legislators were also influenced by the weight of history and demands from Black constituents outside of their districts, as well as the connection of Black legislators' electoral fortunes to local party and race politics.

NOTES

Authors are listed alphabetically.

1. These oral histories were originally recorded by the Avoice Virtual Library Project of the Congressional Black Caucus Foundation in 2007. The CBC Foundation's Avoice Project sought to record still-living CBC founders. C-SPAN later obtained these interviews to air and include in the Video Library.

2. We thank research assistant Nicole Bouye for her transcription of the oral histories.

3. The Cardiss Collins oral history was recorded by the National Visionary Leadership Project (http://www.visionaryproject.org/collinscardiss/). Including it improved our discussion of gender and machine politics. To our knowledge, the CBC Avoice Virtual Library Project, the National Visionary Leadership Project, and C-SPAN are the only depositories of oral histories of Black MCs.

4. In 1966, Representative Adam Clayton Powell Jr. (D-NY) was elected for his 12th term. Based in part on political scandal in New York, and on accusations that he had abused the prerogatives of office, Powell was denied by the House of Representatives the opportunity to take the oath of office in January of 1967. Powell sued House Speaker John W. McCormack and other House leadership in federal district court. The case eventually made its way to the Supreme Court, which determined in *Powell v. McCormack* (1969) that Powell, having been duly elected and satisfying constitutional requirements, had been illegally excluded from taking the oath of office in the 90th Congress. Powell once again won reelection in 1968 and was sworn in in January 1969; however, the House stripped him of seniority and chairmanship of the powerful Education and Labor Committee.

REFERENCES

Allen, R. L., Dawson, M. C., & Brown, R. E. (1989). A schema-based approach to modeling an African-American racial belief system. *American Political Science Review, 83*(2), 421–441. http://dx.doi.org/10.2307/1962398

Arnold, R. D., (1990). *The logic of congressional action.* New Haven, CT: Yale University Press.

Baxter, S., & Lansing, M. (1983). *Women and politics: The visible majority.* Ann Arbor: University of Michigan Press.

Bositis, D. A. (1994). *The congressional black caucus in the 103rd Congress.* Lanham, MD: University Press of America.

Bowen, D.C., & Clark, C.J. (2014). Revisiting descriptive representation in Congress: Assessing the effect of race on the constituent-legislator relationship. *Political Research Quarterly, 67*(3), 695–707.

Bratton, K.A., & Haynie, K. L. (1999). Agenda setting and legislative success in state legislatures: The effects of gender and race. *Journal of Politics, 61*(3), 658–679. http://dx.doi.org/10.2307/2647822

Bratton, K. A., Haynie, K.L., & Reingold, B. (2006). Agenda setting and African American women in state legislatures. *Journal of Women, Politics & Policy, 28*(3/4), 71–96. http://dx.doi.org/ 10.1300/J501v28n03_04

Broockman, D.E. (2013). Black politicians are more intrinsically motivated to advance Blacks' interests: A field experiment manipulating political incentives. *American Journal of Political Science, 57*(3), 521-536.

Brown, N. E. (2014). *Sisters in the statehouse: Black women and legislative decision making* [Oxford Scholarship Online version]. New York, NY: Oxford University Press. http://dx.doi.org/10.1093/acprof:oso/9780199352432.001.0001

Burden, B. (2007). *Personal roots of representation.* Princeton, NJ: Princeton University Press.

Capeci, D. J. (1977). From different liberal perspectives: Fiorello H. La Guardia, Adam Clayton Powell, Jr., and civil rights in New York City, 1941–1943. *Journal of Negro History, 62*(2), 160–173. http://dx.doi.org/10.2307/2717176

Canon, D. T. (1999). *Race, redistricting, and representation: The unintended consequences of Black majority districts.* Chicago, IL: University of Chicago Press.

Casellas, J. P. (2009). *Latino representation in state Houses and Congress.* New York, NY: Cambridge University Press.

Clay, W. L. (1993). *Just permanent interests: Black Americans in Congress 1870–1992.* New York, NY: Amistad Press, Inc.

C-SPAN (Producer). (2009a, October 24). *Walter Fauntroy oral history interview* [online video]. Available from http://www.c-span.org/video/?289322-1/walter -fauntroy-oral-history-interview

C-SPAN (Producer). (2009b, October 25). *Louis Stokes oral history interview* [online video]. Available from http://www.c-span.org/video/?289321-1 /louis-stokes-oral-history-interview

C-SPAN (Producer). (2009c, October 31). *John Conyers oral history interview* [online video]. Available from http://www.c-span.org/video/?289427-1/john -conyers-oral-history-interview

C-SPAN (Producer). (2009d, November 1). *Charles Rangel oral history interview* [online video]. Available from http://www.c-span.org/video/?289426-1/charles -rangel-oral-history-interview

C-SPAN (Producer). (2011, January 2). *Yvonne Brathwaite Burke oral history interview* [online video]. Available from http://www.c-span.org/video/?297086-1 /yvonne-brathwaite-burke-oral-history-interview

Dawson, M. (1994). *Behind the mule: Race and class in African American politics.* Princeton, NJ: Princeton University Press.

Erie, S. P. (1990). *Rainbow's end: Irish-Americans and the dilemma of urban machine politics, 1840–1985.* Berkeley: University of California Press.

Fenno, R. F. (1978). *Homestyle: House members in their districts.* London, UK: Longman Publishing Group.

Fenno, R. F. (2003). *Going home: Black representatives and their constituents.* Chicago, IL: University of Chicago Press.

Gamble, K. L. (2007). Black political representation: An examination of legislative activity within U.S. House committees. *Legislative Studies Quarterly, 32*(3), 421–447. http://dx.doi.org/10.3162/036298007781699663

Gay, C. (2004). Putting race in context: Identifying the environmental determinants of Black racial attitudes. *American Political Science Review, 98*(4), 547–562. http:// dx.doi.org/10.1017/S0003055404041346

Grimshaw, W. J. (1992). *Bitter fruit: Black politics and the Chicago machine, 1931–1991.* Chicago, IL: University of Chicago Press.

Grose, C. R. (2011). *Congress in Black and White: Race and representation in Washington and at home.* New York, NY: Cambridge University Press.

Gurin, P., Hatchett S., & Jackson, J. (1989). *Hope and independence: Blacks' response to electoral and party politics.* New York, NY: Russell Sage.

Hamilton, C. V. (1991). *Adam Clayton Powell Jr.: The political biography of an American dilemma.* New York, NY: Atheneum.

Harris-Lacewell, M. (2004). Barbershops, bibles, and BET: Everyday talk and Black political thought. Princeton, NJ: Princeton University Press.

Harris-Perry, M. V. (2011). *Sister citizen: Shame, stereotypes and Black women in America.* New Haven, CT: Yale University Press.

Haynie, K. L. (2001). *African American legislators in the American states.* New York, NY: Columbia University Press.

Hero, R. E., & Tolbert, C. J. (1995). Latinos and substantive representation in the U.S. House of Representatives: Direct, indirect, or nonexistent? *American Journal of Political Science, 39*(3), 640–652.

Hutchings, V. L., McClerking, H. L. & Charles, G. (2004). Congressional representation of Black interests: recognizing the importance of stability. *Journal of Politics, 66*(2), 450–468.

King-Meadows, T. D. (2011). *When the letter betrays the spirit: Voting rights enforcement and African American participation from Lyndon Johnson to Barack Obama.* Lanham, MD: Lexington Books.

Mansbridge, J. (1999). Should Blacks represent Blacks and women represent women? A contingent "yes." *Journal of Politics, 61*(3), 628–657. http://dx.doi .org/10.2307/2647821

Mayhew, D. (1974). *Congress: The electoral connection.* New Haven, CT: Yale University Press.

Minta, M. D. (2009). Legislative oversight and the substantive representation of Black and Latino interests in Congress. *Legislative Studies Quarterly, 34*(2), 193–218. http://dx.doi.org/10.3162/036298009788314336

Minta, M. D. (2011). *Oversight: Representing the interests of Blacks and Latinos in Congress.* Princeton, NJ: Princeton University Press.

Minta, M. D, & Brown, N. (2014). Intersecting interests: Gender, race and congressional attention to women's issues. *Du Bois Review: Social Science Research on Race, 11*(2), 253–272. http://dx.doi.org/10.1017/S1742058X14000186

Minta, M. D., & Sinclair-Chapman, V. (2013). Diversity in political institutions and congressional responsiveness to minority interests. *Political Research Quarterly, 66*(1), 127–140. http://dx.doi.org/10.1177/1065912911431245

Mishler, E. G. (1999). *Storylines: Craftartists' narratives of identity*. Cambridge, MA: Harvard University Press.

National Visionary Leadership Project. (n.d.). Oral history archive: Cardiss Collins. Retrieved from http://www.visionaryproject.org/collinscardiss/

Nelson, W. E., Jr. (1987). Cleveland: The evolution of Black political power. In M. B. Preston, L. J. Henderson Jr., & P. Puryear (Eds.), *The new Black politics: The search for political power* (2nd ed., pp. 172–179). London, UK: Longman Publishing Group.

Ochs, E., & Capps, L. (2001). *Living narrative: Creating lives in everyday storytelling*. Cambridge, MA: Harvard University Press.

Powell v. McCormack, 395 U.S. 486 (1969). Retrieved from https://supreme.justia .com/cases/federal/us/395/486/case.html

Preuhs, R. R. (2006). The conditional effects of minority descriptive representation: Black legislators and policy influence in the American states. *Journal of Politics, 68*(3), 585–599.

Price, M. T. (2009). *Dreaming blackness: Black nationalism and African American public opinion*. New York, NY: NYU Press.

Reingold, B. (2000). *Representing women: Sex, gender and legislative behavior in Arizona and California*. Chapel Hill: University of North Carolina Press.

Shelby, T. (2005). *We who are dark: The philosophical foundations of Black solidarity*. Cambridge, MA: Harvard University Press.

Spence, L. K. (2011). *Stare in the darkness: The limits of hip-hop and Black politics*. Minneapolis: University of Minnesota Press.

Swain, C. M. (1993) *Black faces, Black interests: The representation of African Americans in Congress:* Cambridge, MA: Harvard University Press.

Swers, M. L. (2002). *The difference women make*. Chicago, IL: University of Chicago Press.

Tajfel, H. (1981). *Human groups and social categories*. Cambridge: Cambridge University Press.

Tate, K. (2003). *Black faces in the mirror: African Americans and their representatives in the U.S. Congress*. Princeton, NJ: Princeton University Press.

Tate, K. (2014). *Concordance: Black lawmaking in the U.S. Congress from Carter to Obama*. Ann Arbor: University of Michigan Press.

Tillery, A. B. (2011). *Between homeland and motherland: Africa, U.S. foreign policy, and Black leadership in America*. Ithaca, NY: Cornell University Press.

Turner, J. C., Hogg, M. A., Oakes, P. J., Reicher, S. D., & Wetherell, M. S. (1987). *Rediscovering the social group: A self-categorization theory*. New York, NY: Blackwell Publishing.

Wallace, S. J. (2014). Representing Latinos: Examining descriptive and substantive representation in Congress. *Political Research Quarterly, 67*(4), 917–929.

Walters, R. (2007). Barack Obama and the politics of Blackness. *Journal of Black Studies, 38*(September), 7–29.

Walton, H. (1985). *Invisible politics.* Albany: State University of New York Press.

Walton, H. (1988). *When the marching stopped: The politics of civil rights regulatory agencies.* Albany: State University of New York Press.

Whitby, K. J. (1997). *The color of representation: Congressional behavior and Black interests.* Ann Arbor: University of Michigan Press.

CHAPTER **8**

"MOM-IN-CHIEF" RHETORIC AS A LENS FOR UNDERSTANDING POLICY ADVOCACY: A THEMATIC ANALYSIS OF VIDEO FOOTAGE FROM MICHELLE OBAMA'S SPEECHES

Ray Block Jr.
Christina S. Haynes

And I say all of this tonight not just as First Lady ... and not just as a wife. You see, at the end of the day, my most important title is still "Mom-In-Chief." My daughters are still the heart of my heart and the center of my world.
— FIRST LADY MICHELLE OBAMA, 2012 DEMOCRATIC NATIONAL CONVENTION

In many respects, Michelle Obama's rousing speech at the 2012 Democratic National Convention was the culmination of an ongoing effort by members of the Obama campaign and administration to manage public perceptions. Whether the First Lady of the United States (FLOTUS) is primarily responsible for this perception management process, or if it originated among her husband's handlers, is up for debate (compare, e.g., Dillaway & Paré, 2013, to Erbe, 2009). However, there is a consensus among scholars and journalists that the image transformation is strategic (i.e., a deliberate attempt to control narratives about the FLOTUS), that it started during the 2008 Democratic primaries, and that the goal of this transformation is to "soften" Michelle Obama's persona so that she may broaden her appeal among ideologically moderate, White, and female voters (see Harris-Perry, 2011, for a comprehensive discussion).

This image transformation process in general, and the use of motherhood rhetoric[1] in particular, is a source of controversy among pundits and bloggers alike. Some critics take exception to the First Lady making this rhetorical move, for they view it as a selling out to electoral pressure, or, worse yet, a veiled attack on feminist values (Belkin, 2012; Campbell, 2012; Cottle, 2013; Traister, 2008). Harris-Perry (2013) defends Mrs. Obama's decision to prioritize her family over her career, seeing it as a testament to the First Lady's desire to transcend negative stereotypes of African American women. In a televised reading of her letter to Michelle Cottle, a Washington reporter for *The Daily Beast,* host Harris-Perry argues that FLOTUS is pushing against the "Mammy" stereotype:

> But when she calls herself mom-in-chief, she is rejecting a different stereotype—the role of Mammy. She is saying that her daughters—her vulnerable, brilliant, beautiful black daughters—are the most important thing to her. The First Lady is saying, "You, Miss Ann, will have to clean your own house, because I will be caring for my own." Instead of agreeing that the public sphere is more important than Sasha and Malia, she buried Mammy and embraced being a mom on her own terms.[2] (Harris-Perry, 2013)

In this chapter, we inform the debate over the political implications of the First Lady's discursive strategies. Rather than replacing her activism or perpetuating traditional (read: nonprogressive) gender roles, we believe that motherhood rhetoric has the potential to extend the FLOTUS's audience and heighten support for her initiatives, and we explore more systematically the interconnections between race, gender, and rhetoric. In so doing, this chapter paves the way for future research that investigates the First Lady's use of Mom-In-Chief oratory when discussing policy.

Like Kahl (2009), we credit much of Michelle Obama's success as a policy advocate to her ability to employ what many have dubbed "Mom-In-Chief"

TABLE 8.1   *Understanding the First Lady's Signature Policies: Details about* Let's Move *and* Joining Forces

	Let's Move	Joining Forces
Established	February 2010	April 2011
Founder(s)	Michelle Obama	Jill Biden and Michelle Obama
Objective(s)	Reduce the nation's childhood obesity rate to 5% by 2030 (the same rate it was in the late 1970s)	Honor and support America's troops and their families
Action Step(s)	Prenatal care services, easier access to health/nutrition information, healthier school lunches and snacks, cheaper and more accessible healthy food outside of school	Maximize wellness, education, and employment opportunities

DATA SOURCES: White House (2010a, 2010b).

rhetoric (see, e.g., Carmon, 2012; Drexler, 2009; Edwards & Call, 2009; Malmsheimer & Weiss-Meyer, 2014; Traister 2008; Zacka, 2014). Kahl characterizes such rhetoric as a "nuanced, rhetorical strategy" designed to boost support for family-related policies (Kahl 2009, p. 317), and we extend Kahl's arguments to analyze the rhetorical artifacts found in two of the First Lady's signature policy initiatives: the "Let's Move" campaign against childhood obesity and the "Joining Forces" program for military families. "Let's Move" is a partnership forged in 2010 between state-level officials, health care professionals, community organizers, celebrities, religious leaders, and members of the private (for-profit and nonprofit) sectors designed to, by 2030, reduce the nation's childhood obesity rate to 5 percent, which was its rate in the late 1970s, before childhood obesity emerged as a problem (White House, 2010b). Founded in 2011 by Michelle Obama and Jill Biden, "Joining Forces" is a nationwide invitation for Americans to rally around troops, veterans, and their loved ones and support them through wellness, education, and employment opportunities (White House, 2010a).[3] Table 8.1 provides a summary of these two policy initiatives.

   To explore the linkages between race, gender, rhetoric, and policy support, we combine a careful reading of the Michelle Obama literature with a qualitative thematic analysis of video footage from a sample of her speeches. This approach allows us to compare the scholarly conversation about policy advocacy with the First Lady's own voice. Consistent with Kahl (2009), the evidence from our thematic analyses points to three "rhetorical moves" that the First Lady incorporates into her discussions of "Let's Move" and "Joining Forces." Specifically, Michelle Obama seeks to cultivate policy support by (1) giving prominence to notions of family and motherhood as unifying dimensions of identity; (2) reassuring constituents that, despite her professional accomplishments and political stature, she is no different from (or better than) other moms and spouses; and (3) obscuring the lines between her public title as First Lady and her private role as a spouse and parent. We conclude this chapter with a call for continued scholarship on the impact of Mom-In-Chief rhetoric on policy perceptions.

DECODING MOTHERHOOD RHETORIC

In an essay titled, "First Lady Michelle Obama: Advocate for Strong Families," Mary Kahl (2009) summarizes the logic behind the First Lady's use of Mom-In-Chief rhetoric. We find the following passage particularly insightful:

> Mrs. Obama has identified her primary role in the White House as "Mom-in-Chief," maintaining that raising her children is her full-time job and first priority. Her focus on the family functions on several levels, not the least of which are to insulate her from criticism, to demystify her racial heritage, and to lend credibility to her image. Because mothering is a profoundly "foundational" and "universal" occupation, Michelle's focus on her family—and on the families of others—affords her a nuanced rhetorical platform that is nonthreatening, wholesome, and comprehensible. It is the female equivalent of "No Drama Obama"; steady, nurturing, and proactive. (Kahl, 2009, p. 317)

This passage fascinates us, not only because of what Kahl says in it, but also because of the author's rationale for communicating what she does about First Lady Michelle Obama. For instance, if we assess the "rhetorical context" by employing the SOAPSTone strategy often taught to reading and writing students—a strategy used to analyze texts for speaker, occasion, purpose, subject, and tone; see Morse (2006) for details—we notice that the *author* (Professor Kahl) selects a particular *occasion* (Michelle Obama's recent decision to refer to herself as "Mom-In-Chief") while targeting her intended *audience* (readers interested in race, gender, and political communication) for the specific *purpose* of discussing the effectiveness of this "nuanced rhetorical platform." Moreover, the scholarly *tone* Kahl takes in the passage lends to her arguments a measure of credibility (which, by extension, gives the author "ethos"), and she marshals sufficient evidence to support her claims (i.e., the messages themselves have quality, or "logos"). Despite the academic genre within which Kahl operates, we can infer that she respects the wisdom behind the FLOTUS's decision, and, while appealing to the emotions of her readers (pathos), the author goes as far as to liken the Mom-In-Chief move to the "No-Drama Obama" leadership approach made famous by Barack Obama during the 2008 presidential campaign (Kellner, 2009; Rudalevige, 2012; Simba, 2009).

Following recommendations from Leach (2000), we break down the Kahl passage, sentence by sentence, to place her words into richer context. For instance, Kahl begins the passage by explaining to her audience that the "Mom-In-Chief" move necessitates the First Lady choosing to identify primarily as a parent, rather than a politician. Whether it be by emphasizing her parental status and/or de-emphasizing her political status, this rhetorical move invites voters to regard Michelle Obama as something other than a FLOTUS: in this case, as a wife and mother who happens to reside in the White House. By doing so, Kahl (2009) argues that Michelle Obama blurs the boundaries between her political role and family duties.[4]

In the second sentence, Kahl maintains that the First Lady derives three political benefits from employing this rhetorical strategy. Specifically, Kahl argues that the "Mom-In-Chief" move protects Michelle Obama from criticism, demystifies her racial background, and makes her appear to be more trustworthy. The FLOTUS seeks these benefits precisely because her intersectional (race/gender) identity is a liability in the Oval Office, and her goal is to reassure constituents that she is not an "outsider" (see Block & Haynes, 2014; Guerrero, 2011).

According to the third sentence, motherhood is a cross-cutting identity to which numerous Americans, regardless of demographic and political background, can relate. Additionally, notions of motherhood (and family more generally) are both universal and noncontroversial in the sense that, by emphasizing this set of identities, the First Lady becomes more accessible to voters. Put differently, when Kahl uses the words *nonthreatening, wholesome,* and *comprehensible* to describe the impact of the First Lady's rhetorical platform on voter perceptions, the author is suggesting that, if not for the Mom-In-Chief move, many people would view Michelle Obama as being hostile, unethical, and unintelligible. We agree with Kahl's word choice here, and our own research on stereotypical media depictions of Michelle Obama (Block & Haynes, 2014) corroborates this claim.

To summarize, Kahl's passage suggests that the First Lady adopted a rhetorical platform that not only strengthens the control she exerts over her image (perhaps by counteracting race–gender stereotypes), but also allows her to advance both her own and her husband's political agenda. Therefore, the effectiveness of this rhetorical platform, based on our understanding of Kahl, hinges upon Michelle Obama's ability to (1) emphasize family/motherhood as a unifying identity; (2) reassure the public that she is "just like everyone else"; and (3) blur the lines between her private life and her public persona.

If it is indeed the case that the First Lady is using this platform, then we should find evidence of her making these rhetorical moves in her "Joining Forces" and "Let's Move!" speeches. Borrowing a phrase from qualitative researchers, Kahl (2009) gives us an outline of the "deductive codes" that we can apply to this corpus of text—where *text* is a generic term we use that includes transcripts, audio files, and video footage (Morgan, 2014).

Evidence from the C-SPAN Archives' online Video Library lends support to this coding approach. A recent search yielded 15 Michelle Obama speeches in which variations of the keywords "Let's Move" and "Joining Forces" appeared. As shown in Table 8.2 (pp. 172–173), the First Lady addresses her audiences in a host of venues (most of which are located in various rooms throughout the White House), and the duration of her speeches range from several minutes to over an hour. The earliest of the speeches in our sample appeared in the fall of 2009, and the most recent of these speeches transpired in the fall of 2012.

With help from a team of assistants, we converted the videos meeting our search criteria into MPEG-4 files and stored them in Dedoose,[5] a cloud-based computer program that allows users to synchronize textual, audio, and video files while analyzing them using techniques that are common to mixed-methods researchers. Following guidelines recommended by Dimitrova et al. (2002), our research team coded excerpts of each video based on a list of themes. In particular, we took note of any allusions the First Lady makes to the aforementioned deductive codes ("family/motherhood as a unifying identity," "I am just like you," and "blurring public with private") while she discusses policy. Dedoose includes a training center where collaborators can practice coding and compare decisions, and the software automatically calculates several intercoder reliability statistics. We provide further details about the program and our procedures in the appendix to this chapter.

Table 8.3 (p. 174) reports a raw count of the rhetorical strategies that the First Lady employs. The cells in this table represent the frequency with which a particular theme appears in either a "Let's Move" or a "Joining Forces" speech, and we include column and row totals of the overall results. It is clear from the table that Michelle Obama often seeks to convince her audiences that she is just like everyone else. This pattern holds true irrespective of policy area, for this rhetorical strategy appears in three of the seven "Let's Move" speeches in our sample, and five of the eight "Joining Forces" speeches. The remaining two strategies appear considerably less often, albeit with similar frequency, no matter the policy: The ratios of "Let's Move" speeches containing allusions to unifying motherhood identity and blurred lines are 2/7 and 2/7, respectively, and those respective ratios are comparably low (at 2/8 and 1/8, respectively) for "Joining Forces" speeches.

In addition to confirming the presence of the three rhetorical strategies suggested by Kahl, the results in Table 8.3 suggest that the First Lady employs these strategies with varying frequency when discussing her policies. That said, we are interested not only in how often these strategies occur but also in how Mom-In-Chief rhetoric is being used, and examining raw counts tells us little about the actual content within these rhetorical strategies. Accordingly, in Table 8.4 (p. 175), we outline the types of rhetorical moves our analysis uncovered (organized by row and sorted by the three deductive codes), while presenting this information across policy areas (sorted by column). In the following sections we provide sample excerpts from those speeches to put these rhetorical practices into fuller perspective.

Family/Motherhood as a Unifying Identity

"Family/motherhood as a unifying identity" is the first of the three strategies we discuss. Specifically, there are several instances in which the First Lady uses notions of motherhood as a rallying cry—one that imbues her constituents with a sense of shared identity. Michelle Obama tends to make this rhetorical move by signaling to her audience, often in a whimsical manner, that she is a mother and a spokesperson for issues that involve families. In fact,

TABLE 8.2 *Descriptive Information about the Michelle Obama Speeches We Use in Our Analyses*

Hosting Organization	Location	Event Type	Date	Duration	Title	Policy Area
National Governors Association	Washington, DC	Public affairs	2/20/2010	1:40:11	Childhood Obesity	Let's Move
White House	Oval Office, White House	Speech	2/9/2010	1:41	Memorandum on Childhood Obesity	Let's Move
White House	White House	Speech	12/13/2010	26:53	Child Nutrition Bill Signing	Let's Move
White House	Washington, DC	Speech	1/28/2010	46:59	First Lady Michelle Obama on Obesity	Let's Move
White House	White House	Speech	2/9/2010	1:03:53	Childhood Obesity Prevention	Let's Move
Office of the First Lady	Washington, DC	Speech	5/27/2014	8:05	First Lady Michelle Obama on Nutrition	Let's Move
White House	Washington, DC	Meeting	5/11/2010	46:35	Task Force on Childhood Obesity	Let's Move
White House	East Room, White House	Speech	1/24/2011	33:47	Military Family Support Programs	Joining Forces
ServiceNation	Washington, DC	Speech	11/11/2009	33:29	Mission serve Initiative Launch	Joining Forces
White House	Washington, DC	Speech	2/28/2011	20:23	Military Families	Joining Forces

DATA SOURCE: C-SPAN Video Library (http://www.c-spanvideo.org/videoLibrary/).

Continued.

TABLE 8.2 *Descriptive Information about the Michelle Obama Speeches We Use in Our Analyses—cont'd*

Hosting Organization	Location	Event Type	Date	Duration	Title	Policy Area
White House	Washington, DC	Speech	2/28/2011	20:23	Military Families	Joining Forces
Office of the First Lady	Washington, DC	Speech	1/26/2010	37:53	2010 Budget and Military Families	Joining Forces
National Park Foundation	Pennsylvania	Ceremony	9/11/2010	1:52:11	September 11 Remembrance Ceremony for Flight 93	Joining Forces
White House	East Room, White House	Speech	11/28/2012	12:35	Michelle Obama Remarks to Military Families	Joining Forces
White House	East Room, White House	Speech	5/6/2011	23:41	Military Spouse Appreciation Day	Joining Forces
White House	East Room, White House	Speech	4/12/2011	54:29	Military Families Initiative	Joining Forces

DATA SOURCE: C-SPAN Video Library (http://www.c-spanvideo.org/videoLibrary/).

TABLE 8.3 *A Raw Count of the Rhetorical Strategies the First Lady Uses, Sorted by Theme and Policy Area*

Theme	Policy Area		Total
	Let's Move	Joining Forces	
Family/motherhood as a unifying identity	2	2	*4*
FLOTUS is "just like everyone else"	3	5	*8*
Blurring private life with public persona	2	1	*3*
Total	*7*	*8*	*15*

NOTE: Table entries are frequencies (counts). We organized the content of these video speeches using Dedoose (http://www.dedoose.com/).
DATA SOURCE: C-SPAN Video Library (http://www.c-spanvideo.org/videoLibrary/).

a raw count of the key phrases reveals that the terms *mom, mother, children,* and *family* appear more than 50 times in this subset of speeches. A particularly intriguing instance of mom-signaling occurs on February 9, 2010, when Michelle Obama joined Tiki Barber, a former professional football player turned television broadcaster, to discuss her anti–childhood obesity initiative (C-SPAN, 2010c).[6] While acknowledging the athletic prowess of the Watkins Hornets, a DC area Pop Warner football team that had recently won a national championship, Mrs. Obama teased the young men about being "bored" and reminded them playfully that things could be worse, for they could be in school. Her chiding was only partly lighthearted: Several members of the Watkins Hornets team were talking amongst themselves and fidgeting in their seats, and the attention she drew to them ensured that they would give the FLOTUS their full attention from then on. Similarly, while hosting an event in the White House on November 28, 2012, to honor Military Families, the FLOTUS coaxed laughter from members of her audience after she invited them to "touch some stuff," so long as they promised not to break anything (C-SPAN, 2012).

In addition to her folksy "mom-isms," the First Lady appeals to her audiences by linking her policy advocacy to her status as a mother and spouse. During a televised dialogue with local students on April 7, 2010, Michelle Obama explained that she "came to this issue [of childhood obesity] as a mom" first and that her decision to advocate for family wellness stemmed

TABLE 8.4 *A Summary of Some of the Rhetorical Strategies the First Lady Employs, Sorted by Theme and Policy Area*

Theme	Policy Area	
	Let's Move	Joining Forces
Family/motherhood as a unifying identity	I came to this issue as a mom	Love of family = love of country
	Stand up 'cause I know you're bored	Touch some stuff, just don't break anything
FLOTUS is "just like everyone else"	Been there, done that	My father served in the Army before I was born
	I get embarrassed when people applaud me	Military moms have embraced me, even though I am not a blue or gold star mom
	The solution isn't going to come from just Washington alone	I am in awe of the heroism of my fellow citizens
		I am in awe of the sacrifices that military families make
		The people who aren't in uniform "serve too"
Blurring private life with public persona	Barack would be sleeping on the couch if he didn't support this bill	Thank your husband for keeping my husband safe
	Nice job … now get to work!	

NOTE: Table entries are summary descriptions of the ideas expressed in Michelle Obama's speeches. We organized the content of these video speeches using Dedoose (http://www.dedoose.com/).
DATA SOURCE: C-SPAN Video Library (http://www.c-spanvideo.org/videoLibrary/).

from there (C-SPAN, 2010f). Furthermore, the FLOTUS often accentuates the universality of motherhood by regaling her constituents with stories of military families who have overcome incredible odds. These stories are compelling because they make explicit the consonance between "loving one's family" and "loving one's country." The First Lady's phrasing in the following excerpt from a White House event on January 24, 2011, illustrates this country–family correspondence:

> Stories like these—and stories like those of so many in this room—are a reminder of what words like "service," "strength," and "sacrifice"—what those words look like in real life. They're a reminder of the love that keeps us together—*the love of family, the love of country* [emphasis added]. And so, for me and for Jill, this isn't about just understanding your concerns. It's about addressing your concerns. It's about telling your stories throughout the country, but more importantly, giving you a voice with decision-makers. But most of all, it's about getting something done. It's about making real, lasting changes that make a real difference in your lives. (C-SPAN, 2011a)

The FLOTUS Is "Just Like Everyone Else"

There is plenty of evidence of Michelle Obama's attempts to reassure citizens that she is just like everyone else. This second rhetorical strategy can entail, among other things, efforts by the First Lady to elevate the status of spouses and mothers, people who are seldom involved in policy decisions. This strategy is particularly prevalent in Michelle Obama's speeches about military families. When she remarked at a National Governor's Association meeting on February 28, 2011, that "the people who aren't in uniform serve too," the FLOTUS recognized the many challenges that soldiers endure in service to their country, and, equally importantly, she acknowledged the often overlooked struggles that the loved ones of these soldiers face, often with grace and without complaint.[7]

On November 11, 2009, while attending an event at George Washington University to launch "Mission Serve" (a program that coordinates the efforts of military and civilian volunteers corps), Michelle Obama revealed that she was awestruck by the heroism, dedication, and selflessness of military families:[8]

> One of the greatest privileges that I have as First Lady is the chance to meet with veterans, and to meet with service members, and their families all across America. And I have to tell you, I always come away from every single visit with this sense of pride, and gratitude—but also with a sense of awe. True awe. I'm in *awe* of sacrifices they make.

… I'm in *awe* of the men and women that I meet who have been wounded—and some very seriously—who will tell you that all they think about is not their injuries but about the folks that they left behind; and all they want to do is to be back in their unit, serving this country again. I'm in *awe*.

And I'm in *awe* of the military families that I meet: spouses who play the role of both parents, trying to juggle getting to baseball games and ballet recitals, doing it all; grandparents who step in to care for the children when a single mom or dad in uniform is away; people who find the strength to carry on after those they love most have made the ultimate sacrifice. (C-SPAN, 2009; emphasis added)

The fact that she repeats the word *awe* four times in this passage demonstrates that this rhetorical move is important to the First Lady, for it is clear that she sought to convey a level of commitment to—and appreciation for—common men and women. By celebrating their hard work and generosity, Michelle Obama reminds her audience that it is they who are special, not she. In essence, the First Lady edifies the standing of her constituents, and this has the net effect of putting the FLOTUS on level footing with her audience (and thus making the First Lady like everyone else).

In addition to praising them, Michelle Obama likes to include her constituents in the policy-making process. On May 11, 2010, when sharing the results from the Childhood Obesity Task Force Report, the First Lady reminds her audience they too are participants in the "Let's Move" initiative. She mentions that solving the nation's obesity problem "isn't going to come from just Washington alone"; rather, it will require efforts from both governmental and nongovernmental entities (C-SPAN, 2010g). Here, Michelle Obama is drawing people in, telling them that they too can contribute to the solution.

But elevating her audience to partners is not the only rhetorical strategy the First Lady employs when she shows her audience that she and they are alike. When necessary, she can also endear herself to her constituents by downplaying her own political status. For instance, she comes across as "one of the wives" during the National Governor's Association Winter Meeting about childhood obesity on February 20, 2010 (see C-SPAN, 2010e). The FLOTUS speaks from experience when acknowledging how physically and emotionally demanding life can be for the spouses of public officials:

I would be remiss if I didn't thank all the spouses who are here for all the things you have to put up with. The long hours. Absolutely. You all are making the same kind of sacrifices, putting up with long hours and late-night crises, all I can say is, "been there, done that," I know how you feel. (C-SPAN, 2010e)

Similarly, while attending an event in Alexandria, Virginia, sponsored by the YMCA to discuss her plan to beat childhood obesity, the First Lady admits (in a humorous and self-deprecating manner) to feeling awkward when receiving applause from the audience (C-SPAN, 2010b).

Finally, by evoking a sense of shared experience with her audience, the FLOTUS can downplay her political stature and show constituents that she is indeed "one of them." Mrs. Obama sometimes signals that she is able to identify (even if only indirectly) with the challenges that all mothers and spouses face. During a Military Spouse Appreciation Day event on May 6, 2011, the First Lady admits that military moms have embraced her, even though she is not a "blue star" or "gold star" mom (i.e., the parent of a child who has served in, is currently serving in, or was honorably discharged from the United States armed forces) (C-SPAN, 2011d). Despite not experiencing firsthand what members of military families often endure, the First Lady explains during a televised launch of the "Joining Forces" initiative on April 12, 2011, that this program is, among other things, her attempt to understand more fully what life is like for troops and the loved ones who support them:

And I have to admit that I haven't always realized it myself. My father served in the Army, but he served before I was born, so I didn't grow up in a military family. I always revered our troops, but like many Americans, I didn't see firsthand just how much our military families sacrifice as well. And that's why we're joining forces. (C-SPAN, 2011c)

Blurring Private Life With Public Persona

A third strategy we confirmed based on Kahl's work is that Michelle Obama can blur the boundaries between her public persona and her private life when advocating for policy. By "blurring," we mean that the First Lady sometimes incorporates "Let's Move" and "Joining Forces" into her discussions of work–life balance. This rhetorical strategy is especially noticeable when she interacts with President Obama, for she lets her audience know that she and Barack are like other married couples who rely on each other's support—and sometimes give each other a nudge to get things accomplished (be it around the house or across the nation).

At the January 16, 2010, Joint Armed Forces Officers' Wives' Luncheon (JAFOWL) at Bolling Airforce Base, the FLOTUS begins her discussion of the proposed budget provisions affecting military families by honoring a member of the audience whose husband is the commander of the Air Force District of Washington, DC, and is, therefore, responsible for Barack Obama while he travels in Air Force One. Michelle wanted to thank the woman's husband for keeping her spouse safe:

> And I'm going to be especially nice to Holly because her husband commands the Air Force district of Washington. So he not only keeps the skies of Washington safe, but he's responsible for when my husband comes back on Air Force One. So Holly, you and me, we've got to get together and get this thing worked out. (C-SPAN, 2010a)

There is even evidence of Barack, rather than Michelle, blurring the lines. On February 9, 2010, President Obama signed a memorandum that was part of a national campaign led by First Lady Michelle Obama on combating childhood obesity. Immediately after adding his signature, Barack smiles and says: "It's done, honey." Michelle quipped: "Nice job. Now get to work!" (C-SPAN, 2010d). A similar exchange between the spouses takes place on December 13, 2010, when the president signed the Healthy, Hunger-Free Kids Act of 2010 bill into law (Pub. L. No. 111-296), which expanded the federal school lunch program by 115,000 students.[9] Michelle Obama attended an event commemorating this bill signing, and Barack joked that he would be "sleeping on the couch" had he failed to support this federal statute (C-SPAN, 2010i).

To summarize, we find evidence of Kahl's (2009) proposed rhetorical strategies in our sample of Michelle Obama speeches. The most common rhetorical move (particularly when discussing military family policy) is for the First Lady to connect herself to rank-and-file citizens by conveying that, despite her high political station, she is ultimately a mother and spouse like many of her peers. While employed less frequently, rhetoric that emphasizes family and motherhood as universal identities seems to be another effective strategy. These approaches often combine humorous "mom-isms" with symbolic gestures that enliven conversations about military service and childhood wellness with the imagery of love, commitment, and familial closeness. Also present in our sample of speeches is rhetoric that blurs the lines between Barack and Michelle Obama (as spouses and parents) and the First Family (as political partners). By allowing voters a glimpse into her married life, Michelle Obama adds a human element to her policy advocacy, one with which many Americans can identify.

CONCLUSION

In this chapter we explored the First Lady's motherhood rhetoric as a potential vehicle for garnering support for two of her signature policy areas: "Let's Move" and "Joining Forces." As such, our study fits within a long line of social science research that explores the link between elite-level discourse and mass-level perceptions,[10] and, as we note in the introduction, the FLOTUS's policy advocacy activities provide an ideal case study for exploring this widely documented link. A careful reading of the Michelle Obama research—particularly Kahl (2009)—inspires us to consider three rhetorical strategies: one emphasizing family/motherhood as a unifying identity, another designed to reassure constituents that she is just like everyone else, and a third that muddies the borders between the First Family's private lives and public personas. Using a computer-assisted analysis of the content within a sample of Michelle Obama speeches we obtained from the C-SPAN Video Library, we learned a fair amount about the First Lady's rhetorical strategies.

Beyond offering guidelines for making sense of her speeches, we hope to open a much needed space for scholarly conversations about Michelle Obama's rhetoric and her policy advocacy. These conversations, we argue, require us to take an unflinchingly honest look at race and gender relations in the United States. Elsewhere (Block & Haynes, 2014), we argue that Michelle Obama has made numerous media appearances since the 2008 election to neutralize the hostility visited upon her by individuals who are either reluctant to accept her political success or are downright resistant to the idea of having an

African American family in the White House (see also Harris-Perry, 2011). On May 9, 2015, during her commencement address at Tuskegee University, the First Lady speaks candidly about the toll that race and gender stereotypes have taken on the Obama administration:

> Back when my husband first started campaigning for President, folks had all sorts of questions of me: What kind of First Lady would I be? What kinds of issues would I take on? Would I be more like Laura Bush, or Hillary Clinton, or Nancy Reagan? And the truth is, those same questions would have been posed to any candidate's spouse. That's just the way the process works. But, as potentially the first African American First Lady, I was also the focus of another set of questions and speculations; conversations sometimes rooted in the fears and misperceptions of others. Was I too loud, or too angry, or too emasculating? [Applause.] Or was I too soft, too much of a mom, not enough of a career woman?
>
> Then there was the first time I was on a magazine cover—it was a cartoon drawing of me with a huge Afro and machine gun. Now, yeah, it was satire, but if I'm really being honest, it knocked me back a bit. It made me wonder, just how are people seeing me.
>
> Or you might remember the on-stage celebratory fist bump between me and my husband after a primary win that was referred to as a "terrorist fist jab." And over the years, folks have used plenty of interesting words to describe me. One said I exhibited "a little bit of uppity-ism." Another noted that I was one of my husband's "cronies of color." Cable news once charmingly referred to me as "Obama's Baby Mama."
>
> And of course, Barack has endured his fair share of insults and slights. Even today, there are still folks questioning his citizenship. (White House, 2015, para. 28–31)

Reading the First Lady's recounting of these instances is both affirming and disheartening. On the one hand, it is difficult for us, as scholars of color, to witness the unfolding of such events. On other hand, the very fact that these types of "slights" and "insults" are a common feature of the Obama-era political climate (Hutchings, 2009)—and, more generally, that Michelle Obama's image transformation was arguably a necessary response to racial and gendered animus[11]—confirms the need for continued conversations about race, gender, respectability, and the Office of the First Lady. Our goal in this chapter was to explore the processes by which Michelle Obama uses media exposure to advocate for policy, and evidence from our analyses suggests that the First Lady can deploy Mom-In-Chief rhetoric to counteract—and perhaps transcend—negative stereotypes of African American women while advancing her political causes. We hope that future research on these and related topics will benefit from our efforts.

NOTES

We wish to thank Nicole Bouye for assistance with transcribing the oral histories.

1. Readers should note that the "motherhood rhetoric" we explore here concerns Michelle Obama's appeal to other women and mothers; it has nothing to do with the FLOTUS's actual or perceived parenting skills.

2. Interestingly, this debate is taking place within both liberal and conservative media outlets. As a case in point, Fox News contributors Jim Pinkerton, Lauren Ashburn, and Howard Kurtz weigh in on the feminist implications of Michelle Obama's Mom-In-Chief rhetoric during the December 1, 2014, episode of "Spin Cycle" (https://www.youtube.com/watch?v=HshhUfbahCo).

3. The First Lady has a third signature policy, "Reach Higher" (White House, 2014; http://www.whitehouse.gov/reach-higher), which encourages America's youth to earn a high school diploma and pursue postsecondary education, but this policy area is very recent (launched in 2014) and is not included in our analysis.

4. Kahl elaborates on this particular idea on p. 319 of her essay.

5. Dedoose Version 6.0.19, web application for managing, analyzing, and presenting qualitative and mixed method research data (2014). Los Angeles, CA: SocioCultural Research Consultants, LLC (www.dedoose.com).

6. For a transcript of this speech, see C-SPAN (2010c; http://www.c-span.org/video/?292017-3/childhood-obesity-prevention).

7. For a transcript, see C-SPAN (2011b; http://www.c-span.org/video/?298232-2/military-families). The idea that the families of troops "serve too" is a common turn of phrase, one that not only appears throughout her speeches (we counted 19 usages of it in this subset of speeches) but is also featured prominently on the official Web page

for "Joining Forces" (White House, 2010a; http://www.whitehouse.gov/joiningforces).

8. She expresses a similar sentiment on September 11, 2010, during her visit to Shanksville, Pennsylvania, to speak at the commemoration of what would become the site of a 9/11 memorial: the crash location of United Airlines Flight 93 (C-SPAN, 2010h; http://www.c-span.org/video/?295418-1/september-11-remembrance -ceremony-flight-93).

9. For details, visit http://www.fns.usda.gov/school-meals/healthy-hunger -free-kids-act.

10. Gabel and Scheve (2007) make this point eloquently in their working paper, "Estimating the Effect of Elite Communications on Public Opinion Using Instrumental Variables":

> The relationship between mass and elite opinion is a central issue to the study of voting behavior, parties and elections, public opinion, and representation in democratic systems. For a variety of theoretical reasons, scholars expect elite opinion to affect mass attitudes and behavior. The literatures on priming, persuasion, and cue-taking all offer theoretical accounts about how elite opinion shapes how voters approach public policy issues and what attitudes they adopt. In contrast, much of the theoretical literature on representation and electoral competition tells the opposite story: party and elite policy positions respond to voter policy preferences. (p. 1)

11. It is not surprising that Kristina Schake, the former White House aide who helped Michelle Obama's image, was hired to assist with Hillary Clinton's 2016 presidential bid (Evans, 2015).

REFERENCES

Belkin, L. (2012, September 5). Michelle Obama: What does she mean by "mom in chief"? [Huffington Post Web log post]. Retrieved from http://www.huffington post.com/lisa-belkin/obama-mom-in-chief_b_1858440.html

Block, R., Jr., & Haynes, C. S. (2014). Taking to the airwaves: Using content analyses of survey toplines and filmographies to test the "Michelle Obama image transformation" (MOIT) hypothesis. *National Political Science Review, 16,* 97–114.

Campbell, K. (2012, September 13). Why mom-in-chief doesn't work for me [Huffington Post Web log post]. Retrieved from http://www.huffingtonpost .com/kristy-campbell/why-mominchief-doesnt-wor_b_1879293.html

Carmon, I. (2012, September 4). Michelle Obama: Beyond mom-in-chief. Retrieved from Salon Web site: http://www.salon.com/2012/09/05/michelle_obama_not_just_mom_in_chief/

Cohen, J. (1988). *Statistical power analyses for the social sciences* (2nd ed.). Hillsdale, NJ: Lawrence Erlbaum.

Cottle, M. (2013, November 21). Leaning out: How Michelle Obama became a feminist nightmare. *Politico Magazine.* Retrieved from http://www.politico.com/magazine/story/2013/11/leaning-out-michelle-obama-100244.html#.VKskKivF98E

C-SPAN (Producer). (2009, November 11). *Mission serve initiative launch* [online video]. Available from http://www.c-span.org/video/?289961-1/mission-serve-initiative-launch

C-SPAN (Producer). (2010a, January 26). *2010 Budget and military families* [online video]. Available from http://www.c-span.org/video/?291656-1/2010-budget-military-families

C-SPAN (Producer). (2010b, January 28). *First Lady Michelle Obama on obesity* [online video]. Available from http://www.c-span.org/video/?291702-2/first-lady-michelle-obama-obesity

C-SPAN (Producer). (2010c, February 9). *Childhood obesity prevention* [online video]. Available from http://www.c-span.org/video/?292017-3/childhood-obesity-prevention

C-SPAN (Producer). (2010d, February 9). *Memorandum on childhood obesity* [online video]. Available from http://www.c-span.org/video/?292017-1/memorandum-childhood-obesity-

C-SPAN (Producer). (2010e, February 20). *Childhood obesity* [online video]. Available from http://www.c-span.org/video/?292184-2/childhood-obesity

C-SPAN (Producer). (2010f, April 7). *Michelle Obama on childhood obesity prevention* [online video]. Available from http://www.c-span.org/video/?292891-1/michelle-obama-childhood-obesity-prevention

C-SPAN (Producer). (2010g, May 11). *Task force on childhood obesity* [online video]. Available from http://www.c-span.org/video/?293445-1/task-force-childhood-obesity

C-SPAN (Producer). (2010h, September 11). *September 11 remembrance ceremony for Flight 93* [online video]. Available from http://www.c-span.org/video/?295418-1/september-11-remembrance-ceremony-flight-93

C-SPAN (Producer). (2010i, December 13). *Child nutrition bill signing* [online video].

Available from http://www.c-span.org/video/?297052-1/child-nutrition-bill -signing

C-SPAN (Producer). (2011a, January 24). *Military family support programs* [online video]. Available from http://www.c-span.org/video/?297666-1/military-family -support-programs

C-SPAN (Producer). (2011b, February 28). *Military families* [online video]. http:// www.c-span.org/video/?298232-2/military-families

C-SPAN (Producer). (2011c, April 11). *Military families initiative* [online video]. Available from http://www.c-span.org/video/?298984-1/military-families -initiative

C-SPAN (Producer). (2011d, May 6). *Military spouse appreciation day* [online video]. http://www.c-span.org/video/?299368-2/military-spouse-appreciation-day

C-SPAN (Producer). (2012, November 28). *Michelle Obama remarks to military families* [online video]. Available from http://www.c-span.org/video/?309658-4 /michelle-obama-remarks-military-families

Dillaway, H. E., & Paré, E. (2013). A campaign for good motherhood? Exploring media discourse on Sarah Palin, Hillary Clinton, and Michelle Obama during the 2008 presidential election campaign. In Kohlman, M. H., Krieg, D. B., & Dickerson, B. J. (eds.), *Notions of family: Intersectional perspectives* (Advances in Gender Research, Volume 17, pp. 209–239). Bingley, UK: Emerald Group Publishing Limited.

Dimitrova, N., Zhang, H., Shararay, B., Sezan, I., Huang, T., & Zakhor, A. (2002). Applications of video-content analysis and retrieval. *IEEE MultiMedia, 9*(3), 42–55. http://dx.doi.org/10.1109/MMUL.2002.1022858

Drexler, P. (2009, May 11). There's something about Michelle [Huffington Post Web log post]. Retrieved from http://www.huffingtonpost.com/peggy-drexler/theres -something-about-mi_b_185631.html

Erbe, B. (2009, May 11). Michelle Obama's mom-in-chief image is a cave to poli-tics and stereotypes [U.S. News & World Report Web log post]. Retrieved from http://www.usnews.com/opinion/blogs/erbe/2009/05/11/michelle-obamas-mom -in-chief-image-is-a-cave-to-politics-and-stereotypes

Edwards, R., & Call, K. (2009). *Michelle Obama: Mom-in-chief.* New York, NY: Grosset & Dunlap.

Evans, S. J. (2015, April 4). Ex-White House aide who transformed Michelle Obama into an all-American "everywoman" hired to help Hillary Clinton become the next president. Retrieved from Daily Mail Web site: http://www.dailymail.co.uk

/news/article-3025637/Ex-White-House-aide-transformed-Michelle-Obama
-American-everywoman-hired-help-Hillary-Clinton-president-overcome-email
-scandal.html

Gabel, M., & Scheve, S. (2007). Estimating the effect of elite communications on public opinion using instrumental variables. *American Journal of Political Science, 51*(4), 1013–1028. http://dx.doi.org/10.1111/j.1540-5907.2007.00294

Guerrero, L. 2011. (M)Other-In-Chief: Michelle Obama and the ideal of Republican womanhood. In R. Gill & C. Scharff (Eds.), *New femininities: Postfeminism, neoliberalism, and identity* (pp. 68–82). New York, NY: Palgrave Macmillan.

Harris-Perry, M. (2013, November 23). Michelle Obama a "feminist nightmare"? Please. Retrieved from MSNBC Web site: http://www.msnbc.com/melissa-harris-perry/michelle-obama-no-ones-feminist-nightmare

Harris-Perry, M. V. (2011). Michelle. In M. V. Harris-Perry (Ed.), *Sister citizen shame, stereotypes, and Black women in America* (pp. 270–281). New Haven, CT: Yale University Press.

Hutchings, V. L. (2009). Change or more of the same? Evaluating racial attitudes in the Obama era. *Public Opinion Quarterly, 73*(5), 917–942. http://dx.doi.org/10.1093/poq/nfp080

Kahl, M. L. (2009). First Lady Michelle Obama: Advocate for strong families. *Communication and Critical/Cultural Studies, 6*(3), 316–320. http://dx.doi.org/10.1080/14791420903063794

Kellner, D. (2009). Barack Obama and celebrity spectacle. *International Journal of Communication, 3,* 715–742. Retrieved from http://ijoc.org/index.php/ijoc/article/view/559/350

Krippendorff, K. (2006). Reliability in content analysis. *Human Communication Research, 30,* 411–433.

Leach, J. (2000). Rhetorical analysis. In M. W. Bauer & G. Gaskell, G. (Eds.), *Qualitative researching with text, image, and sound: A practical handbook* (pp. 207–227). Thousand Oaks, CA: Sage.

Malmsheimer, T., & Weiss-Meyer, A. (2014, June 24). Michelle Obama is leveraging her power as "mom-in-chief." Retrieved from New Republic Web site: http://www.newrepublic.com/article/118335/michelle-obama-working-families-summit-i-am-mom-chief

Morgan, D. L. (2014). Integrating qualitative and quantitative methods: A pragmatic approach. Thousand Oaks, CA: Sage.

Morse, O. (2006). SOAPSTone: A strategy for reading and writing. Retrieved from CollegeBoard Web site: http://apcentral.collegeboard.com/apc/public/preap /teachers_corner/45200.html

Rudalevige, A. (2012). "A majority is the best repartee": Barack Obama and Congress, 2009–2012. *Social Science Quarterly, 93*(5), 1272–1294. http://dx.doi.org/10.1111 /j.1540-6237.2012.00910.x

Simba, M. (2009). The Obama campaign 2008: A historical overview. *Western Journal of Black Studies, 33,* 186–191.

Traister, R. (2008, November 18). The momification of Michelle Obama. Retrieved from Salon Web site: http://www.salon.com/2008/11/12/michelle_obama_14/

White House. (2010a). Joining forces: When our troops serve, their families are serving, too. It's time to do our part. Retrieved from http://www.whitehouse.gov /joiningforces

White House. (2010b). Let's move! America's move to raise a healthier generation of kids. Retrieved from http://www.letsmove.gov/

White House. (2014). Reach higher: complete your education. Own your future. Retrieved January 6, 2014, from http://www.whitehouse.gov/reach-higher

White House. (2015). Remarks by the First Lady at Tuskegee University commencement address. Retrieved from https://www.whitehouse.gov/the-press-office /2015/05/09/remarks-first-lady-tuskegee-university-commencement-address

Zacka, M. (2014, January 23). Despite partisan differences in America, the job of raising children rises above [Huffington Post Web log post]. Retrieved from http:// www.huffingtonpost.com/michael-zacka/despite-partisan-differen_b_2078697 .html

APPENDIX
Using Dedoose as Our
Data Management Software

We performed the thematic analyses reported in this chapter using Dedoose, an intuitive, inexpensive cloud-based mixed-methods program designed to handle semi- and nonstructured data.[1] Unlike most statistical analysis packages, which use flat file database structures containing records with no structured relationships, Dedoose is a relational database. A generalized description of the Dedoose database appears in Figure 8.A.1.[2]

The structure of Dedoose makes it ideal for analyzing Michelle Obama's speeches. Essentially, we imported our "resources" (in our case, footage stored in .MP4 format), linked these multimedia files to "descriptors" that recorded source-related characteristics (e.g., the names of the coders, length of the video, the size of .MP4 files, the date and venue of the FLOTUS's speech), and added codes ("tags") to excerpts of the content in each speech. We based our code tree (i.e., the spreadsheet in Dedoose's relational database recording

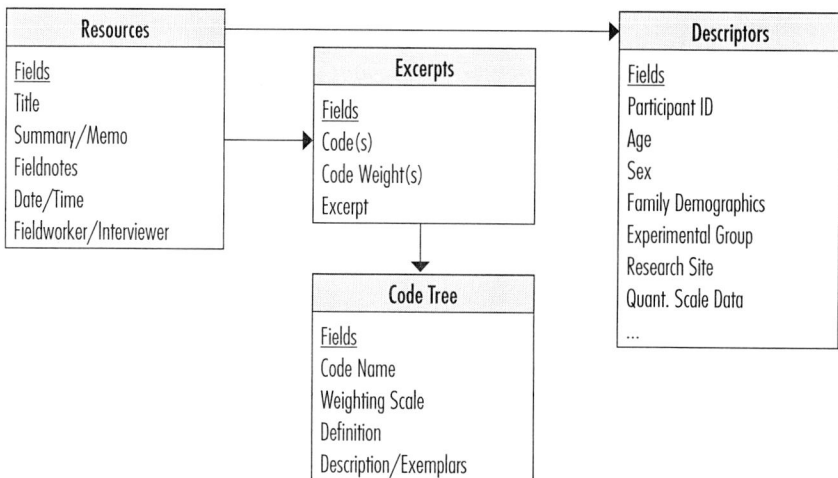

FIGURE 8.A.1 Dedoose database generalized description. *(From Dedoose Version 6.1.11, web application for managing, analyzing, and presenting qualitative and mixed method research data. [2015]. Los Angeles, CA: SocioCultural Research Consultants, LLC [www.dedoose.com]. With permission.)*

the coding procedures) on the insights provided by Kahl (2009). The codes/ tags we applied to the video excerpts helped to facilitate our attempts to organize the First Lady's rhetorical strategies across policy domains, and these domain-specific summaries serve as the basis for our analyses.

Coding Michelle Obama Speeches

To begin, the coauthors and a team of researchers coded segments of each video based on predetermined themes. The research team then generated a random subsample of video footage that each of us coded independently. We calculated inter-rater reliability statistics based on this subsample (see Cohen, 1988, and Krippendorf, 2006) and discussed any problems that arose during the encoding process. When necessary, we modified our codebook to reflect these discussions. After reaching acceptable levels of agreement across coders, each member of the research team received copies of all 15 video speeches, and we coded the first half of them independently. Like before, we met to compute reliability estimates, reconcile coding differences, and reedit the codebook. Once satisfied with the process, each of us did the entire set of videos. Figure 8.A.2 (p. 190) summarizes our procedures.

Notes

1. Dedoose Version 6.0.19, web application for managing, analyzing, and presenting qualitative and mixed method research data (2014). Los Angeles, CA: SocioCultural Research Consultants, LLC (www.dedoose.com).

2. Additional details are available in the Dedoose User Guide (http://userguide .dedoose.com/).

References

Cohen, J. (1988). *Statistical power analyses for the social sciences* (2nd ed.). Hillsdale, NJ: Lawrence Erlbaum.

Kahl, M. L. (2009). First Lady Michelle Obama: Advocate for strong families. *Communication and Critical/Cultural Studies, 6*(3), 316–320. http://dx.doi .org/10.1080/14791420903063794

Krippendorff, K. (2006). Reliability in content analysis. *Human Communication Research, 30*, 411–433.

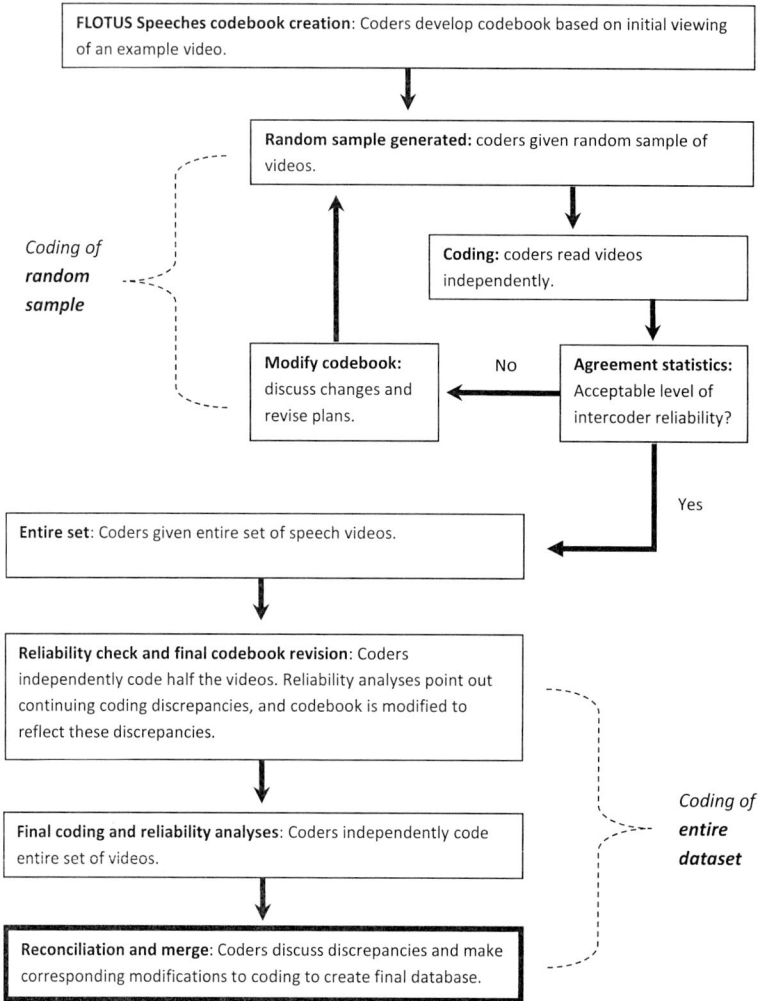

FLOTUS Speeches codebook creation: Coders develop codebook based on initial viewing of an example video.

Random sample generated: coders given random sample of videos.

Coding of *random sample*

Coding: coders read videos independently.

Modify codebook: discuss changes and revise plans.

No

Agreement statistics: Acceptable level of intercoder reliability?

Yes

Entire set: Coders given entire set of speech videos.

Reliability check and final codebook revision: Coders independently code half the videos. Reliability analyses point out continuing coding discrepancies, and codebook is modified to reflect these discrepancies.

Final coding and reliability analyses: Coders independently code entire set of videos.

Coding of *entire dataset*

Reconciliation and merge: Coders discuss discrepancies and make corresponding modifications to coding to create final database.

FIGURE 8.A.2 FLOTUS speeches codebook procedures.

CHAPTER **9**

THE PERFORMANCE OF ROLL CALL VOTES AS POLITICAL COVER IN THE U.S. SENATE: USING C-SPAN TO ANALYZE THE VOTE TO REPEAL "DON'T ASK, DON'T TELL"

Christopher Neff

The need for political cover and the forms that it takes present important questions to legislative studies and public policy. Political cover is defined as the tactical protection measures that politicians use or that are afforded to them when they feel their vote or public viewpoint on an issue could result in a political penalty that may reduce their ability to hold onto their office or further their ambitions. This penalty renders elected officials most vulnerable (Matthews, 1984) when they are of a different party or issue position than that of their local or state constituencies. The tactics to relieve these dangers to political survival (Bueno de Mesquita, Morrow, Siverson, & Smith, 1999; Mayhew, 1974) and gain protection may take many forms, including changing voter opinions to align with theirs through support by popular elites, endorsements by organizations (Arceneaux & Kolodny, 2009), reports by government investigations or departments (Editorial, 2006), editorials by newspapers (Kahn & Kenney, 2002), and domestic and international legal rulings (Allee

& Huth, 2006). While much of this protection may blatantly occur on many political playing fields, the United States Senate is different.

In the collegial nature of the Senate where its own "Senatique" rules apply, political cover is often obtained or provided as a subtle maneuver. It is something that often occurs behind the scenes. Colleagues deliberate on legislation and political dangers in members-only cloakrooms, their private hideaway offices in the Capitol building, and party caucus meetings, which often shield the public from private negotiations. I argue that one of the deals being brokered is how to use the voting process to mitigate controversial issues that come before the Senate and limit the harm a member's vote may have on their chances of reelection.

In this chapter I suggest that political cover is hiding in plain sight through the performance of roll call votes in which senators position themselves in the act of casting a vote relative to certain key colleagues (i.e., before, after, or with). An examination of C-SPAN video during these votes allows for an emerging methodological tool to retrospectively examine senator behavior. To conduct this analysis, I review the historic vote to repeal Don't Ask, Don't Tell (DADT) in December 2010. This Senate action remains the most pro–lesbian, gay, bisexual, and transgender (LGBT) legislative action in American history, with a 65–31 vote in the chamber.

The use of C-SPAN for retrospective analysis of floor behavior in the Senate is important for a number of reasons. First, one is able to view the characteristics of political behavior in an established environment. Senators have known that members of the press have been viewing their behavior since the 1840s (Ritchie, 2009), and the Senate Press Gallery was established in 1859. Daily television viewing of Senate procedures has been ongoing for nearly 30 years, beginning with C-SPAN2 on June 2, 1986 (C-SPAN, 1986). Second, this retrospective view allows for a better understanding of political vulnerabilities and alliances that may not have been known at the time of a vote. For instance, senators may be the only ones who know that they are going to retire before the next election and before casting a key vote, and the resulting lack of political penalty may influence their tactics and their vote. Third, in this chapter I attempt to document a known strategy in Senate protocol. It is understood by insiders that Senate floor behavior includes waiting to go on the floor to vote until a result is obvious to limit or facilitate negotiations on the floor, as well as skipping difficult votes entirely.[1] An inquiry into the performative nature of senator voting is therefore greatly assisted through examination of C-SPAN video.

The Congressional Research Service (CRS) notes the special nature of the Senate and senators' last-minute dealings with each other. Its report acknowledges the floor as a focal point for peer influence based on the actions of senatorial colleagues, stating:

> During a roll call vote, the clerk calls the names of all Senators in alphabetical order, and then reads the names of those voting in the affirmative followed by those voting in the negative. Thereafter, when another Senator wishes to vote, he or she comes to the well (the open area between the rostrum and Senators' desks); the clerk calls the Senator's name and then repeats the Senator's vote. Senators coming to the well frequently consult tally sheets kept at the tables staffed by Republican and Democratic floor aides in order to observe how their colleagues are voting. (Rybicki, 2013, p. 22)

I argue that these actions constitute *the performance of voting* where senators act as political cover seekers and political cover givers. As *cover seekers,* senators locate their vote relative to certain colleagues and thresholds of activity to reduce political penalties or vulnerabilities. This can include voting early or voting late. What matters are the relative orders of the voting, which often correspond to timing. For instance, voting before other senators is consistent with voting early, but the political value is in highlighting a vote ahead of, and apart from, others rather than in being quick. Voting after other senators can be politically valuable because it makes a single vote less visible, but not if a separate group waits until the end, or later. In short, cover seekers are looking first at who is doing what, then when.

Senators function as *cover givers* when their votes create a threshold level of support in favor of or against an issue; the votes reduce the potential political penalty for another; and the votes precede or take place at the same time as the votes of a vulnerable member. It is important to note that not all votes matter in this analysis because not all votes provide cover. A critical mass of the right mix of votes is needed. Moreover, political cover can be provided intentionally or unintentionally. Cover-seeking Senators may strategically look at how other unwitting senators vote and use that vote and its location for cover. Intentional actions provide a range of utilities. I suggest three functions of political cover in roll call votes. These are (1) creating a masking threshold, (2) utilizing a penalty-mitigating order, and (3) establishing an affirmative visible statement.

First, the quantity of votes in a certain direction is a key variable because the accumulation of yea or nay votes creates a threshold effect for those seeking political cover. A great number of yea votes downplays and masks the importance of any one yea vote, making the use of this vote as a penalty against a senator less potentially effective. Second, I suggest that there is a penalty-mitigating order to sequences whereby senators wait to vote until the opposing party votes in favor of an issue (that they will vote for) because this lessens the utility of using the vote as a political weapon. In addition, a penalty-mitigating order can involve senators waiting for colleagues who face similar penalties, such as senior senators or ideological counterparts (i.e., moderates—Blue Dog Democrats), to vote before acting. Third, there are several ways to highlight a position as a means of decreasing political peril. Senators can announce their stance before a vote begins, vote before their colleagues, vote from their desk as a sign of importance, and announce their vote in the chamber publicly. In all, this analysis is about the way senators position themselves in front of, behind, or with certain senators or groups of senators to provide or receive political cover on highly salient votes. The goal in establishing this order is to use the voting process as a way to favor reelection.

This research is consistent with the recent research of Box-Steffensmeier, Ryan, and Sokhey (2015) on cue taking and cue giving in the U.S. Senate. Box-Steffensmeier et al. present a quantitative look at the way senators use the timing and votes of other senators as an informational shortcut to inform vote taking. They build on the cue-taking theories of Matthews & Stimson (1975) and voting behavior noted by Kingdon (1973) by arguing that cueing effects do occur and that these can be seen in specific situations, with party leaders and committee chairpersons providing cue-giving roles (Box-Steffensmeier et al., 2015). Here, a key similarity is that the timing of senators' actions is used as a way to analyze the votes. However, rather than examining the way senators use voting cues and timing to compensate for information overload (Box-Steffensmeier et al., 2015, p. 21), I examine the way they align themselves around other votes to increase their sense of political cover regarding potential political penalties to a highly salient vote.

In this chapter I use the DADT repeal vote in December 2010 to highlight Senate behavior. I move forward by briefly reviewing the background of the Senate on the issue of gays in the military and DADT, note the methodology used in this analysis, analyze the positioning of votes by focusing on 19 senators, and review the factors that may account for the sequence of voting and clustering. I conclude this chapter by suggesting future methodological avenues and the implications of this vote for our understanding of political cover. However, it is also important to note the limitations of this research. Given the small sample size, qualitative methods were utilized. While useful, these methods lack statistical causal indicators. This analysis therefore provides a snapshot of an emerging methodological tool based on a review of one key vote and provides an additional step forward in demonstrating the value of utilizing C-SPAN in political science research.

GAY RIGHTS AND THE U.S. SENATE

The United States Senate's relationship with gay rights issues is complex. I selected the vote to repeal DADT for analysis because of its place as one of the most controversial issues to come before the Senate in the 1990s (Brewer, 2008, p. 3; Miller, 1998) and also the most pro-LGBT roll call vote in Senate history, with 65–31 votes in favor of repeal. The rise of DADT as a legislative issue has been noted in previous literature (Neff & Edgell, 2013). Neff and Edgell highlight four phases of legislative consideration of "gays in the military" from "radioactive, contested, emerging, and viable" (p. 233). The first begins with the introduction of the policy in 1993, when senators vigorously debated the issue on the Senate floor and lengthy hearings were held by the Armed Services Committee (Williams, 1994). President Clinton introduced the policy of "don't ask, don't tell" as a compromise. The political trauma from this debate in Congress, however, left the issue as largely radioactive, and members were unwilling to engage on the topic until a controversy erupted over the firing of gay Arabic linguists from the Defense Language Institute following the September 11, 2001, terrorist attacks (Frank, 2009). The idea of openly gay service was then contested between 2002 and 2005 as activists organized around the idea. The issue emerged between 2005 and 2009 as party leaders supported repeal but opposition from President Bush made lifting the ban a challenge. The most recent viable phase followed the 2008 presidential and congressional elections and actions by President Obama and key senators.

These contextual factors are important because the previous legislative votes in the Senate on gay rights issues had startlingly different outcomes. The 1994 amendment to the National Defense Authorization Bill (NDAA) to support openly gay service in the military offered by Senator Boxer (D-CA) was soundly defeated with a vote of 33–63. In 1996, the Senate vote on the Employment Non-Discrimination Act (ENDA) also failed 49–50. Indeed, the bipartisan Defense of Marriage Act (DOMA) overwhelmingly passed in 1996 with a Senate vote of 85–14. The fear of such a repeated legislative failure kept many LGBT issues off the Senate agenda for more than a decade. In 2009, the first pro-LGBT Senate amendment to become law was the Matthew Shepherd and James Byrd Jr. Hate Crimes Prevention Act, which passed 63–28 on a cloture vote to the 2010 NDAA (Eleveld, 2009). The next issue to come up would be DADT.

When the issue of DADT came before the Senate in 2010, there were both ideological arguments against it and partisan arguments regarding violations of Senate procedure (Brady, 2010). Repeal had been left out of the NDAA "base bill" offered by the Pentagon and was added by amendment in the markup of the Senate Armed Services Committee. Yet from there it failed to gain the votes needed to bring it to the floor and pass cloture. On September 21, 2010, it failed to achieve the 60 votes needed with a vote of 56–43. Again on December 9, 2010, a cloture motion on the bill failed, 57–40. The modern conception of the Senate as one gridlocked by procedure (Saeki, 2009) was evidenced, and it was unclear that repeal could pass the body.

Following these filibusters, the lead sponsors, Senators Lieberman (I-CT) and Collins (R-ME) immediately reintroduced the bill as a stand-alone measure for consideration as the Don't Ask, Don't Tell Repeal Act. The CRS summary of H.R. 2965, the Don't Ask, Don't Tell Repeal Act of 2010, notes that the bill "provides for repeal of the current Department of Defense (DOD) policy concerning homosexuality in the Armed Forces." With the bill no longer tied to the Defense Authorization Act, it was possible to make progress toward an up-or-down vote on the measure. On December 18, 2010, the Senate brought the repeal bill to floor and began the final debate. Cloture was filed and passed by a vote of 63–22 and an agreement was reached for a final vote to begin at

3:00 p.m. on the same day. The stage was set for the largest vote on gay rights in American history in the most deliberative body in the world. A simple majority of 51 votes was needed for passage.

METHODS

Three chief observations are considered in looking at the behavior of senators during the DADT repeal vote: the clerk, the clock, and the senators themselves. First, Senate rules state the way votes are publicly announced in the chamber by the clerk and the timing of these announcements. Second, the sequence of senators' actions over the 30-minute roll call vote is documented in Table 9.1 in the next section. C-SPAN video of the Senate floor (see Box-Steffensmeier et al., 2015; Mixon et al., 2001) is used to record this process. The methodology for using C-SPAN as a retrospective tool includes looking at senators' behavior in the well of the Senate during the vote on DADT repeal (Figure 9.1), signaling their intent to vote to the clerk (Figure 9.2), and indicating the vote itself to the clerk (Figure 9.3). The staff at C-SPAN helped provide the clipping of the vote for review (see C-SPAN, 2010, at 6:17:40).

Third, I reviewed other variables that might influence senators' vote positioning: party affiliation, the presence of a primary challenger, the percentage of previous electoral victory, an interest group's 2004 predicted vote count for DADT repeal, and a different interest group's scorecard on senators' voting history on LGBT issues. In particular, Edgell and I examined an organizational vote count for the Servicemembers Legal Defense Network (SLDN) in 2004/2005 (Neff & Edgell, 2013) that highlighted 19 senators in 2010 listed as either undecided, leaning yes, leaning no, yes, or no in the vote count. This was useful because a review found that "in the Senate, 69% of members from 2004 were still in the Senate for the repeal vote in 2010. Of those predicted to vote yes or leaning yes, 100% voted in favor while 89.1% of predicted no votes voted against repeal in 2010" (Neff & Edgell, 2013, p. 246). In addition, I compared the Human Rights Campaign Scorecard for 110th Congress against the DADT repeal vote. These variables are combined in Table 9.2 in the next section. However, it should be noted that two senators included in this analysis, Scott Brown and Blanche Lincoln, were not on the 2004–2005 list.

DECEMBER 18, 2010

Senate Session

Senators met to vote on the Development, Relief and Education for Alien Minors (DREAM) Act, the "Don't ask, Don't tell" policy in the military and the Strategic Arms Reduciton Treaty (START).

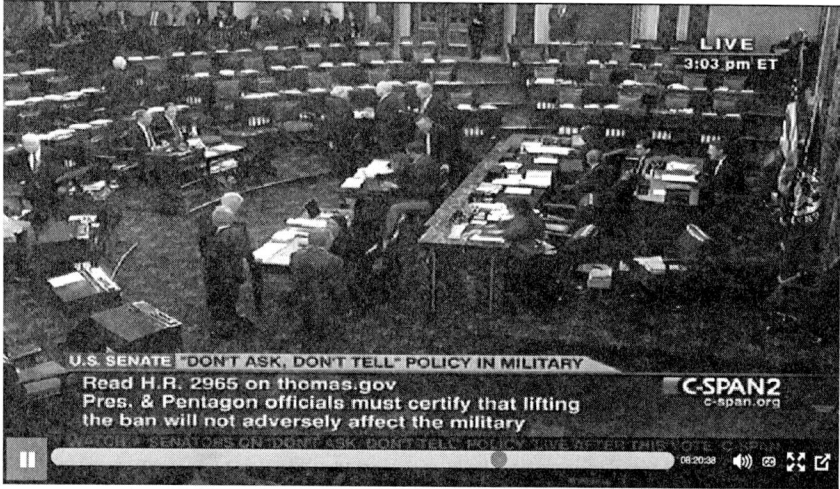

FIGURE 9.1 Senate voting procedure in the well.

DECEMBER 18, 2010

Senate Session

Senators met to vote on the Development, Relief and Education for Alien Minors (DREAM) Act, the "Don't ask, Don't tell" policy in the military and the Strategic Arms Reduciton Treaty (START).

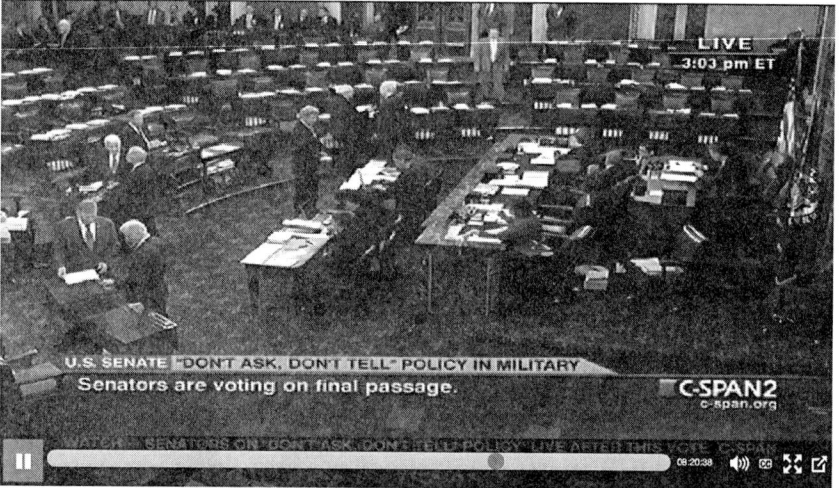

FIGURE 9.2 Senator Kerry indicating a yea vote with a thumbs-up.

DECEMBER 18, 2010

Senate Session

Senators met to vote on the Development, Relief and Education for Alien Minors (DREAM) Act, the "Don't ask, Don't tell" policy in the military and the Strategic Arms Reduciton Treaty (START).

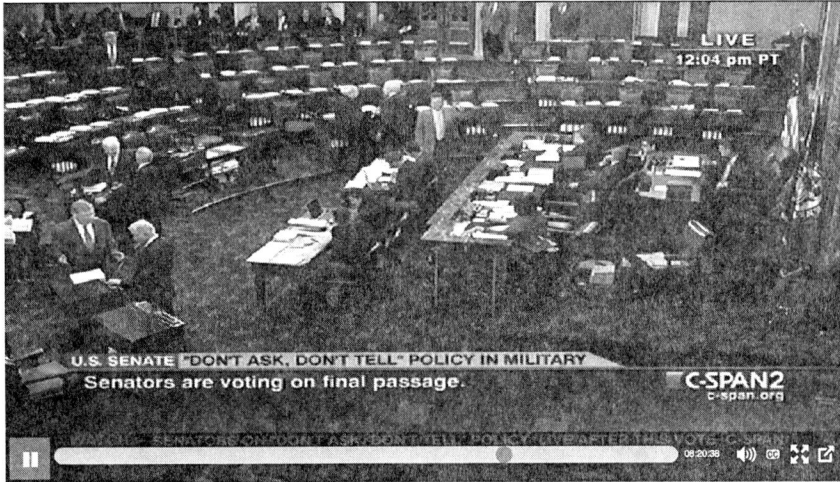

FIGURE 9.3 Senator Webb indicating his intent to vote by raising his hand.

THE CLOCK: EXAMINING THE TIMING OF SENATORS' VOTES

Senators' votes are time stamped using C-SPAN video and the clock that appears on-screen to denote the timing of votes during the 30-minute roll call vote (see Table 9.1, pp. 202–203). The times are listed and the yeas and nays are denoted. Time is a valuable measure to identify the sequencing and positioning of senators. Votes cast at the same time are noted under that time.

It is important to note that the voting period is divided into two parts: the first 10 minutes and the remaining 20 minutes of the vote. This is crucial because the clerk will stop calling the roll at the 10-minute mark, then will stand and read aloud the preliminary results for all in the chamber (and those watching it live on C-SPAN2) to hear. This acts as a signal to other senators. In the remaining 20-minute period, each senator who now approaches the clerk to vote will have his or her name called out and vote announced publicly to the chamber. Senators will also consult with party secretaries to find out how others voted and whether the bill in question will likely pass or fail.

A review of Table 9.1 shows that 40 senators' votes were read aloud at the 3:10 p.m. (10-minute) mark, with 26 yeas and 14 nays. After this period and until the completion of the vote at 3:30 p.m., 56 senators voted, and those votes were recorded and read aloud individually. Table 9.1 lists the yeas and nay votes, their times, and the senator who voted. Two points to note are that Senator Bayh was the acting president pro tempore of the Senate, so his vote is included at the start, and two senators voted twice: Senator Conrad (3:09, 3:13) and Senator Inouye (3:06, 3:18). Their first votes are noted for the purposes of this analysis.

The first senator to vote in favor of repeal was the bill's lead cosponsor, Senator Joe Lieberman (I-CT), and the first Republican to vote in favor of repeal was Senator Scott Brown (R-MA), just before the 10-minute mark. These votes were identified using visual cues from C-SPAN video. Using this retrospective process, one can connect a sequence of events and data points by reviewing the timing of votes and key information (unavailable until after the voting) that informs the level of political vulnerability that senators faced when casting this vote.

THE CLERK: KEY VOTING TIMELINE

The narrative timeline that follows provides a look at the political behavior of 19 senators during the DADT repeal roll call vote. This analysis incorporates data about their record with the interest groups and notes which members had lost primary elections or later decided to retire. A number of additional data points are also added to review their behavior, including their party affiliation and the "blue" (Democratic) or "red" (Republican) nature of their state. These facts and behaviors are annotated as follows.

3:02 p.m. The DADT Repeal Act vote begins and the clerk is directed to begin calling the Senate roll.

3:02 p.m. Senator Lugar (R-IN) votes against repeal. Senator Lugar had a 60 percent rating from the Human Rights Campaign scorecard; however, he was listed on the SLDN vote count as a leaning no. He was up for reelection in 2012 in a red state against a Tea Party primary challenger, to whom he would later lose.

3:09 p.m. Senator Brown (R-MA) is the first Republican to vote in favor of repeal. He was the Republican in the bluest state and he is up for reelection in 2012. He will lose his reelection.

3:10 p.m. Voting pauses while the clerk reads out the existing list of senators who voted. There are 26 yeas and 14 nays announced.

3:12 p.m. Senators Snowe (R-ME), Collins (R-ME), and Burr (R-NC) vote in favor of repeal. Senator Collins was a cosponsor of the repeal bill and up for reelection in 2012. Senator Snowe would later announce her retirement. Senator Burr is the only Republican from a southern red state to vote in favor of repeal. He had just been reelected in 2010 and is up for reelection in 2016.

3:13 p.m. Senators Rockefeller (D-WV) and Conrad (D-ND) vote in favor of repeal. Both Senators would later announce their retirement. This is the second time Senator Conrad has cast a yea vote.

3:15 p.m. Senator Ensign (R-NV) votes in favor of repeal. Senator Ensign had faced recent controversies and would later announce his retirement.

3:16 p.m. Senators Ben Nelson (D-NE) and Voinovich (R-OH) vote in favor of repeal. Senator Voinovich had announced in 2009 that he would not seek reelection. Senator Nelson would later announce his retirement.

3:17 p.m. Senator Mark Kirk (R-IL) votes in favor of repeal. He was up for reelection in 2010 in a Democratic-leaning state and was reelected.

3:17 p.m. Senator Lamar Alexander (R-TN) votes against repeal. Senator Alexander had been viewed as a possible yea vote. He was up for reelection in 2014 against a Tea-Party primary opponent. He was reelected.

3:18 p.m. Senators Nelson (D-FL) and Lincoln (D-AR) voted in favor of repeal. Senator Lincoln was defeated in 2010.

3:19 p.m. Senator Lisa Murkowki (R-AK) voted in favor of repeal. She won reelection in a write-in vote in 2010 and will be up for reelection in 2016.

TABLE 9.1 *Actual Votes With Predicted Vote Count Based on 2004-2005 Votes*

Time	Yeas						
302	Lieberman	Bayh*					
303	Tester	Leahy	Boxer				
304	Kerry	Webb					
305	Franken						
306	Inouye	Mikulski	Bennett (CO)	Casey	Levin	Landrieu	Warner
307	Reed	Bingamon	Schumer				
308	Gillibrand	Shaheen	Cantwell				
309	Hagan	Conrad	*Brown (MA)*	Murray	Reid		
Mid-Vote Tally ⟶							
310	Klobuchar						
311	Durbin						
312	⟨Snowe⟩	*Collins*	*Burr*				
313	Sanders	Harkin	⟨*Rockefeller*⟩	Cardin	⟨Conrad⟩		
314	Brown (OH)	Wyden	Merkley	Begich			
315	Feingold	⟨*Ensign*⟩					
316	Dorgan	⟨*Voinovich*⟩	⟨Nelson (NE)⟩				
317	Johnson	*Kirk*					
318	Akaka	*Nelson (FL)*	Feinstein	Whitehouse	⟨Lincoln⟩		
319	McCaskill	Dodd	*Murkowski*	Menendez			
320	Coons	⟨Specter⟩	⟨Kohl⟩				
321	⟨*Baucus*⟩						
322	Udall (CO)	Stabenow	*Pryor*				
323	Lautenberg						
324	Udall (NM)						
329	*Carper*						
Second Group ⟶							
Final Tally ⟶							

3:20 p.m. Senators Arlen Specter (D-PA) and Herb Kohl (D-WI) vote in favor of repeal. Senator Specter had previously lost his primary race and Senator Kohl would later retire.

3:21 p.m. Senator Max Baucus (D-MT) votes in favor of repeal. He would later retire from the Senate and be named Ambassador to China.

Nays						Yes	No
Barasso	McCain	*Lugar*	Johanns	Isaakson		2	5
Cornyn	Corker	Sessions				3	3
Kyl						2	1
Vitter	Coburn					1	2
Reed	Bingamon	Schumer				7	0
						3	0
						3	0
Roberts	Demint	Cochran				5	3
					→	26	14
						1	0
						1	0
Bond						3	1
						4	0
Lemieux	Brownback					4	2
Graham	Wicker	Risch	Bennett (UT)	Shelby	Grassley	2	6
Crapo	Chambliss					3	2
Alexander	McConnell					2	2
Enzi						5	1
						4	0
Inhofe						3	1
Thune						1	1
						3	0
Hutchison						1	1
						1	0
						1	0
					→	39	17
					→	65	31

Leaning yes (D)   *Leaning yes (R)*   Undecided (D)   *Undecided (R)*   No (R)   ⬭ Not facing reelection

3:22 p.m. Senator Mark Pryor (D-AR) votes in favor of repeal. He was up for reelection in 2014 and was not reelected.

3:30 p.m. The vote is closed and passage is announced 65–31 by the Presiding Officer, Senator Bayh, who voted yea and would later retire.

TABLE 9.2 *Comparing Vote Timing and Contextual Vulnerability*

Timing of Senate Vote	Member 111th Congress	Party	2005 SLDN Predicted Vote Count	HRC Scorecard for 110th	Vote	State Divide
3:02	Lugar	R	No	60	No	Red in red
3:09	Brown (MA)	R		33˙	Yes	Red in blue
3:12	Burr	R	Leaning no	20	Yes	Red in red
3:12	Snowe	R	Leaning yes	70	Yes	Red in blue
3:12	Collins	R	Leaning yes	75	Yes	Red in blue
3:09/3:13	Conrad	D	Undecided	60	Yes	Blue in red
3:13	Rockefeller	D	Undecided	85	Yes	Blue in red
3:15	Ensign	R	Undecided	0	Yes	Red in red
3:16	Voinovich	R	No	60	Yes	Red in red
3:16	Nelson (NE)	D	Leaning yes	65	Yes	Blue in red
3:17	Kirk	R	Leaning yes˙	85	Yes	Red in blue
3:17	Alexander	R	Undecided	20	No	Red in red
3:18	Lincoln	D	Leaning yes	70	Yes	Blue in red
3:18	Nelson (FL)	D	Undecided	90	Yes	Blue in blue
3:19	Murkowski	D	Undecided	20	Yes	Red in red
3:20	Specter	D	Undecided	70	Yes	Blue in blue
3:20	Kohl	D	Undecided	80	Yes	Blue in blue
3:21	Baucus	D	Undecided	80	Yes	Blue in red
3:23	Pryor	D	Undecided	60	Yes	Blue in red

The timeline for the votes with their contextual vulnerability is shown in Table 9.2. This table shows how the interest groups were predicting their vote, the electoral situation, and the outcome. Returning to Table 9.1, we see how knowledge about electoral implications is revealed in the predicted outcome based on the SLDN 2004–2005 vote.

Political Penalty?	Electoral Decision	Election Percentage
Yes—primary	Lost to primary challenger in 2012	87 (2006)
No—Democratic state	Lost in general election in 2012	52 (2010)
Yes—but had just been reelected	Won in general election in 2010	55 (2010)
No—retired	Announced retirement in Feb 2012	74 (2006)
No—blue state	Won general election in 2012	62 (2008)
No—retired	Announced retirement in Jan 2011	69 (2006)
No—retired	Annouced retirement in Jan 2013	64 (2008)
No—retired	Announced retirement in Mar 2011	55 (2006)
No—retired	Annouced retirement in Jan 2009	64 (2004)
No—retired	Announced retirement in Dec 2011	64 (2006)
No—Democratic state	Won general election in 2012	48 (2010)
Yes—primary	Won	67 (2008)
No—lost election	Lost general election in 2010	37 (2010)
No—Obama state	Won general election in 2006	52 (2012)
Yes—but had just been reelected	Won general election in 2010	49 (2010)
No—lost primary	Lost primary in 2010	46 (2010)
No—retired	Announced retirement in May 2011	67 (2006)
No—retired	Annouced retirement in Apr 2013	73 (2008)
Yes—Republican state	Won general election in 2010	79 (2006)

A review of outside variables (see Table 9.2) as possible indicators for their positioning offered limited predictability. For example, the previous electoral winning percentage for senators was not compelling. Senator Lugar had won his previous race by 87 percent and Senator Pryor had won his by 79 percent, and yet both faced different electoral situations in 2010. The

Human Rights Campaign scorecard was also of limited value. For instance, it ranked Senator Ensign at 0, Senator Burr at 20, Senator Murkowski at 20, and all voted for repeal.

SENATORIAL LOSSES AND RETIREMENTS

A retrospective analysis of the repeal vote places senators in two camps: those who faced electoral penalties and those who did not (Tables 9.1). A snapshot that emerges from Table 9.1 is illustrated with circles around those members who would not face reelection. This overlay offers two important data points to inform this narrative. First, 15 of the 17 yea voters faced little political penalty either because they had lost a primary, were not planning to seek reelection, or were a Republican from a Democratic-leaning blue state where the state constituency was likely to support repeal. The only immediate political penalty on the basis of a yea vote in favor of DADT repeal was faced by Senator Pryor. Senators Burr and Murkowski faced potential penalties six years later.

DISCUSSION

In this chapter I have reviewed senatorial behavior during the roll call vote on DADT repeal. I have argued that there is a performative nature to Senate roll call voting. The performance of either seeking cover or providing cover during a roll call vote is designed to protect senators during controversial votes, and this can be seen in the case presented. I find that positioning corresponds to the presence or absence of penalties and that vulnerable officials appear to strategize to seek political cover. The results of my study suggest six initial conclusions with electoral implications.

First, the C-SPAN (2010) video allows for an analysis of senator voting behavior. The voting positioning shows that the Republican in the bluest state and with the greatest political penalty (Senator Brown, R-MA) voted yea earlier. This positioning is consistent with making an affirmative visible statement. Senator Brown's positioning highlights how his particular vote (the 23rd vote cast in favor of repeal) directly contributed to the final result and signaled his support to LGBT voters. In this way, the vote timing provided political cover from the penalty of being a Republican, a party that is not known for its LGBT support, in a solidly Democratic state.

Second, the video shows that the Democratic senator from the reddest state (Senator Pryor, D-AR) voted later, after the result was already determined. Senator Pryor cast the 62nd of the 65 votes in favor. This vote timing is consistent with a masking threshold and penalty-mitigating order because it had the value of taking place after the Republican yea votes and placed Senator Blanche Lincoln (D-AR) before him. Or put another way, it is reasonable to assume that while Senator Pryor was brave and he was going to vote for repeal, he was not going to be the first Arkansas senator to do so. The performative sequence of events in the casting of a roll call vote mattered.

Third, the C-SPAN video allowed the clustered yea voting across both parties to be documented. For Republicans, Senators Collins, Snowe and Burr were clustered as were Democratic Senators Rockefeller and Conrad. Whether planned or spontaneous, this clustering allowed each group of senators a certain degree of political cover on a previously controversial issue.

Fourth, of the 17 senators under review who voted yea in the second 20-minute voting block, Republicans appeared to lead and Democrats appeared to follow. Two explanations are useful here. First, voting in favor of DADT repeal was considered either politically valuable or not costly for 7 senators (5 Republicans and 2 Democrats) who would face reelection. And second, Democrats could have been using Republican votes to provide cover regardless of electoral implications. In addition, it is interesting, but more speculative, to note the impact of nay votes. For instance, voting nay early by Senator Lugar, who had a 60 percent rating on LGBT rights, may have signaled support to his more conservative backers. At the very least, this positioning shows that the Republican in the red state with the greatest political penalty also voted earlier than Democrats facing potential danger. Moreover, I suggest that there is value in noting Senator Lamar Alexander's late nay vote. It is possible, but again speculative, that Senator Alexander waited until repeal was ensured by the votes of others before voting no.

And last, there are a number of key points to consider from this methodological tool. First, there may be randomness to the timing or clustering of voting that is unaccounted for in this analysis. However, this was not a normal vote, and senators and their staff take great care when managing such historic votes. Also, it is important to note that this type of retrospective analysis may not be possible in the future if senators are aware that their behavior is being watched and recorded. The use of C-SPAN video in this way may create a behavioral bias. Furthermore, the access and ability to review outside variables and target key senators is limited. In this case, the availability of inside lobbying tools made this possible. In addition, political penalties and political cover should continue to be studied. We have only just begun to analyze the way votes can be used to provide or take cover. Such analysis is an important aspect of legislative studies, and C-SPAN video, available through the C-SPAN Archives' online Video Library makes this possible.

CONCLUSION

In this chapter I have discussed how I used C-SPAN video of the Senate floor to conduct a retrospective analysis of Senate voting behavior, illustrating how roll call votes may be used to take or provide political cover regardless of party. Party members use the sequencing and clustering of roll call votes to provide political cover for their vulnerable members as a way of addressing controversial political issues within legislative bodies. Where in the order a senator casts his or her vote is as important as how the senator votes (yea or nay). To illustrate this, I reviewed the historic Senate vote on the repeal of DADT. The absence of penalties for many senators may have truly reflected how pro-gay senators are outside of the partisan political machinery. The outcome may also have represented a tipping point because it set a higher bar for bipartisan support in the future. In addition, this vote appears to signal the way political issues may be considered in light of presidential electoral results. In all, this analysis suggests that viewing Senate floor behavior through C-SPAN can be informative and that the positioning of senators' votes can matter in understanding policy outcomes. This chapter demonstrates how C-SPAN video may be a useful retrospective methodological tool in political science. Analyzing the sequencing of member votes relative to each other, peer support on floor, and the implications of these tactics to navigate difficult political issues provides an important understanding of the legislative process.

NOTES

Thanks to the University of Sydney Department of Government and International Relations. A previous draft of this chapter was presented at the Australian Political Studies Association Conference in 2014. Special thanks to Luke Edgell for his previous research on the 2010 DADT vote, as well as David Smith, Senthorun Raj, and David Marsh for their encouragement. A final thanks to the anonymous reviewer, whose feedback greatly improved this chapter.

1. I was a participant observer of Senate procedure as an aide de camp to Senator John Warner from July to October 1999, as a staff assistant to Senator Harry Reid from March 2000 until March 2001, and as a registered lobbyist from November 2002 to July 2005.

REFERENCES

Allee, T. L., & Huth, P. K. (2006). Legitimizing dispute settlement: International legal rulings as domestic political cover. *American Political Science Review, 100*(2), 219–234. http://dx.doi.org/10.1017/S0003055406062125

Arceneaux, K., & Kolodny, R. (2009). Educating the least informed: Group endorsements in a grassroots campaign. *American Journal of Political Science, 53*(4), 755–770. http://dx.doi.org/10.1111/j.1540-5907.2009.00399.x

Box-Steffensmeier, J., Ryan, J. M., & Sokhey, A. E. (2015). Examining legislative cue-taking in the US Senate. *Legislative Studies Quarterly, 40*(1), 13–53. http://dx.doi.org/10.1111/lsq.12064

Brady, J. (2010, December 9). DADT hits senate roadblock. Retrieved from http://www.rollcall.com/news/-201349-1.html

Brewer, P. R. (2008). *Value war: Public opinion and the politics of gay rights.* Lanham, MD: Rowman & Littlefield Publishers.

Bueno De Mesquita, B., Morrow, J. D. Siverson, R. M., & Smith, A. (1999). Policy failure and political survival the contribution of political institutions. *Journal of Conflict*

Resolution, 43(2), 147–161. http://dx.doi.org/10.1177/0022002799043002002

C-SPAN. (1986, June 2). *Senate session* [online video]. Available from http://www
.c-span.org/video/?45919-1/28th-anniversary-tv-cameras-senate

C-SPAN. (2010, December 18). *Senate session* [online video]. Available from http://
www.c-span.org/video/?297168-1/senate-session

Editorial. (2006, December 7). Welcome political cover. *New York Times.* Retrieved
from http://www.nytimes.com/2006/12/07/opinion/07thu1.html?_r=0

Eleveld, K. (2009, July 15). Hate crimes passes, faces veto [Queer Justice League Web
log post]. Retrieved from http://queer-justice-league.blogspot.com.au/2009/07
/hate-crimes-passes-faces-veto-by-kerry.html

Frank, N. (2009). Unfriendly fire: How the gay ban undermines the military and
weakens America. New York, NY: Thomas Dunne Books.

Kahn, K. F., & Kenney, P. J. (2002). The slant of the news: How editorial endorsements
influence campaign coverage and citizens' views of candidates. *American Political
Science Review, 96*(02), 381–394. http://dx.doi.org/10.1017/S0003055402000230

Kingdon, J. (1973). *Congressmen's voting decisions.* New York, NY: Harper and Row.

Matthews, D. (1984). Legislative recruitment and legislative careers. *Legislative Studies
Quarterly,* 547–585.

Matthews, D., & Stimson, J. (1975). Yeas and nays: Normal decision-making in the
U.S. House of Representatives. New York, NY: John Wiley & Sons.

Mayhew, D. (1974). *Congress: The electoral connection.* New Haven, CT: Yale University
Press.

Miller, D. H. (1998). *Freedom to differ the shaping of the gay and lesbian struggle for
civil rights.* New York: New York University Press. Retrieved from http://search
.ebscohost.com/login.aspx?direct=true&scope=site&db=nlebk&db=nlabk&A
N=47796

Mixon, F. G., Hobson, D. L., & Upadhyaya, K. P. (2001). Gavel-to-gavel congressional
television coverage as political advertising: The impact of C-SPAN on legislative
sessions. *Economic Inquiry, 39*(3), 351–364. http://dx.doi.org/10.1093/ei/39.3.351

Neff, C. L., & Edgell, L. R. (2013). The rise of repeal: Policy entrepreneurship and
don't ask, don't tell. *Journal of Homosexuality, 60*(2–3), 232–249. http://dx.doi
.org/10.1080/00918369.2013.744669

Ritchie, D A. (2009). *Press gallery: Congress and the Washington correspondents.*
Cambridge, MA: Harvard University Press.

Rybicki, E. (2013, August 19). *Voting and quorum procedures in the senate* (CRS

Report No. 96-452). Retrieved from Congressional Research Service website: http://www.senate.gov/CRSReports/crs-publish.cfm?pid=%26*2D4QLO9%0A

Saeki, M. (2009). Gridlock in the government of the United States: Influence of divided government and veto players. *British Journal of Political Science, 39*(3), 587–607. http://dx.doi.org/10.1017/S0007123408000550

Williams, K. (1994). Gays in the military: The legal issues. *University of San Francisco Law Review, 28,* 919.

CHAPTER **10**

PUBLIC UNDERSTANDINGS OF WOMEN IN STEM: A PROTOTYPE ANALYSIS OF GOVERNMENTAL DISCOURSE FROM THE C-SPAN VIDEO LIBRARY

Lauren Berkshire Hearit
Patrice M. Buzzanell

In the award-winning television series aired on CBS since 2007, *The Big Bang Theory,* the main characters are men who have careers in science, technology, engineering, and mathematics (STEM), with the exception of an apartment neighbor, Penny, who holds a variety of work positions, including waitress at The Cheesecake Factory, aspiring actress, bartender, community college student, and pharmaceutical sales representative. The men are depicted as obsessed with STEM. For example, they vie for accolades in their profession with particular characters, like Sheldon, who often discusses the higher status of theoretical physics and diminishing applied STEM areas, and Howard, who frequently shares his engineering background. The male characters also fit popular cultural portrayals of STEM as they discuss futuristic science in the original and spinoffs of *Star Trek* and *Back to the Future.* They love video games and comic books. When Penny enters the sitcom as the first non-STEM member of the cast, she brings alternative ways of thinking about and doing everyday life. She offers relationship advice, encourages the men to try new things, and provides a contrast to the men's obsessive STEM-focused world. Amy (Sheldon's friend and eventual girlfriend) and Bernadette (Howard's girlfriend and eventual wife) later join Penny in the cast of *The Big Bang Theory*, but as women whom have STEM careers.

Throughout this sitcom prototypes, or idealized stereotypes, of people interested and working in STEM offer sharp contrasts to socially skilled and relationally oriented non-STEM characters. Although humorous and perhaps true to people's orientations at times (see person–thing orientation, Graziano, Habashi, & Woodcock, 2011), the series draws upon notions of scientists, engineers, and those in related professions as socially awkward and obsessive geniuses attuned to abstraction and not to appearance, relationships, and everyday life. *The Big Bang Theory* and other examples of popular culture coincide with scholarship on prototypes. Prototypes affect understandings and treatment of other people in varied venues, including assumptions about leadership in business and other sectors, qualities associated with gender, racial, and ethnic identity categorizations, and abilities to access and use policies (e.g., Buzzanell & Liu, 2005; Mendez & Busenbark, 2015; Sesko & Biernat, 2010).

Of interest to us are whether and how these prototypes, particularly of women in STEM, surface in policymakers' and other governmental discourses found in the C-SPAN Archives' online Video Library. We also are interested in the possible implications of such discourses and their cultural formations, especially in considering if and how popular culture is associated with governmental discourse. We use discourse with a small "d" to mean the intersections of everyday talk-in-interaction and linguistic choices. We also pay attention to the macro discourses, known as big "D" Discourses that enable conversational and textual understandings and form the basis for politicized decision premises (e.g., see Alvesson & Kärreman, 2000; Fairhurst, 2007; Fyke & Buzzanell, 2013; Putnam & Mumby, 2014). Macro discourse includes societal and cultural knowledge that is often tacit and socialized early in life, such as very young children's understandings of women's and men's appropriateness for particular jobs and how people do and should behave in the workplace (Paugh, 2005). In taking this route, we contribute not only to research linking d/Discourses[1] with consequences on individual, meso (group and organizational), and macro (institutional, global) levels but also to popular culture and policy initiatives designed to encourage women (and men) to pursue education and careers in STEM (e.g., Kisselburgh, Berkelaar Van Pelt, & Buzzanell, 2009).

LITERATURE REVIEW

Van Gorp, Rommes, and Emons (2014) argue that the negative image of the scientist, engineer, and technologist as portrayed in media both through fiction and nonfiction venues contributes to a general lack of interest in STEM-related careers among young people. Although their study is situated in the Netherlands, they draw upon research on prototypes, popular culture, and national as well as global initiatives to promote STEM awareness and careers. The urgency of their work also is apparent insofar as the Netherlands has one of the lowest proportions of women entering STEM-related fields, with the United States located toward the top of international ranking systems with 38 percent of women graduates in STEM fields. These percentages, they argue, require not only educational interventions but also greater understanding of how the popular media may contribute to national and gender disparities in STEM interests and careers.

Using self-to-prototype matching theory, Van Gorp et al. (2014) provide insight into how individuals select and choose professions. Individuals compare themselves to people in different jobs or careers and, if the self-image and occupational prototype (or ideal type; e.g., ideal engineer or scientist) are more similar than different, then people are more likely to select, or at least not discount, particular employment and career possibilities. The comparison process is cognitive and embodied, meaning that prototype schema are activated and produce particular imagery and emotional responses. To examine this process, they asked grade school children to engage in the draw-a-scientist test only to find that scientists (and engineers because of similarities in occupations) were depicted as ugly, not fashionable, and uninterested in their appearance. While there may be a cultural context to these depictions, scholars such as Haynes (2003) looked at prototypes of scientists across different cultural and national contexts, with results informing and supporting Van Gorp and colleagues' findings that scientists are portrayed as alone, isolated, unsociable, and obsessed or completely absorbed by their work. These images are not to-tally unrealistic. As Cech and Blair-Loy (2014) note, their top-ranked STEM faculty overwhelmingly agreed that "the specific research I engage in is an important part of my identity" (90 percent of respondents), often working 60 hours a week, with the majority of time spent on research-related activities, and wishing that they could spend more time on work. Moreover, the images discussed in scholarship surface in U.S. popular media, such as *The Big Bang Theory,* with which we opened our chapter.

Van Gorp et al. (2014) argue that the representation of scientists in nonfic-tion genres (popular media) is the result of conscious or unconscious choices of media producers influenced by these prototypes in fiction (p. 648).[2] They conducted thematic and content analyses of select popular cultural materials from the Netherlands, including items that are commercially available (e.g., books, DVDs readily available in stores, comic books, TV shows), with an eye toward capturing the breadth of stereotypes rather than examining the entire corpus of media representations. They found that scientists in popular media were *always* characterized as white, old men. There were *no* representations of female scientists in the media examined.[3]

In general, the image of the scientist in Dutch media has these charac-teristics: is physically unattractive; does work that often is considered useless and/or unclear for ordinary people; is dedicated and focused, nonsocial, not compliant with societal (or fashion) norms; and is predominantly a white (old) man. They argue that these prototypes and the loneliness of science make the occupation seem less attractive for many girls (see also Rommes, Overbeek, Scholte, Engels, & de Kemp, 2007). Also, the level of dedication of science/STEM may be overwhelming for students who may not feel as though they are *that* dedicated, even if they express interest in the field. Young women and men also may question whether such a lifestyle is conducive to the kinds of career and personal life balance that they desire at present and across their life span (e.g., Mason, Goulden, & Frasch, 2009). If this is how science is depicted in the media, young students might not pick this career and the accompany-ing educational and extracurricular experiences that can ensure success in STEM (e.g., see Buzzanell, Berkelaar, & Kisselburgh, 2011).

Van Gorp et al.'s (2014) findings are similar to others in North America and Western Europe. For instance, the oft-cited findings of Haynes (2003) discuss representations of scientists as bad and dangerous people, findings replicated so often that Haynes refers to them as the master narrative about science and technology. In Haynes's study, she distinguished seven prototypes about scientists' representation in Western literature: evil scientist, noble scientist, foolish scientist, inhuman scientist, scientist as an adventurer, mad scientist, and helpless scientist. Women scientist prototypes were old maid, masculine woman, naive expert, evil plotter, daughter or assistant, and lonely heroine (see also Flicker, 2003). All were negative except the lonely heroine, although the heroine is *lonely*. Popular portrayals indicate that no man wants to be with her because she is smarter than all the men, self-obsessed with work, and unattractive.

More than a decade later, Haynes (2014) found that contemporary women scientists are presented as problem solvers: "Because they are of recent origin and were never part of the alchemist stereotype, female fictional scientists, far from being mad or evil, usually resolve problems, despite attacks on their work and their integrity" (p. 11). Moreover, scientists and engineers are displaying greater variation in contemporary representations: In the Discovery Channel's *MythBusters,* each character is unique with the woman presented as heavily tattooed with crazy hair; in *The Big Bang Theory,* the men adhere to the scientist–engineer stereotypes in their characterizations but also show personal and relational development, often through their interactions with Penny and, later in the series, their other relational partners. Likewise, Amy, Sheldon's female counterpart, grows through friendships and attraction to Penny's and Bernadette's feminine qualities and interactive styles. Thus, there are variations of STEM characters in popular media, despite the dominance of certain STEM prototypes.

In short, prototypes of scientists and engineers are depicted in the discourses and portrayals of STEM occupations in fiction and nonfiction of varied media and popular cultural materials. These prototypical portrayals, such as Sheldon the physicist on *The Big Bang Theory,* have consequences for occupational recruitment and retention as well as public demands for services and products. These prototypes are both perpetuated and changeable because of connections between micro discourses and macro discourses (d/Discourses) and human action in different life realms (Fairhurst, 2007).

Our research question asks how these prototypes and other ideal images surface in governmental discourses, particularly the discourses of women and men who testify on behalf of bills, policy changes, and funding initiatives and for other purposes in archived hearings, deliberations, public affairs, and federal government proceedings captured in the C-SPAN Video Library. Not only might the matching of professional prototypes against personal interests and lifestyle aspirations prompt less (or more) interest in particular occupations, but also they establish seemingly unrealistic notions of the nature and meaning of the occupational work itself. For instance, crime scene investigation personnel not only express their frustrations that most people who consume media depictions of their work have increased demands for action and unrealistic timelines and expectations, but they also express these interactions as opportunities to educate the public (see Huey, 2010).

Thus, prototypes in popular fictional and nonfictional discourse are embedded in contexts that might attract and/or dissuade occupational entry and long-term careers. These prototypes have national importance because they seem to be associated with the recruitment and retention of women and men, particularly women in STEM majors and careers. To our knowledge, federal discourse in the C-SPAN Video Library has not been examined for the popular understandings and prototypes of engineers and scientists expressed by political elites. Possible consequences of gendered occupational discourses and images might be funding and policy changes that perpetuate rather than change traditional strategies designed for increasing numbers of women in STEM.

METHOD

We began by searching the C-SPAN Video Library using the keywords "science, technology," "engineering, women," "engineering, women, education," "technology, women," and "science, women." Video segments on these topics, as well as "mentions" of these keywords, were compiled into one larger data set.

A total of 103 videos and clips were collected for this analysis. The videos ranged in length from a few minutes to several hours. Within the data set, mentions of women in STEM ranged from only a brief comment to an entire session (e.g., 40 minutes) on the discussion of women in STEM fields and careers. The videos were from 1988 to 2014. The video that had the most views, 4,069, was *Book Discussion on* The Immortal Life of Henrietta Lacks, which originally aired on March 19, 2010. The video that had the least number of views from within the Video Library was *Open Phones,* where viewers called in and commented on the news of the day. This video had only 16 views and originally aired on March 10, 2005.

After these videos were compiled, we gathered transcripts from closed captioning contained in the C-SPAN Video Library. We viewed videotapes in two ways: for content accuracy and for chronological ordering. First, we viewed the video sessions and compared the closed-captioned record against the recordings to ensure accuracy of our data and to insert the names and political affiliations or other institutional affiliations of speakers and groups. Second, we viewed the videos and took notes on the video content chronologically from 1988 to 2014. This ordering allowed us to gain a sense of the temporal nature of the discourse surrounding women in STEM by policymakers and to better understand how the d/Discourse changed over time. As we engaged in the content accuracy and chronological analysis of the C-SPAN discourse, we eliminated videos and clips that did not relate directly to this study on the discourses surrounding policymaking regarding women in STEM fields. From the total 103 videos collected, 27 were flagged as relating to women in STEM prototypes. We then began to individually take notes on what was happening within the video segments as well as the larger society with regard to women in STEM policymaking, what was happening with regard to the exigencies (e.g., context underlying Discourses) from which these discourses probably emerged, and the actual wording (e.g., everyday linguistic choices in discourse) about these topics and why this d/Discourse seemed to emerge.

After multiple conversations and re-viewings of videos (and transcripts), once we felt confident that we had achieved not only a representative, if not complete, corpus of video and textual data around our keywords but also a verified database with contextual notes and memos, we began our data analysis. Using thematic analysis (Owen, 1984), we looked for recurring semantic units, or thought and language units, that related to women in STEM in general, gendered notions about STEM majors and institutions, and policy for, characterizations of, and relevant details about women in STEM. We followed Owen's criteria for themes: recurrence, repetition, and forcefulness. Recurrence is "observed when at least two parts of a report had the same thread of meaning, even though different wording" (p. 275), meaning that there could be implicit mention or reference to gendered prototypes of women (and men) in STEM using varied wording. Repetition involves the "explicit repeated use of the same wording" (p. 275), such as the word *obsessed*. For the third criterion, forcefulness, we examined, as Owen recommended, "vocal inflection, volume, or dramatic pauses which serve to stress and subordinate some utterances from other locutions in the oral reports … [noting that] the assumption here was that participants themselves could and did make sense of their relations evidenced in part by the *form* of their discourse" (pp. 275–276).

We then read and reread the verified transcripts, viewed all of the videos and key segments repeatedly, and sorted out the recurring semantic patterns or themes individually and collaboratively. We discussed and revised our themes until we were satisfied that our thematic process labels and their conceptualizations and textual support captured the main ways in which women in STEM were portrayed in the C-SPAN Video Library. We went back and reexamined our video and textual data to find negative cases that would counterbalance the themes and noted variations and possible exceptions. Thus, our findings focus on the prototypes used within the discourse of policymakers and those that influence policymakers. The examples that follow are exemplars of the overall discourse in the C-SPAN Video Library. We chose particular examples to illustrate broader themes or prototypes found within this data set. These are representative rather than idiosyncratic examples.

RESULTS

To answer the research question "What are the prototypes of women in STEM that emerge through examination of the d/Discourses found in the C-SPAN Video Library?" we identified the theme and corresponding prototypes as our first steps. We incorporated information about contexts to identify how this d/Discourse impacts policies related to women in STEM and STEM careers. The three themes and accompanying prototypes that emerged were women in STEM as (a) exceptional, (b) different, and (c) representative of other women.

Women in STEM as Exceptional

In this theme, we found that the emphasis was on *specific women* whose experiences in STEM represented idealized versions or prototypes of what women could do in these fields. They were depicted as exceptional women in terms of their accomplishments and their gender. As a result they functioned as prototypes for a certain image of women as well as tokens who provide evidence of women's representation and inclusion (for discussions on tokens, see Guttierrez y Muhs, Niemann, Gonzalez, & Harris, 2012). In this theme, women were characterized as (a) trailblazers, (b) firsts, and (c) pioneers, not only in their fields based on their professional contributions but also in breaching gendered occupations in STEM. These characterizations overlapped, but specific content related more so to one prototype than others.

Trailblazers

Amelia Earhart and Dr. Sally Ride are two examples from within the C-SPAN Video Library where the prototype of a woman as a trailblazer was invoked. For example, at an Amelia Earhart exhibit in 2012, remarks about her accomplishments were made by a number of people. In one case, Earhart's value in encouraging STEM participation, especially in aviation, was noted: "Amelia also recognized that there was an opportunity to use her fame as a platform for encouraging and advancing women in aviation and not only aviation but giving women the encouragement to pursue independent lives outside the home" (C-SPAN, 2012c). In this way, her own accomplishments were understood and portrayed as unique but also beneficial to others in providing a role model and path for other women interested in STEM to succeed.

The day after she passed away from pancreatic cancer, Dr. Sally Ride was referred to in the Senate as having "blazed a trail out into the stars" for women in science and technology fields (C-SPAN, 2012b). In this video, it seemed as though Dr. Ride was used as a success story regarding the number of women in science and technology fields. Senator Mikulski (D-MD) spent several minutes discussing Dr. Ride's individual accomplishments, and mentioned repeatedly how Dr. Ride inspired women to go into science and technology fields, or to become an astronaut like she was. In these and other cases, the women are depicted as trailblazers with unusual contributions that they made to STEM fields by being women. The excerpts convey neither these women's lived experiences and societal realities nor the complexities of gender in STEM disciplines. Regardless, both Amelia Earhart and Dr. Ride were considered trailblazers and lauded within multiple governmental and policy-making platforms: Amelia Earhart as a woman aviator and Sally Ride within the Senate for her accomplishments as an astronaut. In prototypical terms, they both fit the prototypes of women scientists in Western literature: noble scientist and scientist as an adventurer.

Firsts

Women who are firsts—first-generation college student, first to study in a STEM field, first woman to overcome particular barriers, and so on—face challenges that other women, and men, might not face because there are no role models to follow and the normalized discourse of exclusion and lack of women's fit in STEM occupations is perceived as normal and natural (see Guttierrez y Muhs et al., 2012).

When former Health and Human Services Secretary (under President Clinton, 1993–2001) Donna Shalala began her PhD studies in political science, she was told by her department chairperson that no fellowship would be available to her because investing in women was a bad idea—namely that the return on investment was doubtful at best because women interrupted their careers for marriage and children (displaying both gendered, economic, and career Discourses).[4] Then, during her first job, she was told, "Even though you've published more than all the men in our department, we've never tenured a woman and we never will" (C-SPAN, 2005e). The explicit use of "we never will" illustrated the failures to fully recognize talent and ability in gendered structures and institutions. Moreover, the discourse also implied that the lack of women was natural, and that there was no need to create a pipeline.

For women noted as firsts in different institutions and roles, there was no funding, often no recruitment and selection process, and no job security, even when claims of exceptional performance were empirically supported, for example in Shalala's case. There also was no desire for change within institutions because women pursuing a career in STEM were firsts or unusual cases. Stories of exclusion and deliberate attempts to prevent women from achieving career success or even getting into a promotion and tenure track seemed all too common in the C-SPAN and other popular and academic discourse in previous years.

Shalala used her specific story as an exceptional woman to introduce a conference focused on increasing women in STEM and to illustrate the importance of creating an ad hoc committee designed to examine gender data across all fields of science and engineering. In this talk, National Academy of Engineering President Bill Wulf acknowledged that issues regarding the full participation of women in engineering and engineering within academia was a major issue that required further policies and research. Shalala stressed that since the National Science Foundation Authorization and Science and Technology Equal Opportunities Act (Pub. L. No. 96-516) passed 25 years earlier, not enough progress had occurred and "academic institutions are not fully utilizing the pool of women we've produced" (C-SPAN, 2005e).

Shalala cited statistics, such as how the proportion of women in tenure-track faculty positions at the top 50 U.S. universities was only 3 to 15 percent, and that women who did obtain academic employment were less likely than men to get tenure-track positions and be tenured in those positions (C-SPAN, 2005e). From this discussion it was clear that the number of women earning degrees in STEM fields was increasing (e.g., women now earn half of the PhDs in biomedical fields), yet the rate of women at high-productivity research universities did not reflect this trend. As this issue was sent to an ad hoc committee, the major issue reiterated by all the speakers in this session was the need to better understand how to retain and promote women in STEM tenure-track academic positions.

This action—sending this issue to an ad hoc committee to study—would be appropriate for firsts, but not for those who have followed over the last few decades. The action delayed a potential response and created some passivity regarding the critical gender inequities and labor force shortages, potentially for several years. While this committee alone cannot solve the problem of advancement of women in science, creating and maintaining the pipeline from firsts through adequate numbers is a multistep process because career phenomena are more complex than the pipeline metaphor indicates. Even so, the action of studying issues is consistent with d/Discourses of firsts and their roles in the prototypical solution of studying and building a pipeline.

Pioneers

The frontier, pioneer spirit, and masculine heroic quests to go where others dare not go are prevalent in U.S. popular culture, from politicized and gendered images of Sarah Palin to images of the moon as a human frontier in President John F. Kennedy's talks, and advertising using iconic imagery of lone western cowboys (e.g., Gibson & Heyse, 2014; Harter, 2004). Therefore, it is not surprising that the pioneer would also be a prototypical image for C-SPAN content on women in STEM. The pioneer often also invoked the language of firsts and trailblazers, but with some variation.

When speaking about Shirley Ann Jackson to the House of Representatives in 2005, Bob Ney (R-OH) said the following:

> She is … the first African-American woman to lead a national research university. She has been a pioneer in many of her other endeavors as well. She is the first African-American woman to receive a doctorate (M.D.) from M.I.T., the first African-American to become a commissioner and chairman of the U.S. Nuclear Regulatory Commission. (C-SPAN, 2005b)

Jackson was up for an appointment to the Board of Regents to the Smithsonian. In framing Ms. Jackson's career in this way, the representative implies that in order to become a successful professional, Ms. Jackson had to be a "pioneer" in science. Then just a few days later, House Concurrent Resolution 96, honoring women in science, was passed with remarks from Representative Judy Biggert (R-IL). Biggert said, "Today, African-American women scientists hold positions at all levels of universities, government, laboratories, and industry. … The women we are honoring in House Concurrent Resolution 96 aren't just pioneers, they are role models" (C-SPAN, 2005c). The word *pioneer* was used an additional four times in five minutes to describe African American scientists. Additionally, solutions to increasing the number of African American scientists or PhDs were not offered; rather, speakers simply acknowledged in their speeches that this condition was "a shame."

Similarly, John Hall (D-NY) also used pioneer language when honoring Dr. Frances E. Allen, calling her a pioneer and role model for other women in technology:

> Frances has been a pioneer in advancing the role of computer science. The goal is to increase participation of women in all aspects of technology. She worked tirelessly to help more women enter the field and served as a role model for women and men hoping to make new breakthroughs in computing. (C-SPAN, 2007a)

Hall's quote identified a variation of the pioneer prototype. Rather than the trailblazer who was a specific adventurer and unique contributor, the first who was breaking new ground (for herself primarily, but also often in ways that benefit other women), the pioneer, like those of the western frontier or other planets in *Star Trek,* establishes paths for others to follow. In this metaphor, exceptional women work for each other's inclusion. They are not lauded for intellectual brilliance and accomplishments; rather, as pioneers they are people who have faced and overcome obstacles, typically winning or surviving against incredible odds. Thus, women in STEM who were depicted as pioneers were not unique trailblazers in their disciplines and accomplishments but were those who by gender and/or racial and ethnic identity categorizations opened paths for others.

Women in STEM as Different

In this theme, women in STEM fields were portrayed as different not only from men but also from other women. The d/Discourses of difference did not focus on specific unique women and their accomplishments (trailblazers) or their place in the STEM pipeline (firsts) or role in creating a path for others (pioneers) as in the prior theme of exceptional women. Instead, difference was aligned with varied prototypes, often aligned with images in popular culture. The prototypes of difference identified were (a) outsiders within, (b) obsessive scientists, (c) engineers first, women second, and (d) team players on the bench (implying squandered talent).

Outsiders Within

Although the women were members of STEM fields, they perceived themselves or were portrayed and/or treated as outsiders, different from men in STEM. The prototypical outsider within presented personal narratives about her own experiences. In a 2006 book discussion on *Sisters in Science,* narratives from 30 to 50 years ago emerged when describing women entering graduate school in STEM fields and the fight for gender equity. For example, one woman discussed how as a graduate student, it was oftentimes assumed that she was a maid or teacher:

> I was in my science department at Michigan State, and, you know, some science buildings are kind of dark and the hallways are kind of dark and dingy. … I am walking through and this black gentleman stops me and he says … "Have you cleaned the toilet?" … And then

as I turned slightly, he saw my backpack. And he realized [I was a student]. (C-SPAN, 2006)

This narrative demonstrates how these women in science, particularly women who were minorities in STEM fields, found themselves treated as if they were not legitimate students or members of their STEM career field. To gain recognition of her status and entrée into the world of science, this woman needed a particular material artifact to signify her status and to disrupt the man's stereotypical response. Perhaps women require materialities, such as backpacks or technical gear, to symbolically and materially provide evidence that they deserve inclusion in the "STEM club." Paretti, McNair, and Leydens (2014) found that

> texts such as reports, work orders, budgets, graphs, and charts become tools not only for allocating resources, awarding power, and making critical decisions. Understanding the ways in which these texts operate is part of what new engineers learn as they enter the workplace, and part of what enables individuals to exert access control over their own work. (p. 613)

Understanding how materialities or written texts allow for power within the workplace and women "into the STEM club" enables us to identify the way prototypes of difference, especially the outsider within prototype, seep into the day-to-day interactions of women in STEM.

Obsessive Scientists

The obsessive scientist is an insider within STEM fields because she exhibits the obsession, genius, unconventional, and perhaps asocial eccentricities often ascribed to men of STEM and documented in research. Yet, the obsessive woman scientist was portrayed as one not attuned to relationships and nurturing, as would befit the stereotypical women in contemporary societies. In discussing the book *Obsessive Genius: The Inner World*, the host called both Madame Curie and the two women who joined the discussion, Lynn Sherr and Barbara Goldsmith, "trailblazing women," but the more prevalent theme as indicated by the book title and the video material available through the C-SPAN Video Library was that of obsession. Marie Curie and, by extension, women in STEM were obsessive scientists and engineers (C-SPAN, 2005a). Marie Curie was "obsessed with discovery … to find things that nobody else had found … to measure things that nobody else had measured" (C-SPAN, 2005a). The book discussants argued that Marie Curie's husband, her father, and her father-in-law allowed, enabled, and encouraged her obsession with science, even to the point that her father-in-law took over raising her two daughters. This story seemed to indicate that women in STEM (e.g., Marie Curie) required men's permission, encouragement, and support for career success. Whereas all people need educational, familial, or social/financial support, regardless of race, gender, or ethnicity, by noting that women need such resources, women are positioned as different. Indeed, men scientists often have partners and others who raise their children and care for the home so that they can work. This book discussion leads listeners to the conclusion that not only was Marie Curie obsessive but also she was atypical insofar as her support structures were concerned. While this book discussion does not necessarily create policy, it is an example of how within the C-SPAN Video Library selections, prototypes emerge from within the larger video corpus associated with government and policymakers by its offering through C-SPAN.

Engineers First, Women Second

In *The Evolving Workforce* from May 15, 2007, Joanne Maguire, the Lockheed Martin Space Systems executive vice president, said, "But as … young women entering engineering, I would hope that there would be a very strong impetus to think of themselves as engineers first and women second" (C-SPAN, 2007b). She then claimed that at Lockheed Martin, others were more interested in her brain and her thoughts as opposed to her gender. She expressed satisfaction that she was valued for her intellect and expertise, thus admitting that scientist and woman, expertise and femininity, were not fused in the way that man + scientist are normative for men.

In campus discussions not recorded by C-SPAN but pertinent to our analysis, Ellen Pollack (2014) recounted to a campus audience at a public talk sponsored by Purdue University how such prioritization of identities such as engineer first/woman second can impact a woman's feelings. Pollack's experiences as the sole woman interested in physics in her high school and then later at Yale University offered the impetus for her current research. She recounted a U.S. cultural truism that women who do science, engineering, and similar activities are not feminine or sexy, a popular idea that has been viewed as a significant deterrent to women's continued interests in STEM (Park, Young, Trois, & Pinkus, 2011).

The engineer or scientist first/woman second theme is recurring in *The Big Bang Theory.* As the non-STEM woman, Penny is sexy, fun, and attractive. Amy, the neuroscientist, in particular is depicted as dumpy and unattractive but very intelligent. The implied "choice" for women is to pursue STEM or to attend to appearance and relationships. By being a scientist first, especially in initial episodes, Amy had forsaken her feminine side and eliminated family possibilities. This subtheme and prototype of engineer and scientist first/woman second indicated that women could not have both a career and a personal life and, therefore, must compartmentalize and prioritize particular identities.

Team Players on the Bench

The metaphor of "team" emerged from the C-SPAN Video Library discourse. President Obama, at the 2014 White House Science Fair, had this to say:

Fewer than three in 10 workers in science and engineering are women. That means we've got half the field—or half our team we're not even putting on the field. We've got to change those numbers. These are the fields of the future. This is where the good jobs are going to be. And I want America to be home for those jobs. (C-SPAN, 2014)

As President Obama noted, women are sidelined by the very metaphor intended to be inclusionary. To sideline team players indicates not only that the United States cannot compete but also that talent is squandered.

In a House Session in May 2005, Lynn Woolsey (D-CA) spoke about a House rule that prevented a vote on her bill regarding women in STEM fields:

We are debating an issue that has long been important to me and I consider critical to our country's future. That is, the lack of women and girls in science, math, engineering, and technology. My amendment would have helped school districts increase girls' interest in studying these careers and in these areas. … A recent G.A.O. study, Mr. Chairman, found that men still outnumber women in nearly every field in science. In his recent article, "It's a flat world after all" and new book, "The World is Flat," *The New York Times* writer Thomas Friedman explains America's historical economic advantages have disappeared now that the world is flat and anyone with smarts, access to Google and a cheap wireless laptop can join the innovation fray. … Mr. Friedman's and others' remedy is to attract more men and women to science and engineering. It will be impossible four [sic] our country to continue to lead the world in innovation as long as more than half of our population are steered away from intentionally—or not—from studying and working in the field from where that innovation will come. … The biggest issue facing women in science and engineering is squandered talent. (C-SPAN, 2005d)

This discussion about increasing the number of women in STEM fields seemed hollow not simply because of the decades of research and implementations directed toward this goal but also because individuals, such as Representative Woolsey, failed to provide any measures to increase women's STEM participation outside of passing a bill to increase funding for school districts. While this is more substantive than many of the other congressional discussions, it still fell short.

In sum, this theme of difference was observed in governmental discourse aligned with prototypes. Women were seen as obsessive, eccentric, unattractive, or uncaring about their feminine side or personal life, and not team players.

Women in STEM as Representative

This theme of representativeness encompassed women in STEM as representative of other women by being (a) storytellers and (b) supporters. This theme needs more explanation, as it seems to contradict the previous two themes.

Storytellers

In the C-SPAN Video Library, women would be called upon to tell stories that supposedly represented (all) women's experience with only some variations in personal details. Women functioned as representative cases to argue for the creation of new educational initiatives.

Based on the content of our data, there was much policymaking regarding women in STEM in the mid to late 1990s. Many of the House and Senate sessions during which the commissions and laws were passed to encourage an increase in women in STEM fields occurred in 1996, 1998, and so on, but since then, the discussion seems to have become focused around women describing their experiences in STEM fields. Committees would explore the issues by, for example, bringing in four women to discuss the state of the STEM disciplines and the state of early education in STEM subjects, particularly in elementary and middle schools, but little follow-up in terms of new policies and substantive policy change seemed to happen.

This is not to say that there have not been policies or laws passed since the 1990s, but the discourses surrounding STEM in the last 10 to 15 years seem to have reverted to understanding women's experiences, investigating the factors contributing to the lack of women in STEM fields, and/or portraying the current experiences of women in engineering and science. These narrative data then are used to educate the majority, or dominant, group members in policymaking and related circles.

There was also much discussion in the C-SPAN Video Library about the history of women in STEM fields. For example, in a 2012 video on the History of Women at Harvard University (see C-SPAN, 2012a), panelists discussed at great length the history of women in science and medical professions at Harvard. However, there was a distinctive lack of discussion on the current state of affairs, especially in comparison to the narratives women tell regarding their own personal histories or the histories of other women.

Richard Templeton, CEO at Texas Instruments, testified before the House Science, Space, and Technology Committee on February 6, 2013. He claimed that women who opted into science and technology fields were graduating at higher rates than men because they were actually "sticking with it" at higher rates than men. Once again, the main policy recommendation made was to shift congressional emphasis toward the K–12 educational system as policymakers claimed that this is where children are making decisions, and this will be the only way to increase the number of women in STEM fields (C-SPAN, 2013).

Supporters

Another area of discourse that developed within the theme of women in STEM as representative concerned the support of families and teachers in encouraging women in their academic pursuit of STEM careers. For example, a C-SPAN book discussion on *Sisters in Science* profiled 18 African American women in science careers. Professor Diann Jordan, when talking about her book, shared many examples of issues such as equal pay, racism, finding a mentor, and fairness. Professor Jordan stated, "The women that you meet and sisters in science had a family member that encouraged them or teacher who encouraged them to be all that they could be" (C-SPAN, 2006). As part of the book discussion, she shared about her own job at Alabama State University and said that if she teaches her students about science and how science impacts everyday life, then her students become interested in science. She stressed repeatedly the role of the teacher in nurturing a student's interest in science and STEM careers, a role not surprising given the considerable research documenting the importance of socialization agents and nurturers of interests and talents (e.g., Buzzanell et al., 2011; Jablin, 2001; Jahn & Myers, 2014). In the theme of representation, it was not the STEM prototype that emerged, but that of woman as storyteller and supporter, roles that use "soft" data to make arguments and the stereotypical characteristics of support and nurturing to encourage women to pursue a STEM education and career.

DISCUSSION

Prototypes are person schema that capture the meaning of a category and serve as symbols or reference points for the category (Fiske & Taylor, 2013). Because governmental discourses invoke prototypical images of women, attitudes toward these women as individuals are of less importance than attitudes toward career women in the United States' science, technology, engineering, and math (STEM) realm. This means that the male–female dichotomy continues to be played out in media and governmental reports, such as on C-SPAN and in everyday conversations. The prototype references may disguise underlying issues—namely, how both men and women evaluate women, particularly women in male-dominated professions; why funding for the recruitment, retention, and promotion of women in STEM continues to require argument, providing evidence for the notion that such ideas are still controversial; and how prototypes might symbolize the continuing tensions and double binds experienced by women in the public sphere.

Our research question asked how ideal images surface in governmental d/Discourses. While prototypical images emerge in popular culture, the concern becomes whether these prototypes impact the funding, recruitment, or retention of women in STEM fields. Our findings contribute to greater understandings about women in STEM portrayals as well as initiatives to encourage more women in these areas. Specifically our themes of extraordinary, different, and representative women with accompanying prototypical depictions indicate that women still are not included as viable and appealing members of STEM fields. These prototypes emerged in the discourses of the women and men who, for example, testify on behalf of bills, policy changes, and funding initiatives. According to these prototypes, the women in STEM are different from other women, and both similar to and different from the men in STEM, because of their qualities: they must be exceptional; they are obsessive, unattractive, alone, and courageous; they are focused on STEM rather than their personal life; and so on. A consequence of these prototypes (both male and female) is that the imagery of scientists and engineers needs to be reworked to make such careers more appealing to children and adolescents.

Returning to the beginning of our chapter about prototypical representations of scientists and engineers that emerge in popular culture such as *The Big Bang Theory* and *MythBusters:* Van Gorp et al. (2014) proposed that the imagery of scientists and engineers be reworked so that they are considered as either doubters or puzzlers, given that both could be perceived as alternate prototypes with positive connotations. The puzzler could use the systematic collection of clues to work out a puzzle, like a mystery detective, and reframe the dominant narrative about scientists (and engineers) as essential research to promote STEM careers for youth in the Netherlands as well as other parts of the world. Moreover, popular media could also show variations in women and men in STEM fields. For instance, both Leonard and Amy in *The Big Bang Theory* have become more attuned to personal and social considerations throughout the series, thus representing more complex and nuanced characterizations of men and women in STEM.

The danger of presenting members of STEM fields only as characters such as Sheldon is that it reinforces stereotypical images that those interested in STEM must be obsessive or nerdy or only like certain aspects of popular culture (e.g., *Star Wars* or *Star Trek*). When individuals are interested in STEM yet sense that they do not match with the prototypes they have encountered on shows like *The Big Bang Theory* or *MythBusters,* they may self-select out of the field. As these prototypes emerge in governmental discourse—as evidenced by many of the videos collected from the C-SPAN Video Library—these prototypes become perpetuated in yet another public realm. If we do not show variations in women and men in STEM fields or move away from these prototypes to more nuanced, positive prototypes like the "puzzler" or the "doubter," gendered discourse likely may continue to impact funding and recruitment/retention policies and laws that are enacted by the government.

We examined the talk-in-interaction and Discourses of policymakers and other relevant materials available through the C-SPAN Video Library. Of concern to us is that, if stereotypes and their more idealized form, prototypes, are not attractive to youth and do not match with children's and adolescents' interests and self-image, then these future members of the U.S. labor force might self-select out of particular occupations and careers in STEM. While these stereotypes and prototypes have emerged within the U.S. popular media (e.g., Haynes, 2014), the danger is how media may impact laypersons as well as governmental policymakers. Zorn, Roper, Weaver, and Rigby (2010) found that laypersons were influenced by scientists, *and* scientists were influenced by laypersons (p. 12). They specifically found that laypersons were influenced by dialogue with experts *and* dialogue with nonexperts, and vice versa. The implications of this finding are stark when considering the discussions in many of the videos we watched in the C-SPAN Video Library. As congressmen and congresswomen bring in both scientists and laypersons (e.g., a former athlete turned doctor) to discuss their experiences as women in STEM, not only are the prototypes of women as trailblazers or women in STEM are different perpetuated, but policymakers' decisions may be impacted—for better or for worse—by this testimony. By examining the three themes that emerged from the data and associated prototypes indicating that women in STEM are extraordinary, different, and representative, we encourage enlargement and enrichment of language and portrayals in popular cultural and governmental materials. It appears that the prototypes and stereotypes that pervade popular culture in television shows like *The Big Bang Theory* influence the public dialogue occurring in Congress and in Washington. The danger of these prototypes and stereotypes influencing the public dialogue lies in the gendered, limiting discourse used, which can influence policies, recruitment, and retention of women in STEM.

LIMITATIONS AND FUTURE DIRECTIONS

This study, while among the first to examine the prototypes in governmental discourse and discuss how these prototypes influence policymakers and policymaking, has several limitations. While the cases used in this chapter were specifically chosen as exemplars that provide key examples or specific discourse that was representative of the larger corpus of data, it is important to remember that discussion at a book talk through C-SPAN BookTV is different from a House or Senate Committee meeting or deliberations on the floor of Congress.

Future research in this area or extensions of this study may consider further connecting how popular media impacts policymaking regarding STEM (and not just women in STEM, but men and women in STEM). Additionally, looking only at policymaking and the discourse used within policymaking deliberations and the potential proposed solutions to the "leaking STEM pipeline" may prove useful in understanding how the U.S. governmental discourse aligns with the recruitment and retention of women in STEM fields.

NOTES

1. Fairhurst and Putnam (2014) define discourse studies as "a broad class of approaches that focuses on the constitutive effects of language; processes of text production, distribution, and consumption; and reflexive, interpretive analysis aimed at deciphering the role of discourse in a socially constructed reality" (pp. 271–272). In echoing Fyke and Buzzanell's (2013) work, our "engagement with 'small d' *and* 'big D' avoids the dichotomization of discourse levels present in many discourse studies" as we examine the tensions inherent with the stereotypical and prototypical d/Discourse in STEM (p. 1621). Alvesson and Kärreman (2000) originally distinguished little "d" from big "D" discourse to differentiate between a language-centric view of discourse research (little "d" discourse) and a larger view of discourse (big "D" discourse), rooted in sociohistorical systems of thought (Fairhurst, 2007; Fairhurst & Putnam, 2014). Fairhurst and Putnam (2014) claim this distinction is unnecessary as scholars embrace either or both views "to examine the multiple levels at which organizational discourse operates" (p. 271).

2. These prototypes also operate in news coverage of women politicians and women in the public sphere whereby women are assumed not to fit within the realm

of politics, power, and masculine enterprise, such that women struggle for legitimacy and access (e.g., Byerly & Ross, 2006; Meeks, 2012).

3. As an example of how these prototypes have manifested in fiction and nonfiction media, Van Gorp et al. (2014) discuss a nonfiction news article about Bill Gates that portrayed him as a mad scientist: "Is the American super-nerd really a devilish, power-hungry person? Gates is portrayed as a tyrant with Mankind as his victim. Gates is the devil personified, a power-hungry person who wants to take over the world, a monopolist taking delight in the destruction of his competitors" (p. 654). Competing images portray Gates as a smart man who has revolutionized the technology industry and has established philanthropy foundations to research and battle diseases and other challenging situations on a grand scale.

4. The department chair's argument about "bad" investments in women's education and careers is commonplace and inconsistent with empirical data that demonstrates that women return to work with the same employer within a year after giving birth, especially if they are guaranteed a job (e.g., Lyness, Thompson, Francesco, & Judiesch, 1999). Moreover, Fox and Quinn (2015; see also Buzzanell & Liu, 2005) note the ways that stigmatized interactions as well as other factors affect women's turnover.

REFERENCES

Alvesson, M., & Kärreman, D. (2000). Varieties of discourse: On the study of organizations through discourse analysis. *Human Relations, 53*(9), 1125–1149. http://dx.doi.org/10.1177/0018726700539002

Buzzanell, P. M., & Liu, M. (2005). Struggling with maternity leave policies and practices: A poststructuralist feminist analysis of gendered organizing. *Journal of Applied Communication Research, 33*(1), 1–25. http://dx.doi.org/10.1080/0090988042000318495

Buzzanell, P. M., Berkelaar, B., & Kisselburgh, L. (2011). From the mouths of babes: Exploring families' career socialization of young children in China, Lebanon, Belgium, and the United States. *Journal of Family Communication, 11*(2), 148–164. http://dx.doi.org/10.1080/15267431.2011.554494

Byerly, C., & Ross, K. (2006). *Women and media. A critical introduction.* Malden, MA: Blackwell.

Cech, E., & Blair-Loy, M. (2014). Consequences of flexibility stigma among academic scientists and engineers. *Work and Occupations, 41*(1), 86–110. http://dx.doi.org/10.1177/0730888413515497

C-SPAN (Producer). (2005a, March 13). *Book discussion on* Obsessive Genius: The Inner World of Marie Curie [online video]. Available from http://www.c-span .org/video/?185824-1/book-discussion-obsessive-genius-inner-world-marie -curie.

C-SPAN (Producer). (2005b, April 19). *House session* [online video]. Available from http://www.c-span.org/video/?186343-2/house-session&start=3610

C-SPAN (Producer). (2005c, April 26). *House session* [online video]. Available from http://www.c-span.org/video/?186456-2/house-session

C-SPAN (Producer). (2005d, May 4). *House session.* Retrieved from http:// www.c-span.org/video/?186558-1/house-session

C-SPAN (Producer). (2005e, December 9). *Women and science careers* [online video]. Retrieved from http://www.c-span.org/video/?190264-1/women-science-careers

C-SPAN (Producer). (2006, July 15). *Book discussion on* Sisters in Science [online video]. Available from http://www.c-span.org/video/?193254-1/book-discussion -sisters-science

C-SPAN (Producer). (2007a, May 1). *House session* [online video]. Available from http://www.c-span.org/video/?197881-2/house-session

C-SPAN (Producer). (2007b, May 18). *The evolving workforce* [online video]. Retrieved from http://www.c-span.org/video/?198124-1/evolving-workforce

C-SPAN (Producer). (2012a, July 5). *History of women at Harvard* [online video]. Available from http://www.c-span.org/search/?searchtype=All&query=history +of+women+at+harvard

C-SPAN (Producer). (2012b, July 24). *Senate session, part 1* [online video]. Available from http://www.c-span.org/video/?307225-1/senate-session -part-1&start=8157&transcriptQuery=sally

C-SPAN (Producer). (2012c, September 23). *Amelia Earhart exhibit* [online video]. Available from http://www.c-span.org/video/?308058-1/amelia-earhart-exhibit

C-SPAN (Producer). (2013, February 6). *Science and technology enterprise* [online video]. Retrieved from http://www.c-span.org/video/?310849-1/science -technology-enterprise

C-SPAN (Producer). (2014, May 31). *2014 White House science fair* [online video]. Available from http://www.c-span.org/video/?319581-1/president-obama -addresses-science-fair

Fairhurst, G. T. (2007). *Discursive leadership: In conversation with leadership psychology.* Thousand Oaks, CA: Sage.

Fairhurst, G. T., & Putnam, L. L. (2014). Organizational discourse analysis. In L. L.

Putnam & D. K. Mumby (Eds.), *The SAGE handbook of organizational communication: Advances in theory, research, and methods* (3rd ed., pp. 271–295). Los Angeles, CA: Sage

Fiske, S., & Taylor, S. (2013). *Social cognition: From brains to culture* (2nd ed.). Thousand Oaks, CA: Sage.

Flicker, E. (2003). Between brains and breasts—women scientists in fiction film: On the marginalization of scientific competence. *Public Understanding of Science, 12*(3), 307–318. http://dx.doi.org/10.1177/0963662503123009

Fox, A., & Quinn, D. (2015). Pregnant women at work: The role of stigma in predicting women's intended exit from the workforce. *Psychology of Women Quarterly, 39*(2), 226–242. http://dx.doi.org/10.1177/0361684314552653

Fyke, J., & Buzzanell, P. M. (2013). The ethics of conscious capitalism: Wicked problems in leading change and changing leaders. *Human Relations, 66*(12), 1619–1643. http://dx.doi.org/10.1177/0018726713485306

Gibson, K. L., & Heyse, A. L. (2014). Depoliticizing feminism: Frontier mythology and Sarah Palin's "the rise of the mama grizzlies." *Western Journal of Communication, 7*(1), 97–117. http://dx.doi.org/10.1080/10570314.2013.812744

Graziano, W., Habashi, M., & Woodcock, A. (2011). Exploring and measuring differences in person–thing orientation. *Personality and Individual Differences, 51*(1), 28–33. http://dx.doi.org/10.1016/j.paid.2011.03.004

Guttierrez y Muhs, G., Niemann, Y., Gonzalez, C., & Harris, A. (2012). *Presumed incompetent: The intersections of race and class for women in academia.* Logan: Utah State University Press.

Harter, L. M. (2004). Masculinity(s), the agrarian frontier myth, and cooperative ways of organizing: Contradictions and tensions in the experience and enactment of democracy. *Journal of Applied Communication Research, 32*(2), 89–118. http://dx.doi.org/10.1080/0090988042000210016

Haynes, R. (2003). From alchemy to artificial intelligence: Stereotypes of the scientist in Western literature. *Public Understanding of Science, 12*(3), 243–253. http://dx.doi.org/10.1177/0963662503123003

Haynes, R. D. (2014). Whatever happened to the "mad, bad" scientist? Overturning the stereotype. *Public Understanding of Science, 23,* 1–14. http://dx.doi.org/10.1177/0963662514535689

Huey, L. (2010). "I've seen this on CSI": Criminal investigators' perceptions about the management of public expectations in the field. *Crime Media Culture, 6*(1), 49–68. http://dx.doi.org/10.1177/1741659010363045

Jablin, F. (2001). Organizational entry, assimilation, and disengagement/exit. In F. M. Jablin & L. L. Putnam (Eds.), *The new handbook of organizational communication: Advances in theory, research, and methods* (pp. 732–818). Thousand Oaks, CA: Sage.

Jahn, J. S., & Myers, K. K. (2014). Vocational anticipatory socialization of adolescents: Messages, sources, and frameworks that influence interest in STEM careers. *Journal of Applied Communication Research, 42*(1), 85–106. http://dx.doi.org/10.1080/00909882.2013.874568

Kisselburgh, L., Berkelaar Van Pelt, B., & Buzzanell, P. M. (2009). Discourse, gender, and the meanings of work: Rearticulating science, technology, and engineering careers through communicative lenses. In C. Beck (Ed.), *Communication yearbook 33* (pp. 258–299). New York, NY: Routledge.

Lyness, K. S., Thompson, C. A., Francesco, A. M., & Judiesch, M. K. (1999). Work and pregnancy: Individual and organizational factors influencing organizational commitment, timing of maternity leave, and return to work. *Sex Roles, 41*(7–8), 485–508. http://dx.doi.org/10.1023/A:1018887119627

Mason, M., Goulden, M., & Frasch, K. (2009, January–February). Why graduate students reject the fast track. Retrieved from http://www.aaup.org/article/why-graduate-students-reject-fast-track#.UUpTH4Xku0b

Meeks, L. (2012). Is she "man enough"? Women candidates, executive political offices, and news coverage. *Journal of Communication, 62*(1), 175–193. http://dx.doi.org/10.1111/j.1460-2466.2011.01621.x

Mendez, M., & Busenbark, J. (2015). Shared leadership and gender: all members are equal ... but some more than others. *Leadership & Organization Development Journal, 36*(1), 17–34. http://dx.doi.org/10.1108/LODJ-11-2012-0147

Owen, W. F. (1984). Interpretive themes in relational communication. *Quarterly Journal of Speech, 70*(3), 274–287. http://dx.doi.org/10.1080/00335638409383697

Paretti, M. C., McNair, L. D., & Leydens, J. A. (2014). Engineering communication. In A. Johri & B. M. Olds (Eds.), *Cambridge handbook of engineering education research* (pp 601–633). New York, NY: Cambridge University Press.

Park, L. E., Young, A. F., Trois, J. D., & Pinkus, R. T. (2011). Effects of everyday romantic goal pursuit on women's attitudes toward math and science. *Personality and Social Psychology Bulletin, 37*(9), 1259–1273. http://dx.doi.org/10.1177/0146167211408436

Paugh, A. L. (2005). Learning about work at dinnertime: Language socialization in dual-earner American families. *Discourse & Society, 16*(1), 55–78. http://dx.doi .org/10.1177/0957926505048230

Pollack, E. (2014, November 4). *One and a half strikes and you may be out: Intersectionality in science, math, and engineering.* Paper presented at the Women, Gender, and Sexuality Studies Fall 2014 Lecture Series, Purdue University, West Lafayette, IN.

Putnam, L. L., & Mumby, D. K. (Eds.). (2014). *The Sage handbook of organizational communication: Advances in theory, research, and methods* (3rd ed). Thousand Oaks, CA: Sage.

Rommes, E., Overbeek, G., Scholte, R., Engels, R., & de Kemp, R. (2007). "I'm not interested in computers": Gender-based occupational choices of teen-agers. *Information, Communication & Society, 10*(3), 299–319. http://dx.doi .org/10.1080/13691180701409838

Sesko, A. K., & Biernat, M. (2010). Prototypes of race and gender: The invisibility of Black women. *Journal of Experimental Social Psychology, 46,* 356–360. http://dx .doi.org/ 10.1016/j.jesp.2009.10.016

Van Gorp, B., Rommes, D., & Emons, P. (2014). From the wizard to the doubter: Prototypes of scientists and engineers in fiction and non-fiction media aimed at Dutch children and teenagers. *Public Understanding of Science, 23,* 646–659. http://dx.doi.org/10.1177/0963662512468566

Zorn, T. E., Roper, J., Weaver, C. K., & Rigby, C. (2010). Influence in science di-alogue: Individual attitude changes as a result of dialogue between layper-sons and scientists. *Public Understanding of Science, 21,* 1-17. http://dx.doi .org/10.1177/0963662510386292

CHAPTER **11**

IF A PICTURE IS WORTH A THOUSAND WORDS, WHAT IS A VIDEO WORTH?

Bryce J. Dietrich

Congressional sponsorship–cosponsorship relationships have been shown to be important predictors of many variables of interest, ranging from legislative influence to party polarization. Generally, in these studies cosponsorship matters because it is indicative of an underlying working relationship (Fowler, 2006a, 2006b). However, many of the dependent variables in these studies are not social in nature (Tam Cho & Fowler, 2010; Waugh, Pei, Fowler, Mucha, & Porter, 2011). Indeed, legislative influence is certainly affected by the degree to which a member of Congress is connected, but a number of things predict whether a representative can pass amendments on the House floor. Similarly, the polarization of roll call votes certainly has a social component, but, at the same time, polarization can occur for a variety of reasons, none of which have to do with interpersonal relationships. Given that, in the study discussed in this chapter I ask a simple, yet important, question: Do sponsorship–cosponsorship relationships predict polarized social interactions on the House floor?

For network analysis scholars this question is of particular import since it is often assumed that sponsorship–cosponsorship ties capture the underlying "social fabric" of Congress (Tam Cho & Fowler, 2010). However, to date these relationships have not been used to predict actual social interactions in the U.S. House of Representatives. Even though network studies are more interested in quantifying social connectedness as opposed to predicting it, one would imagine that if sponsorship–cosponsorship relationships have a social component then they are likely to be correlated with something as simple as the degree to which Republicans and Democrats talk with one another. In this way, measuring actual social interactions may give us new insights into resolving one of the fundamental problems when using sponsorship–cosponsorship relationships as a proxy for social interactions: at best, these relationships capture a social interaction that took place days, if not months, prior. At worst, these relationships have little to no social component and instead are grounded entirely in other political considerations, such as reelection and making good public policy. If these ties are shown to reasonably predict social interactions on the House floor, then it suggests that cosponsorship can be used to capture important interpersonal dynamics.

Fortunately C-SPAN gives us a way to answer this question. Since its launch in 1979, C-SPAN has gone to great lengths to give viewers the opportunity to observe the intricacies of the House floor. With the advent of the C-SPAN Archives' online Video Library, C-SPAN programming became increasingly accessible, which is why it is peculiar that no scholar has taken the opportunity to analyze the dynamics captured in these videos. The question becomes, why analyze floor videos? Simply put, these videos contain the social interactions network legislative scholars have been seeking to measure since Caldeira and Patterson's (1987) influential work on political friendship in the legislature. These authors found that members of legislatures tend to flock together, at least in terms of their demographic characteristics. What I will show in this chapter is that members of Congress actually flock together on the floor of the U.S. House of Representatives, and do so in a meaningful way. In the next two sections I will explain why this relationship is not only understandable but entirely predictable given what we know about sponsorship–cosponsorship relationships and video motion.

SPONSORSHIP–COSPONSORSHIP

Members of Congress cosponsor legislation for a variety of reasons, many of which are not social. For example, Fenno (1973) argues that legislators pursue three main goals: reelection, influence with the legislature, and pursuing good public policy. Campbell (1982) later argued that each of these goals can influence cosponsorship activity. However, most cosponsorships are attached to legislation that never makes it to the House floor, suggesting that ultimately cosponsorship could be purely symbolic (see, for example, Mayhew, 1974). Wilson and Young (1997) go as far as to say that cosponsorship is an overrated cue that, at best, signals one's expertise, meaning it is has no real effect on the legislative process.

More recently, scholars have begun to slowly revise this view. For example, bills with a large number of cosponsors are more likely to receive committee consideration, even though ultimately floor success is difficult to demonstrate (Browne, 1985; Krutz, 2005). Similarly, cosponsorship can send a strong signal within the House about one's ideological leanings that can then be used by one's colleagues to infer information about the content of legislation (Alemán, Calvo, Jones, & Kaplan, 2009; Kessler & Krehbiel, 1996). Along these same lines, Koger (2003) argues that cosponsorship can be used by members of Congress to signal their legislative priorities to their constituents. Thus, it is not too surprising that the characteristics of a legislator's constituency (Hall, 1996; Rocca & Sanchez, 2008) and electoral margin (Koger, 2003) are important predictors of whether he or she will cosponsor a bill. Collectively, this means that cosponsorship can be used as a commitment device, meaning that if members of Congress renege on their cosponsorship obligations, future legislative success could be jeopardized (Bernhard & Sulkin, 2013).

Although these scholars would certainly admit that some personal contact happens, for the most part the social aspect of cosponsorship has been left to the network sciences (for a review, see Ward, Stovel, & Sacks, 2011). Here, when members of Congress solicit cosponsors they often send "Dear Colleague" letters in which sponsors of bills attempt to recruit potential cosponsors whom they think would help their bill's success in the legislature. Given that, "the closer the relationship between a sponsor and a cosponsor, the more likely it is that the sponsor has directly petitioned the cosponsor for support. It is also more likely that the cosponsor will trust the sponsor or owe the sponsor a favor, both of which increase the likelihood of cosponsorship. Thus, the push and pull of the sponsor–cosponsor relationship suggest that even passive cosponsorship patterns may be a good way to measure the connections between legislators" (Fowler, 2006b, p. 455). In essence, this means that individuals who sponsor and cosponsor together are more likely to have a meaningful working relationship as compared to those who do not.

From this, scholars have used sponsorship–cosponsorship networks to study a variety of phenomena, such as an individual legislator's influence (Fowler, 2006a,b) and a legislature's ability to be generally productive (Tam Cho & Fowler, 2010). Of these, the use of these relationships to predict polarization is of particular import for this study (Zhang et al., 2008). Here, at a basic level these relationships are very intuitive. If bills have more cosponsorships from the opposition, then polarization is probably less likely. However, using network structures, researchers have uncovered an underlying social connectedness which both predicts and shapes partisan structures, giving us additional insights into how polarization changes over time (Waugh et al., 2011).

However, do sponsorship–cosponsorship relationships actually predict social interactions on the House floor? The answer to this question gets at the very nature of cosponsorship. At one extreme, if cosponsorship signals to the legislature one's position, then a bill that contains a lot of partisan cosponsors would send a very strong signal to the House floor about the nature of partisanship within the chamber. In essence, these bills may be viewed as being intentionally divisive, making bipartisan interactions less likely in this environment. At the other extreme, if sponsorship–cosponsorship relationships contain a social element, then they are indicative of the actual "social fabric" of the legislature, implying that more bipartisan cosponsors would be indicative of a more collegial environment in which walking across the aisle and talking to the opposition is encouraged. Either way, cosponsorship matters when it comes to the actual social interactions on the House floor.

Fortunately we can regularly observe these types of encounters on C-SPAN. Figure 11.1 shows a single frame from one of the videos I used for this study. This image shows the mingling that takes place after many floor votes. Later in this chapter I will demonstrate how one can predict the movement within this video by knowing the number of cosponsors from the opposing party. However, measuring video motion is easier said than done. From my understanding of the basic nature of video dynamics, I was convinced that

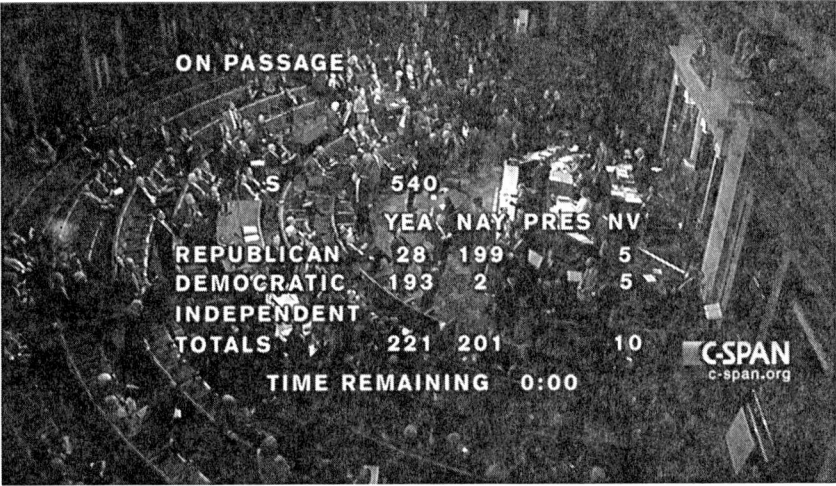

FIGURE 11.1 Overhead shot of members of Congress mingling after a roll call vote on the House floor.

some patterns should emerge, but the types of patterns were difficult to predict a priori. Thus, to help formulate testable hypotheses, I created an agent-based model (see the appendix to this chapter).

FORMULATING TESTABLE HYPOTHESES

In this simulation, members of Congress either seek out members of the opposition (bipartisanship) or they seek out members of their own party (polarization). All of these simulated interactions were recorded, then analyzed. Here, variations in pixel intensity are particularly useful. Specifically, how much do the pixels change from one frame to the next? Although this measure has never before been used to analyze motion in political science, variations of this measure have been employed by scholars in other fields, such as computer science (for a review see Zhan, Monekosso, Remagnino, Velastin, & Xu, 2008). Although unfamiliar, the measure itself is fairly easy to understand. If videos represent a series of pixel matrices, then the difference between one matrix and the next would indicate the degree to which a video changes from one frame to the next since each matrix represents a frame. If we assume more change is indicative of more motion, then tracking

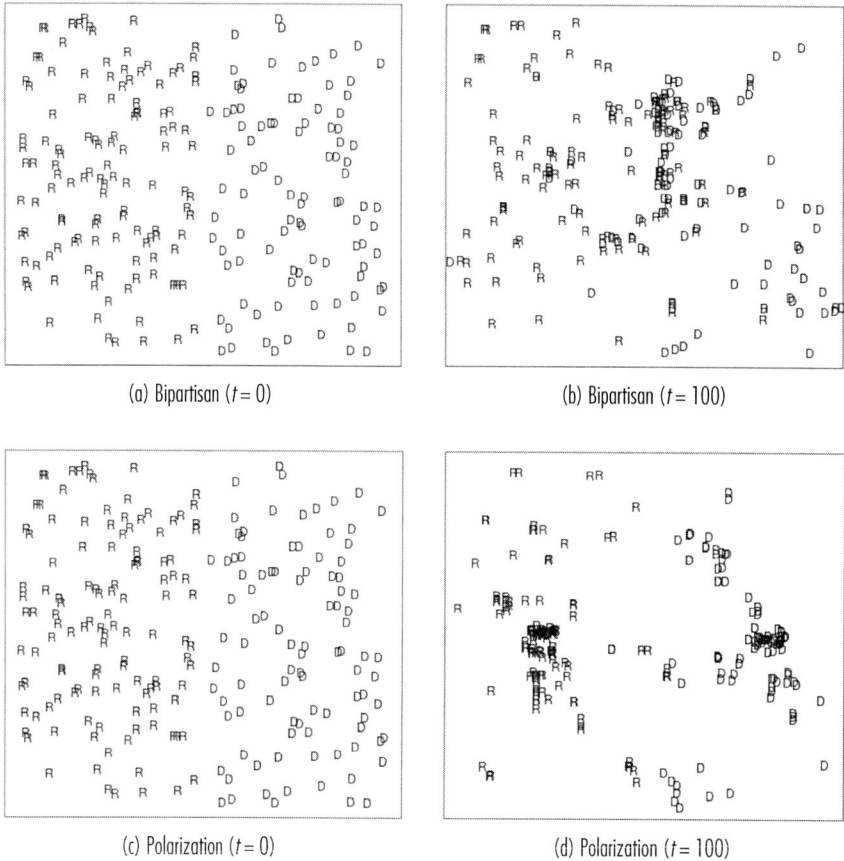

(a) Bipartisan ($t = 0$)

(b) Bipartisan ($t = 100$)

(c) Polarization ($t = 0$)

(d) Polarization ($t = 100$)

FIGURE 11.2 Images of initial and final states of each agent-based simulation. NOTE: Panels A and B represent where the agents began and ended after 100 time steps in the bipartisan simulation. Panels C and D show the same for the polarization simulation. In each, "D" and "R" represent Democratic and Republican members of Congress, respectively. Each representative was randomly placed when $t = 0$.

the change in the average pixel intensity as the agents move throughout the simulation would be useful for understanding the video dynamics produced by bipartisan versus polarized interactions.

With this in mind, consider Figure 11.2. Here, I show the initial and final positions of an agent-based model after 100 time steps. The details of this model can be found in the appendix to this chapter. The first thing to note is how the Democratic (represented by a "D") and Republican (represented by an "R") agents are positioned on either side of the board. In the Senate, this is formalized in the seating chart. In the House there are no assigned seats, but seats are, by tradition, divided by party, with Democrats sitting to the Speaker's right and the Republicans sitting to the Speaker's left. This is why in the simulation Democrats begin on the right and Republicans begin on the left. As you can see, the same distribution of agents appears for both the bipartisan and polarization simulations. This is because each simulation uses the same initial conditions.

The question then becomes, how did the agents move during the course of the simulation? Videos of the simulations can be found online,[1] but for the purposes of this chapter let us consider how the average pixel intensity changed from one frame to the next. This is shown in Figure 11.3. Here, each frame of the bipartisan and polarization simulations are compared directly. Positive values imply that more change exists in the bipartisan simulations than in the polarization simulations. For example, at the 20th time step, the average change in pixel intensity was about 4 percent greater in the bipartisan simulation than in the polarization simulation. With this in mind, when comparing the bipartisan to polarization simulations, in the former, on average, pixel intensity changes more, suggesting more movement is present in the bipartisan simulation. This is not too surprising given where the agents began and where they ended. In the U.S. House, Democrats and Republicans sit on opposite sides of the aisle: If a Democrat wants to talk to a Republican, or vice versa, that person literally has to walk across the aisle. Given that, videos of bipartisan interactions should produce more motion than videos of partisan interactions, since less physical ground has to be covered in the latter.

Ultimately, this was the main theoretical drive behind this project, but the simulation revealed additional dynamics that I was not initially expecting. First, note the trajectory of the change in pixel intensity in Figure 11.3. Here we see a rapid increase in bipartisan motion early on, but the system eventually stabilizes. This also makes intuitive sense on the House floor. Although generally videos of bipartisan interactions include more motion, this motion happens early on as Republicans get out of their chairs and move to the other side of the aisle to interact with Democrats. Conversely, this same type of motion exists early on when observing partisan interactions, but instead of moving to the opposite side of the room, Republicans are remaining in their immediate neighborhood. However, the end result is the same: people standing around talking to one another. This is essentially what we see in the simulation. A rush of immediate movement, then stabilization.

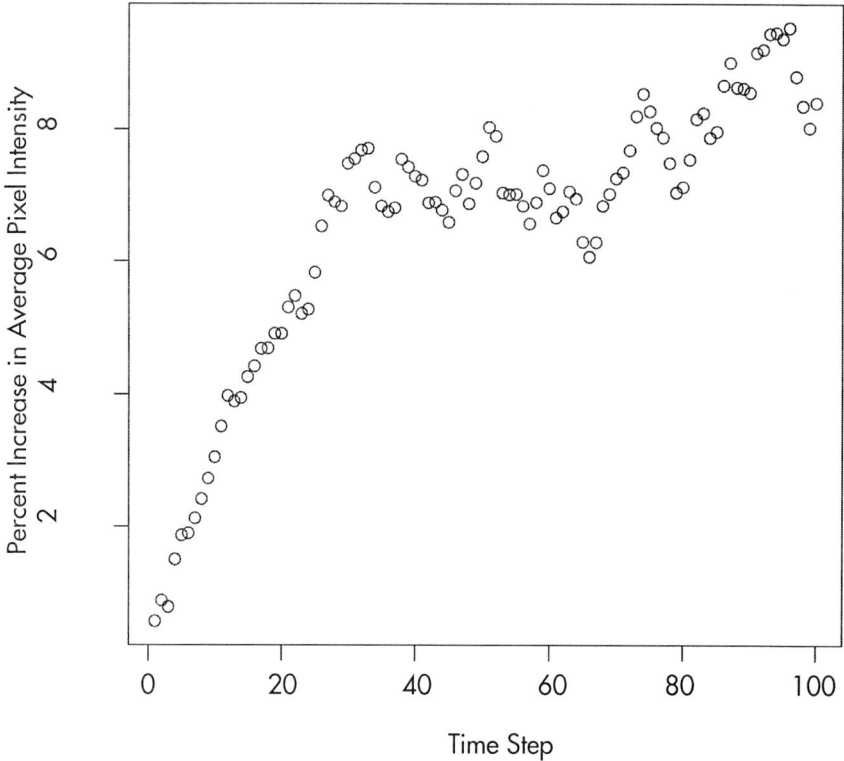

FIGURE 11.3 Results from an agent-based model of bipartisan versus polarized social interactions on the House floor. NOTE: This plot shows changes in pixel intensity from one frame to the next. Specifically, each point represents bipartisan pixel intensity minus polarized pixel intensity divided by bipartisan pixel intensity. Thus, positive values indicate that at that time step there was a greater change in pixel intensity in the bipartisan simulation as compared to the polarized simulation. Negative values would imply the inverse is true.

Finally, the end points of each simulation also reveal another unanticipated dynamic. This can be seen in panels B and D in Figure 11.2. Here, we see that the bipartisan simulation produces one large centralized cluster, whereas the polarization simulation produces two clusters on either side of the board. Again, this makes intuitive sense. If Democrats are moving toward Republicans and Republicans are moving toward Democrats, they are likely to meet in the middle of the room since both are beginning on opposite sides. Certainly, some may wander all the way to other side, but, for the most part, this is irrational since the goal is to interact with members of the opposition. This is most likely to happen right in the middle of the House floor. Thus, when we observe bipartisan interactions, Republicans do not cross the aisle to talk to Democrats. Rather, Republicans and Democrats meet with each other in the aisle itself. Conversely, partisan interactions are more likely to take place away from the aisle because this is the easiest place for a given to party to congregate since this location minimizes the distance between all party members.

Collectively, the results from this simulation imply that videos of bipartisan interactions are more likely to produce motion than videos of partisan interactions. On a very basic level, this has to do with the positioning of Democrats and Republicans in the U.S. House of Representatives. If they typically sit on opposite sides of the aisle, then a bipartisan environment will tend to produce more motion because members of Congress have to cover a greater distance on the House floor. Similarly, in these instances, the interactions are more likely to be clustered toward the center of the video, whereas partisan interactions are more likely to be clustered toward either side. In both instances, these relationships are going to be more pronounced toward the beginning of the video as compared to the end, since the beginning of the video captures the initial sorting which eventually stabilizes once conversations begin. Thus, if sponsorship–cosponsorship ties can predict social polarization, then we should find evidence of the following relationships when it comes to video motion.

Hypothesis 1: Videos associated with bills that have more cosponsors from the opposite party as compared to the sponsor's party should have, on average, a greater change in pixel intensity than videos associated with bills where the inverse is true. This general relationship should be more pronounced toward the beginning of the video.

Hypothesis 2: Videos associated with bills that have more cosponsors from the opposite party as compared to the sponsor's party should have, on average, more centralized pixel clustering than videos associated with bills where the inverse is true. Again, this general relationship should be more pronounced toward the beginning of the video.

DATA AND MEASURES

To test these hypotheses, a research assistant captured videos similar to the one shown in Figure 11.1 using C-SPAN's Video Library. To make the starting and ending point of each video more definable, the video was stopped once the House cameras moved away from this overhead shot. On average, this took place after 2 minutes and 30 seconds. Although we plan to obtain video for every floor vote in the 113th U.S. House of Representatives, for an initial demonstration I decided to find bills in which every cosponsor was from the opposition. Unsurprisingly, these were quite rare, but I was able to find 6 bills of this nature. Once these were found, I then examined the number of cosponsors each had. For the most part, these bills only had a couple of cosponsors each. With this in mind, I then looked for bills that had no cosponsors from the opposite party. To make these bills similar, I only considered bills that had fewer than 10 cosponsors. This yielded the bills outlined in Table 11.1.

All of the bills listed in Table 11.1 are sponsored by Republicans. This is partially by design. When I examined the bipartisan bills, I found that all of these were sponsored by Republicans and cosponsored by Democrats. Thus, I restricted the partisan bills to those sponsored by Republicans. Ultimately, this only eliminated one bill from consideration (H.R. 338). Excluding this bill did not significantly affect the results, but it should be kept in mind.

For each video, pixel intensity was relatively easy to obtain. Basically, once videos are broken into frames, one can assess the change in pixel intensity by comparing one frame to the next. Here, comparisons were made using the Euclidean distance, calculated by row. A greater Euclidian distance between one frame and the next would indicate greater motion, since the greater distance would imply greater change between the two associated pixel matrices. Ironically, the most difficult part of this calculation was actually dividing the videos into individual frames. This was done using ffmpeg software and resulted in 2,008 images, one for each second of video. From this point, each image had to be compared to every other image in a given video.[2]

To determine whether pixels were clustered centrally, I first partitioned each frame into two distinct clusters using the algorithm outlined in Chapter 2 of Kaufman and Rousseeuw (1990), which can be implemented using the *cluster* package in R software. Then, using the position of each cluster's center, I calculated how far the cluster was from the middle of the frame, again using the Euclidian distance. In this instance, greater values would imply the clusters were further from the middle, whereas smaller values would imply they were more centrally located. Given that, I expected the cosponsorship ratio to be a positive predictor of pixel intensity and a negative predictor of pixel clustering. As suggested in the previous section, I expected these relationships to be more pronounced toward the beginning of the video. Thus,

TABLE 11.1 *Bills Selected for This Study*

Bill Number	Date	Title	Sponsor
Bipartisan Bills			
HR 1067	3/12/2013	To make revisions in Title 36, United States Code	Rep. Bob Goodlatte (R)
HR 1162	3/14/2013	Government Accountability Office Improvement Act	Rep. Darrel Issa (R)
HR 1412	4/9/2013	Department of Veterans Affairs Expiring Authorities Act of 2013	Rep. Mike Coffman (R)
HR 2374	6/14/2013	Retail Investor Protection Act	Rep. Ann Wagner (R)
HR 2747	7/19/2013	Streamlining Claims Processing for Federal Contractor Employees Act	Rep. Tim Walberg (R)
HR 2848	7/30/2013	Department of State Operations and Embassy Security Authorization Act	Rep. Edward Royce (R)
Partisan Bills			
HR 668	2/13/2013	To amend Section 1105(a) of Title 31, United States Code	Rep. Luke Messer (R)
HR 767	2/15/2013	To amend the Energy Policy Act of 2005	Rep. Kevin Cramer (R)
HR 1582	4/16/2013	Energy Consumers Relief Act of 2013	Rep. Bill Cassidy (R)
HR 1911	5/9/2013	Bipartisan Student Loan Certainty Act of 2013	Rep. John Kline (R)
HR 2879	7/31/2013	Stop Government Abuse Act	Rep. Lynn Jenkins (R)
HR 3210	9/2/2013	Pay Our Military Act	Rep. Mike Coffman (R)

NOTE: For bipartisan bills, all of the cosponsors were from the opposition, meaning that since all of these bills were sponsored by Republicans, all of the cosponsors were Democrats. For partisan bills, all of the cosponsors were Republican. The dates indicate when the bill was introduced and the titles were obtained online from the Library of Congress.

these measures were also calculated using the first 10 percent of the video. I expected these relationships to be the same, but the coefficients to be greater in size. Ultimately, even though both variables operate in the predicted direction, greater support is found when comparing pixel intensity, which is where we now turn.

RESULTS

Figure 11.4 shows box plots for average and early pixel intensity for both the bipartisan and partisan bills outlined in the previous section. In each, the solid line represents the median value, and the borders of each box capture the 25th and 75th quantiles. The whiskers extend to the minimum and maximum values. Grey boxes indicate a t-test comparing the bipartisan and partisan bills was statistically significant at the .05 level. For example, the average pixel intensity for bipartisan bills (6.84) is approximately 4 percent higher than the average pixel intensity for partisan bills (6.55). Although this difference is slight, it is statistically significant ($t = -2.23$, $df = 11$, $p \le .05$) which is impressive given that only 12 bills were used.

Similar evidence is found for early pixel intensity. Here, bipartisan bills tended to produce more early motion (7.05) than do partisan bills (6.74). Again, this difference was slight (approximately 5 percent) and statistically significant ($t = -2.33$, $df = 11$, $p \le .05$). Moreover, as predicted, in both instances pixel intensity changed more in the early portions of the video as compared to the video overall. However, this difference was only significant for bipartisan bills ($t = -2.99$, $df = 16$, $p \le .05$), where early motion was approximately 3 percent higher than overall motion. In Figure 11.4 this can be seen using the dashed boxes. These indicate that early motion is significantly ($p \le .05$) higher than average motion. As you can see, even though early motion is higher for partisan bills as compared to overall motion, this difference is not statistically significant at the .05 level ($t = -1.09$, $df = 16$, $p \le .05$). Collectively, these results provide evidence consistent with the first hypothesis.

When I considered pixel clustering a similar story was found. Pixels were more centralized in videos of bipartisan bills, and this relationship was more pronounced early in the video. However, unlike pixel intensity, none of these relationships were statistically significant at the .05 level. This can be seen in

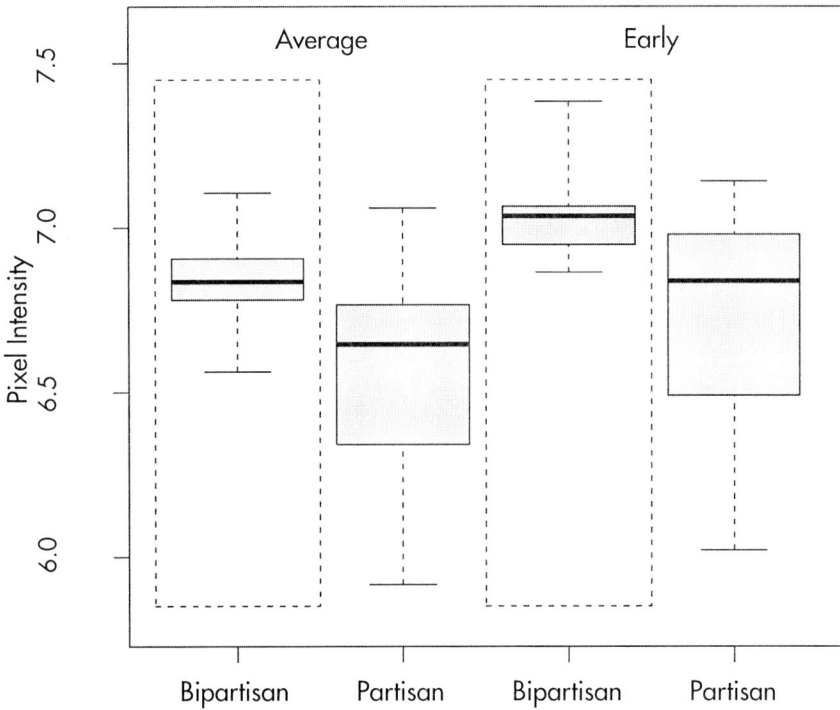

FIGURE 11.4 Comparing pixel intensity in bipartisan versus polarized social interactions on the House floor. NOTE: Grey box plots indicate there is a significant ($p \leq .05$) difference between average and early pixel intensity. Significance was determined using a two-sample t-test where unequal variance was assured.

Figure 11.5. Here, partisan bills produce, on average, less centralized pixel clustering (384.85) as compared to their bipartisan counterparts (378.69). As before, this difference is small (approximately 2 percent), but this time it is not statistically significant ($t = 0.28$, $df = 16$, $p > .05$). The same can be said when I compared early pixel clustering, where again partisan bills produce less centralized clustering, but this slightly larger difference (approximately 8 percent) was still insignificant ($t = 0.85$, $df = 13$, $p > .05$). All of these are consistent with the second hypothesis, but less confidence can be placed in these results.

For those convinced that social interactions matter in the U.S. House of Representatives, these results are important in and of themselves because they suggest bipartisan cosponsorship relationships are more likely to produce bipartisan social interactions as compared to their partisan counterparts.

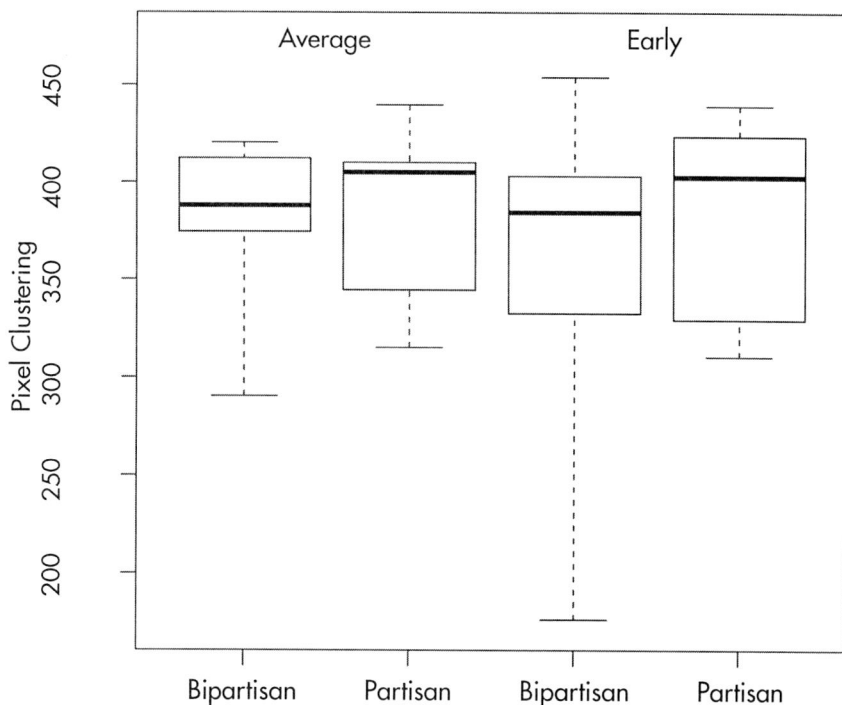

FIGURE 11.5 Comparing pixel clustering in bipartisan versus polarized social interactions on the House floor. NOTE: Grey box plots indicate there is a significant ($p \leq .05$) difference between average and early pixel clustering. Significance was determined using a two-sample *t*-test where unequal variance was assured.

However, others may be skeptical of whether these results are substantively important. In an attempt to convince this latter group, I considered whether pixel intensity and pixel clustering correlated with the number of yes votes each bill received. Here, I took the number of representatives voting yes, divided by the total number of representatives voting for the bill. I then determined the degree to which this measure correlated with those outlined in the previous paragraphs. When this was done, I found that average ($\rho = 0.34$) and early pixel intensity ($\rho = 0.41$) were both positively correlated with the vote margin, with the latter being not only higher but statistically significant at the .10 level ($t = 1.81$, $df = 16$, $p \leq .10$).

When I considered pixel clustering, I found a similar relationship. Again, both average ($\rho = -0.27$) and early pixel clustering ($\rho = -0.49$) were correlated with the number of yes votes, and the latter was statistically significant, but this time at the .05 level ($t = -2.23$, $df = 16$, $p \leq .05$). As explained earlier, the measure of pixel clustering operates differently than the measure of pixel intensity. Here, larger values imply less clustering, making the direction of the correlations consistent with the previous results. Even with this caveat, the direction of causation is difficult to determine since the floor votes happened prior to the videos being analyzed, meaning it is impossible to determine whether bipartisan interactions contribute to more representatives voting yes or the other way around. Thus, more research is needed.

DISCUSSION

Although the techniques used in this study may be unfamiliar to political scientists, the results are very intuitive. If Democrats and Republicans sit on opposite sides of the aisle, then bipartisan interactions simply require more effort because individuals have to stand up and walk to the other side of the room. Conversely, in instances of polarization, members of Congress just stay put, meaning motion is less likely. Although it is impossible to comment about the content of these conversations, these results seem to tell a simple and uncontroversial story: Bipartisan bills are associated with bipartisan social interactions.

For years, network scholars have been using sponsorship–cosponsorship ties to capture the "social fabric" of Congress. Even though many legislative scholars are beginning to accept this argument, others are reluctant to believe that cosponsorship is anything more than a symbolic gesture to win points either within the legislature or within one's own district. This study provides evidence that sponsorship–cosponsorship relationships may contain some social element, at least when it comes to polarization. Note that this is not the same as claiming that sponsorship–cosponsorship ties are indicative of interpersonal relationships since I am unable to determine whether the sponsors of the bills in question actually talked to their cosponsors on the House floor. However, although untested, the results seem to be consistent with this claim.

For legislative scholars, this study is entirely consistent with cosponsorship being important for legislative signaling. Members of Congress know what they are doing when they solicit cosponsors from their own party. They are signaling to the legislature that party matters. Similarly, when members of Congress go out of their way to find cosponsors from the opposition, they are likely attempting to emphasize the importance of bipartisanship. Both of these affect social interactions on the House floor, either directly or indirectly. Directly, bipartisan bills may actually signal to those on the House floor to move across the aisle as a sign of solidarity for an important bipartisan effort. Indirectly, members of Congress know that a partisan bill is coming up for a vote, which is why they choose to stand with each other to demonstrate party unity. Either way, these underline an important social dynamic that many have suspected, but few have actually observed and quantified.

Fortunately C-SPAN gives us the opportunity to begin to test these and other related questions. No scholar has yet used C-SPAN for this purpose. The C-SPAN Video Library is an extraordinary resource, but to date we have only scratched the surface of what we can do with it. Social interactions take place all the time on the House floor. Many scholars argue these matter for a variety of reasons. With this chapter I demonstrate how we can begin to actually measure the extent of these relationships without relying on proxies such as cosponsorship. Does social polarization predict polarization in roll call votes? Did Democrats talk more to Republicans before 2008? How did the Gabrielle Giffords shooting affect the social dynamics on the House floor? I argue that we can begin to answer these types of questions using these videos. Although not perfect, this study provides a useful starting point for these efforts.

NOTES

1. The polarization simulation can be found at https://www.youtube.com/watch?v=lNLzsizM4fY. The bipartisanship simulation can be found at https://www.youtube.com/watch?v=mkrzQQXZtSg.

2. This was done using Amazon's Elastic Computing Cloud.

REFERENCES

Alemán, E., Calvo E., Jones, M. P., & Kaplan, N. (2009). Comparing cosponsorship and roll-call ideal points. *Legislative Studies Quarterly, 34*(1), 87–116. http://dx.doi.org/10.3162/036298009787500358

Bernhard, W., & Sulkin, T. (2013). Commitment and consequences: Reneging on cosponsorship pledges in the U.S. House. *Legislative Studies Quarterly, 38*(4), 461–487. http://dx.doi.org/10.1111/lsq.12024

Browne, W. P. (1985). Multiple sponsorship and bill success in the U.S. State legislatures. *Legislative Studies Quarterly, 10*(4), 483–488. http://dx.doi.org/10.2307/440070

Caldeira, G. A., & Patterson, S. C. (1987). Political friendship in the legislature. *The Journal of Politics, 49*(4), 953–975. http://dx.doi.org/10.2307/2130779

Campbell, J. E. (1982). Cosponsoring legislation in the U.S. Congress. *Legislative Studies Quarterly, 7*(3), 415–422. http://dx.doi.org/10.2307/439366

Fenno, R. F. (1973). *Congressmen in committees.* Boston, MA: Little, Brown.

Fowler, J. H. (2006a). Connecting the congress: A study of cosponsorship networks. *Political Analysis, 14*(4), 456–487. http://dx.doi.org/10.1093/pan/mpl002

Fowler, J. H. (2006b). Legislative cosponsorship networks in the U.S. House and Senate. *Social Networks, 28*(4), 454–465.

Hall, R. L. (1996). *Participation in Congress.* New Haven, CT: Yale University Press.

Kaufman, L., & Rousseeuw, P. J. (1990). *Finding groups in data: An introduction to cluster analysis* [Wiley Online Library version]. New York, NY: Wiley. http://dx.doi.org/10.1002/9780470316801

Kessler, D., & Krehbiel, K. (1996). Dynamics of cosponsorship. *The American Political Science Review, 90*(3), 555–566. http://dx.doi.org/10.2307/2082608

Koger, G. (2003). Position taking and cosponsorship in the U.S. House. *Legislative Studies Quarterly, 28*(2), 225–246. http://dx.doi.org/10.3162/036298003X200872

Krutz, G. S. (2005). Issues and institutions: "Winnowing" in the U.S. Congress. *American Journal of Political Science, 49*(2), 313–326. http://dx.doi.org/10.1111/j.0092-5853.2005.00125.x

Mayhew, D. R. (1974). *Congress: The electoral connection.* New Haven, CT: Yale University Press.

Rocca, M. S., & Sanchez, G. R. (2008). The effect of race and ethnicity on bill sponsorship and cosponsorship in Congress. *American Politics Research, 36*(1), 130–152. http://dx.doi.org/10.1177/1532673X07306357

Tam Cho, W. K., & Fowler, J. H. (2010). Legislative success in a small world: Social network analysis and the dynamics of congressional legislation. *The Journal of Politics, 72*(1), 124–135. http://dx.doi.org/10.1017/S002238160999051X

Ward, M. D., Stovel, K. & Sacks, A. (2011). Network analysis and political science. *Annual Review of Political Science, 14,* 245–264. http://dx.doi.org/10.1146/annurev.polisci.12.040907.115949

Waugh, A. S., Pei, L., Fowler, J. H., Mucha, P. J., & Porter, M. A. (2011, July 25). Party polarization in Congress: A network science approach. Retrieved from http://arXiv:0907.3509

Wilson, R. K., & Young, C. D. (1997). Cosponsorship in the U.S. Congress. *Legislative Studies Quarterly, 22*(1), 25–43. http://dx.doi.org/10.2307/440289

Zhan, B., Monekosso, D. M., Remagnino, P., Velastin, S. A., & Xu, L. (2008). Crowd analysis: A survey. *Machine Vision and Applications, 19*(5–6), 345–357. http://dx.doi.org/10.1007/s00138-008-0132-4

Zhang, Y., Friend, A. J. , Traud, A. L., Porter, M. A., Fowler, J. H., and Mucha, P. J. (2008). Community structure in congressional cosponsorship networks. *Physica A: Statistical Mechanics and Its Applications, 387*(7), 1705–1712. http://dx.doi.org/10.1016/j.physa.2007.11.004

APPENDIX
Simulating Social Interactions
on the House Floor

Videos are extraordinarily complex. Each frame of a video represents a matrix of pixels. When the video is in color, there are actually three matrices that combine to form the image. Given that, most videos are converted to grayscale when analyzed. When this is done, each cell of the matrix represents a pixel that ranges from 0 to 1, where 0 is white and 1 is black. Thus, a grayscale image that is 480 by 640 pixels can be represented by a single matrix of equivalent size. Ultimately, this implies that videos are essentially a time series of matrices, with one image representing a predetermined length of time.

Agent-based models are particularly useful for analyzing video, especially if the video involves crowds (for review see Zhou et al., 2010). Generally, agent-based models are useful for studying systems which contain the following characteristics: (1) the system is composed of interacting agents; and (2) the system exhibits emergent properties—that is, properties arising from the interactions of agents that cannot be deduced by aggregating the properties of the agents themselves (Axelrod & Tesfatsion, 2006). I argue that C-SPAN videos contain each of these characteristics.

First, when Democrats walk across the aisle and talk with Republicans they are, by definition, interacting agents. In fact, social polarization itself is grounded in these interactions. Second, when we watch these encounters on C-SPAN, we are actually observing the result of a complex process that produced the video we see on the screen. Indeed, by simply watching the video from afar it is difficult to deduce who is talking to whom. Given that, not only is an agent-based model useful for understanding the types of video dynamics we should see on the House floor, but from a theoretical standpoint an agent-based model may be the only way to study these dynamics at all.

In the model used for this study, I first created a space in which the agents could move. This space was a simple 250 by 250 matrix. At the beginning of the simulation, I created 218 agents: 122 Republicans and 96 Democrats. This partisan split (which was randomly assigned) was chosen because it closely resembles the 113th U.S. House of Representatives, which was 54 percent Republican. Once this was done, I randomly assigned each agent two vision parameters, one of which allowed the agent to look north and south while the other allowed the agent to look east and west. These vision parameters were randomly drawn from a uniform distribution that ranged from 1 to 200, meaning at one extreme agents could only look one space around them while at the other extreme they could look almost across the room. After this, each agent was assigned a movement parameter, which was randomly drawn from a uniform distribution that ranged from .50 to 1. This variable captured the degree to which an agent was likely to move. Although I wanted to make it more likely than not that an agent would move, I also wanted to allow some agents to be less willing to budge as compared to others. Similarly, I made some agents faster than others, meaning at any given time step some could move more spaces than others. This parameter was also set using a random uniform distribution (min. = 1, max. = 10). Finally, although the goal of this simulation was to mimic social interactions, some agents may be social butter-flies, meaning that instead of just talking to one person they want to mix and mingle. This was captured using a variable randomly drawn from a uniform distribution which ranged from 0 to .25, meaning that on average agents are not going to jump from one agent to another, but some may.

With this initial setup in mind, what are the agents doing in the simulation? In the initial time step of the polarization simulation, each agent first decides whether to move. If the agent chooses to move, it then looks north, south, east, and west for agents around it. The degree to which an agent can see other agents is constricted by its vision. Once it obtains a list of potential targets, it selects only targets that are from its own party, meaning Democratic agents select only Democrats and Republican agents select only Republicans. Then, from these potential targets the agent determines the closest and moves in that direction. This motion is first determined by taking a number of steps north, south, east, and west equal to each agent's speed. Once these potential moves are calculated, the agent selects the move that minimizes the distance between it and the partisan target. After this move is made, the agent then re-cords its position and the ID of the target. In some instances, the agent will be unable to find a target. When this happens, the agent randomly moves (equal to the agent's speed) either north, south, east, or west.

From this point, the simulation continues in a similar fashion in sub-sequent time steps, with two caveats. First, if an agent has already found a target, then it proceeds to move toward that target. This was done because I assume that agents are seeking out their friends in the legislature. Generally, these friendships are stable, meaning they tend to select one friend and stick with that selection. Thus, if the agent does not have a partisan target, then the agent follows the process outlined above to find one. Second, in subsequent time steps the agent can decide if it wants to find a new target. If it does, then its current partisan target is removed from its memory and it finds a new one using the process outlined in the previous paragraph. Of course all of this assumes that the agent has selected to move in the given time step. If the agent has not selected to move, then it stays put. Although somewhat different the bipartisan simulation is essentially the same, except instead of trying to find targets from its own party, each agent is trying to find targets from the opposition, meaning Democratic agents seek out Republicans and Republican agents seek out Democrats.

Undoubtedly, real social interactions on the House floor are more complex than the model presented here, but I think this model can capture some of this complexity. First, embedded within the two simulations is polarization versus bipartisanship. In terms of the former, agents are seeking out members from their own party, whereas in the latter agents are seeking out members from the opposition. In the future, I will vary these two strategies by agent, but in the short-term, this is exactly what I think of when I think of polarized social interactions. Here, members of Congress refuse to talk to the opposition. Conversely, in a bipartisan environment, members of Congress are literally willing to reach (or walk) across the aisle. This model captures some of this dynamic.

Second, although vision seems somewhat silly, this parameter captures a combination of things. Indeed, some people are able to see further than others, but vision primarily captures the degree to which a member of Congress is actually willing to look out onto the House floor and find someone to talk to. In instances where vision is low, an agent is unwilling to look further than its local neighborhood. Conversely, when vision is high, the agent looks beyond its immediate vicinity for potential targets. However, the agent is not irrational, meaning that even if other potential targets are found elsewhere, the agent is not going to expend energy to move toward those targets when perfectly acceptable targets are standing one or two spaces over.

Finally, speed captures both the physical limitations of a given agent and the energy by which an agent is willing to move toward its objective. For example, imagine that a representative is excited about mingling with a member of the opposition: This representative is likely to move toward the member of the opposition with greater purpose than would be a member of Congress who is not excited. The same can be said about polarization: If members of Congress are extremely polarized, then they may move more quickly to their fellow partisans than to others. Thus, speed not only captures the degree to which an agent moves from one space to the next, but also the motivation it has for achieving the objective, be it partisan or bipartisan.

When one observes the videos of the polarization[1] and bipartisan simulations,[2] three patterns emerge. First, the bipartisan simulation produces more motion. This is understandable given the initial starting points and motivations of the agents. In each simulation, Republicans and Democrats begin on opposite sides of the aisle. Thus, to find a member of the opposition, the agents have to cover more ground. This ultimately produces more motion.

Second, at the end of each simulation we see a great deal of clustering, but the locations of the clusters differ. In the partisan simulation, the clustering takes place on either side of the aisle. Conversely, in the bipartisan simulation, the clustering takes place in the middle of the screen. Again, from the agents' perspectives this makes sense. If agents are interested in interacting with members of the opposition, they will walk toward the opposition, but they will actually never cross the aisle since their opponents are doing the same. Thus, they meet in the center. Those in the partisan simulation want to talk only to members of their own party, which makes moving from their present location irrational. Instead, these agents simply want to cluster on their side of the aisle. This is readily apparent from the videos associated with each simulation.

Finally, the endpoint of each simulation is the same: agents standing around talking to one another. Given that, regardless of whether one is observing the bipartisan or the partisan simulation, the majority of the movement happens early on. In these moments, the agents are frantically sorting themselves based on the rules assigned at the beginning of the simulation. Once they find someone to talk with, they have little reason to move. Thus, the general motion and clustering patterns outlined above are more pronounced earlier in the simulation.

I encourage the reader to observe the interactions for themselves. Even though many of these relationships are demonstrated empirically, these videos will help the reader understand each of the hypotheses tested in the associated chapter. Agent-based models are extraordinarily complex, which sometimes makes understanding them difficult. However, in this instance I argue that the agent-based model helps to clarify the results. I hope this appendix helps to achieve this end.

Notes

1. The polarization simulation can be found here at https://www.youtube.com/watch?v=lNLzsizM4fY.

2. The bipartisanship simulation can be found here at https://www.youtube.com/watch?v=mkrzQQXZtSg.

References

Axelrod, R., & Tesfatsion, L. S. (2006). Appendix A: A guide for newcomers to agent-based modeling in the social sciences. *Handbook of Computational Economics, 2*, 1647–1659. http://dx.doi.org/10.1016/s1574-0021(05)02044-7

Zhou, S., Chen, D., Cai, W., Luo, L., Yoke, M., Tian, F., … Hamilton, B. D. (2010). Crowd modeling and simulation techniques. *ACM Transactions on Modeling and Computer Simulation, 20*(4), 2001–2035. http://dx.doi.org/10.1145/1842722.1842725

CHAPTER **12**

REFLECTIONS AND A LOOK AHEAD

Patrice M. Buzzanell

With this second volume in Robert X. Browning's Purdue University series on discovery, learning, and engagement on and using the C-SPAN Archives' online Video Library, the hopes expressed just a year earlier have started to come to fruition. At the time of the first conference and edited collection focused on the C-SPAN Video Library, namely *The C-SPAN Archives: An Interdisciplinary Resource for Discovery, Learning, and Engagement* (Purdue University Press, 2014), there was deep interest in multidisciplinary work that utilized the C-SPAN Archives in novel ways to stimulate further theory, research, methodological innovations in digital archival use, and workshops to draw in students and non-academicians. With this second volume, these interests have grown. Now we see much more complex findings and sophisticated procedures that tell a story about scholars' interests and analytic techniques but, even more so, capture the enthusiasm expressed in the first volume.

Like the first volume, this book is not designed or presented to be the final word on how to conduct C-SPAN archival research, nor are the findings expected to be conclusive. Instead, this volume is designed to focus on and be generative in the area of discovery. The importance of increasing awareness of the C-SPAN Archives as a resource for discovery cannot be understated.

Less than a month before the November 2014 C-SPAN conference that provided a context for C-SPAN researchers to meet at Purdue University, I was in Shanghai at the Global Media Forum hosted by colleagues at Shanghai Jiaotong University. The title of my keynote address was "How Do C-SPAN Archives' Discourse Portray the Chinese Internet? Legitimization Strategies Around US–China Relationships" (see Buzzanell, 2015). At the conclusion of my talk, I was somewhat surprised and hugely encouraged at how many conference attendees and speakers wanted to chat about C-SPAN. Their enthusiasm for the unedited content about government policymaking, special features about life and political figures in the United States, and archived online content was strong. Audience members wanted to know how to access and search the C-SPAN Video Library; they wanted to know the specific steps that they could take to retrieve and analyze data; they wanted to express their fond memories for the programming that was so much a part of their lives while they lived in the United States during visiting scholar or graduate and undergraduate years. Most of all, they wanted to say how much they appreciated the C-SPAN commitment to discourse as it occurred in the moment and without censorship. Still others, including a couple of other keynote address speakers who specialized in media and different communication contexts, remarked that they had not considered analyzing video from the C-SPAN Archives. They started to talk about possible bridges with their own data and research interests. Of importance to these scholars is that the C-SPAN Video Library offers insights into the bases of collective memory that is unfiltered and not nostalgic. In eras in which history is reworked—and all eras demonstrate this capacity for reconstructing and recollecting history and particular events—the C-SPAN Video Library has tremendous import.

REFLECTIONS ON DISCOVERY USING THE C-SPAN VIDEO LIBRARY

In the first volume of Robert Browning's series of edited books featuring the C-SPAN Archives, we see glimmers of several themes that now have come to fruition in this second volume. In the chapters, we see researchers grappling with how to access and analyze data. Although the focus of their work is on academic research consistent with the foci in their disciplines, their inquiry offers contributions in different areas as noted by several recurring ideas or themes within this book. These themes are (1) making sense of recorded events and re-collected memories; (2) changing ways of searching and analyzing data; (3) contributing engaged scholarship; and (4) celebrating difference, telling our stories.

Many chapters have aspects of these different themes. In this final reflection, the following sections do not attempt to cover all of the interconnections but just position some chapters as presenting examples of and/or complexities within particular themes.

Theme 1: Making Sense of Recorded Events and Re-Collected Memories

The basis of the theme "making sense of recorded events and re-collected memories" is researchers' interest in reexamining what actually happened, as recorded for and displayed in the C-SPAN Video Library, in contrast to what was promoted at the time in news media and what now is recalled and part of our collective memory.

Although this theme is central to many chapter authors' work, we see the foregrounding of these processes explicitly in the sole-authored work of Kathryn Cramer Brownell and the collaboration between Alison N. Novak and Ernest A. Hakanen.

In "Going Beyond the Anecdote: The C-SPAN Archives and Uncovering the Ritual of Presidential Debates in the Age of Cable News" (Chapter 1), Kathryn Cramer Brownell is interested in the ways in which presidential debates and memories shape the media construction and the ways the media, along with other coverage, form presidential debates history through news coverage and other media coverage. She revisits news stories that sometimes exaggerated the importance of certain debate aspects. Her work of reconstruction, correction, and analysis provide insights for historians and political scientists, but also for communication scholars and rhetoricians interested in examining the constitutive processes whereby discourse fragments and their materialities become re-collected and re-cognized in collective memory (see Aden et al., 2009; see also Rowlinson, Booth, Clark, Delahaye, & Procter, 2010). Drawing from Aden et al.'s (2009) work and reinterpreting Rowlinson et al.'s (2010) focus on corporate sites of memory and episodic memory studies, we can approach the C-SPAN Video Library as a site of memory around and in which humans engage in different kinds of and motivations for remembering. Even when data are viewed to establish "objective" reports, we admit that being situated in particular spatiotemporal locations affects and is affected by what we experience through the C-SPAN Video Library. As a result, the C-SPAN record is a valuable resource to re-collect and analyze anew with and for each generation. In this endeavor, we can emphasize the importance of the subjective experiences of the people remembering and of the analysts interpreting. As Charmaz (2000) says about grounded theory, all knowledge claims arise out of relationships, meaning that knowledge emerges in the relationship between people and data. People, analyses, and knowledge are situated, making the C-SPAN Video Library invaluable. In particular, how and why these digital fragments of discourse and interaction become negotiated and sedimented into the stories that we now tell is of interest for understanding the values and motivations of particular generations and storytellers—of the Kennedy–Nixon and Ford–Carter presidential debates, for example, as Kathryn Cramer Brownell did.

A different means of engaging in remembering is offered by Alison Novak and Ernie Hakanen. In "Framing Technological Influence through C-SPAN" (Chapter 2), they conduct a frame analysis of *The Communicators'* series episodes from 2005 to the present. Their analysis offers both retrospective and prospective accounts of leaders' views of technology, offering data for further examination of the reshaping of memory regarding past contributions and of the as-yet-to-be-determined foresight that these leaders have. As examples, program guests such as the inventor of the cell phone as well as a former chair of the U.S. Federal Communications Commission (FCC)[1] talk about themselves and their work. They are framing the past, present, and future of technology and who are they in this history. Alison and Ernie provide insights into dialectic tensions surrounding dystopian and utopian views of technology, regulatory policies, and strategic communication implications for engaged scholarship, our third theme in this reflection.

Theme 2: Changing Ways of Searching and Analyzing Data

A second theme is that researchers' sense of how to search and analyze the C-SPAN archival data has changed and continues to change. For instance, at the November 2014 C-SPAN conference Robert Browning, director of the

C-SPAN Archives, described how the records of votes and of speaker order for events are available in the "graphical timeline," where anyone interested in searching the C-SPAN Video Library can find particular remarks. Robert related that, for the first time, records have been organized by the speaker who actually spoke when one searches under People. This responsiveness of the C-SPAN Archives staff is commendable in terms of their interest in and ability to make changes that would benefit scholars, teachers, and other individuals.

Foreshadowing the third theme of engaged scholarship, the theme of "changing ways of searching and analyzing data" underscores that scholars live in an era of mixed method approaches and recognition that the questions of consequence that researchers ask require in-depth studies as well as big data responses. Scholars do their work at a time when innovative procedures and techniques are being designed to utilize the C-SPAN Archives to its fullest and in combination with social media and other data.

Researchers can "scrape" much data, use computational social science, and make accessible the minute variations necessary for visual or video analysis because of the C-SPAN Video Library's free digital accessibility. In light of these qualities, the chapters by Erik P. Bucy and Zijian Harrison Gong, stonegarden grindlife, and David A. Caputo are featured.

In "Image Bite Analysis of Presidential Debates" (Chapter 3), Erik Bucy and Zijian Gong provide a look at the broader and multi-institutional research program on image bites and the way people can infer personality traits and motivations of leaders in mediated contexts. Put simply, they coded for indicators such as emotions, blink rate, individual gaze and posture, and production values in two 2012 debates featuring Barack Obama and Mitt Romney, supplementing the C-SPAN Video Library materials with data from Twitter where possible. Using Twitter, they linked biobehavioral and big data, examining such variables as Twitter volume per minute. They studied displays of defiance and affinity, anger and reassurance, and evasion and neutrality in 30-second increments. Although this synopsis focuses on some of the complex methodological decisions, coding categories, and procedural steps and constraints, the larger questions are the ways in which political leaders and, indeed, most public figures can anticipate stakeholders' responses to even their most minute behaviors.

Similarly, in "Expressive Polarization in Political Discourse" (Chapter 4), stonegarden grindlife explores polarization in appearances in eight years of raw C-SPAN Video Library video—namely, how anger and fear are expressed by talking faster and louder with individual microfluctuations being considered with regard to individuals' baselines. With his data set of over 10,000 speeches, he reports that "the presence of indicators of anger and aggression are not merely random. They are related in consistent ways with the mechanics of a chamber, the level of controversy associated with the debate topic, and party strength."

Finally, in "C-SPAN, MOOCs, and the Post-Digital Age" (Chapter 5), David Caputo describes the depth and force of C-SPAN and its Video Library for U.S. citizens and the world, depicting it as "an elixir that energizes the spirit and recharges the mind." However, he is mindful of the challenges that C-SPAN faces and the need to reconsider ways in which C-SPAN and users might leverage its qualities and enhance its appeal. As one possibility, David suggests how Massive Open Online Courses (MOOCs) might utilize C-SPAN in novel ways to ensure an engaging educational approach. He discusses the idea of an advocacy MOOC involving campaigns and leaves his readers with the opportunity to reflect upon other ideas.

Theme 3: Contributing Engaged Scholarship

This theme of "contributing engaged scholarship" is not simply about promoting the use of the C-SPAN Video Library for engaged scholarship but about the ways in which chapters actually contribute research that is, at its very core, engaged. This theme acknowledges the ways in which researchers' relationships to their data have changed in recent years. Aligning with core responsibilities and standards in the particular epistemological and ontological stances that researchers hold, this theme acknowledges not only that the archive creation process itself provides an exemplar of engaged scholarship but also that chapters in this edited collection illuminate how members of the academy are engaging with the C-SPAN archival data in different ways. In this book, engagement is not always blatant but might be part of the underlying values and/or the strategic use of a results continuum where particular work may be positioned. Before providing an example of engaged scholarship by Mary L. Nucci, I include a discussion of engaged scholarship to situate this work and the value of the C-SPAN Archives and other repositories of people's voices and records of sociocultural and political events. Engaged scholarship using the C-SPAN Video Library encourages new questions about possibilities for and of research in content, form, and values.

Engaged scholarship is a term capturing the profound dynamics within, between, and encapsulating theory, research, and practice. Engaged scholars forge interdisciplinary connections yet recognize the need for arguments about distinct disciplinary contributions. Engaged scholars' work is multi-topic—often not a linear research program—using diverse paradigms (from understanding to critique and transformation) and multiple and mixed methodologies. Engaged scholarship is funded and not funded and micro and/or macro level, but it produces local and global insights about and effective strategies for managing key challenges facing today's world.

As Putnam (2009) noted in her keynote address delivered to the 7th Aspen Conference on Engaged Communication Scholarship entitled "The Multiple Faces of Engaged Scholarship," there are numerous ways of conducting engaged scholarship: "What is clear is that we have a variety of faces for engaged scholarship and simply aligning the term with problem-centered research or the study of practical, real-world problems is not particularly useful for making this construct distinctive." Indeed, she continues, engaged scholarship has a "unique cast that separates it from merely addressing practical problems or focusing on translation or disseminating and making knowledge accessible."

Whereas Putnam argues that the three faces of engaged scholarship are collaborative learning, activism and social justice, and practical theory, we focus on collaborative learning. Here scholars coproduce knowledge about complex problems in sophisticated and nuanced ways. Engaged scholarship is relational insofar as it exists in conversation with diverse stakeholders. The outcomes are knowledge production as well as help for local communities. Dempsey and Barge (2014) focus on the promise of engaged scholarship to model and enact participatory forms of communication, bridging practitioner and academic communities.

Mary Nucci examines data from the C-SPAN Video Library to illuminate the shift in popular cultural and governmental policymakers' discourse about science as a means of solving problems related to questions about science and policy and associated problems about whether people believe in and use scientific evidence for policy. In her chapter, "Using the C-SPAN Archives: Evidence in Policymakers' Discourse on Science" (Chapter 6), Mary positions herself as someone with a non–political science background, invested in science communication, and questioning federal government funding, programs, agencies, and decisions on science. She focuses on legislative committees where nonpartisan actors who are not well versed in scientific procedures and theories decontextualize findings but have tendencies to support certain beliefs in science along partisan lines. In the end, her analysis provides ideas about how the government thinks about science, and how that affects policy and media presentations about science. In using the C-SPAN Video Library, Mary engages with publics to help people understand who is out there and voting (voting records), what science issues are being debated, who is or is not granted expertise, how science is debated by nonscientists, and how science discussions are framed in committees and in offices that have direct bearing on education and national prominence in science.

Theme 4: Celebrating Difference, Telling Our Stories

A fourth and final theme, "celebrating difference, telling our stories," encompasses the idea that there are many ways in which stories from different research projects are extracted and told. Chapters authored by several researchers support this theme. In some cases, this theme presents voices of those either not routinely acknowledged or not part of mainstream political stories (Nadia E. Brown, Michael D. Minta, and Valeria Sinclair-Chapman). In other cases, difference comes to the foreground of the research as participants depicted in C-SPAN archival segments—such as Michelle Obama, gays in the military, and women in STEM (science, technology, engineering, and math)—and the researchers themselves struggle to explain and remedy what they see as a devaluation or oversimplification of their own and others' experiences (Ray Block Jr. and Christina S. Haynes; Christopher Neff; Lauren Berkshire Hearit and me). This theme also encompasses research that is not aligned exactly with celebration but with recognition of polarizations that seem to preserve difference (Bryce J. Dietrich), offering scholarship of hope that visualization and sound analyses can offer insights into oppositional stories and potential imagery for incorporating the voice between.

First, in "Personal Narratives and Representation Strategies: Using C-SPAN Oral Histories to Examine Key Concepts in Minority Representation" (Chapter 7), Nadia E. Brown, Michael D. Minta, and Valeria Sinclair-Chapman talk about how members of the Congressional Black Caucus performed their identities, told their own lived stories, and described how they went to Congress. The voices of five African American members of the Congressional Black Caucus described in their oral histories how they were prepared to link their identities to what they did and how they represented people not only in their own districts but throughout the United States. The oral histories reveal how and why such distinct personalities with very different backgrounds could merge into the Congressional Black Caucus as a collective for social change.

Second, Ray Block Jr. and Christina Haynes describe how Michelle Obama actively created her own image—one bridging public, private, and policy—despite negative depictions in everyday conversations and media reports. Through their chapter, "'Mom-In-Chief' Rhetoric as a Lens for Understanding Policy Advocacy: A Thematic Analysis of Video Footage From Michelle Obama's Speeches" (Chapter 8), they depict the struggles that public figures like the First Lady have with their identity constructions and their efforts to contribute productively to public and private conversations about intersectionalities of race, gender, motherhood, politics, and other politics of import in contemporary society. Ray and Christina center on Michelle Obama's speeches to, interactions with, and advocacy for military families. Discussing family would provide a means of creating identification—that is, ways of making Michelle Obama seem not so different from other mainstream Americans. The military family dialogues became ways to bridge private–public and policy. Through close readings of texts and thematic analyses of video footage of the First Lady's speeches, Ray and Christina find that Michelle Obama utilizes rhetorical moves to stress unifying identities (family and motherhood), situate herself as an ordinary person despite her political stature, and blur boundaries between her public and private roles.

Third, in "The Performance of Roll Call Votes as Political Cover in the U.S. Senate: Using C-SPAN to Analyze the Vote to Repeal 'Don't Ask, Don't Tell'" (Chapter 9), Christopher Neff finds not only that gays in the military were disenfranchised through their social identity and institutional structures and policies but that that the sequencing of votes corresponded to electoral implications. Christopher concludes that "party members use the sequencing and clustering of roll call votes to provide political cover for their vulnerable members as a way of addressing controversial political issues within legislative bodies."

Extending social identity discussions and ways to broaden the participation and inclusion of those whose voices often are not routinely or effectively incorporated in political processes, Lauren Hearit and I offer insight in our chapter, "Public Understandings of Women in STEM: A Prototype Analysis of Governmental Discourse from the C-SPAN Video Library" (Chapter 10). From media representations in popular culture to video footage from the C-SPAN Video Library, Lauren and I build a case for how prototypes are perpetuated in policy discussions, contributing to the relative lack of progress regarding women in STEM. Echoing the theme of engaged scholarship, we argue that three clusters of prototypical representations continue to situate on the numbers, unique characteristics and achievements, and pattern of selective resource allocations for girls and women aligned with STEM. Rather than portraying everyday exclusionary processes and women's skills and talents, arguments legitimizing expenditures for STEM education and related practices focus on increasing STEM expertise for national competitiveness by simply incorporating more women.

As a final example of "celebrating difference, telling our stories," we take a sideways look at the processes underlying this theme. Bryce Dietrich poses the question in his chapter title, "If a Picture Is Worth a Thousand Words, What Is a Video Worth?" (Chapter 11). In response, Bryce illustrates the importance of audio and video for understanding the political processes, particularly cosponsorship. Not only does Bryce provide time series work in the polarization of social networks before, during, and after cosponsorship events, but he also refers to the visual traces that capture Congressional members' motivations—as they look beyond their local neighborhoods to others, act with other agents, and move more or less quickly and eagerly into interactive space for deliberation—as well as implicates findings from other research to trace patterns in policymaking and those involved on the floor, in caucuses, and in other settings. Through Bryce's research, visualization analyses offer additional leverage to answer questions about how polarization can be explained, how the stories about difference can be told differently, and how perspectives between these factions gain greater voice in political processes.

A LOOK AHEAD

The authors' collective goal has been to expand and enrich the use of the C-SPAN Archives' online Video Library in innovative and profound ways. Although an open call in various disciplinary and interdisciplinary venues produced an encouraging number of submissions (22 proposals) for competitive selection into the conference that supported this edited collection, we, as contributors to this volume, look forward to more focused collaborations on the themes presented here. Upon reflecting on commonalities and differences among the themes—making sense of recorded events and re-collected memories; changing ways of searching and analyzing data; contributing engaged scholarship; and celebrating difference, telling our stories—we acknowledge that many of the chapters incorporate different aspects of these themes to greater and lesser extents.

As we look ahead, we ask how we might increase awareness of and knowledge generated through use of the C-SPAN Video Library. We're pleased with the different disciplines and variety of research that have emerged with this conference and edited collection. We are humbled by the visions of particular people, such as Brian Lamb, Robert Browning, Susan Swain, and Rob Kennedy, who produced C-SPAN and the C-SPAN Video Library, and are encouraged by national and global respect for the C-SPAN Archives. As we share our enthusiasm for utilizing the data contained in the Archives, we recognize that they remain underexplored in so many ways. We close by thanking C-SPAN and Purdue's president, Mitch Daniels, for financial support. And we look ahead to the next conference highlighting use of the C-SPAN Video Library.

NOTE

1. See http://www.fcc.gov/what-we-do.

REFERENCES

Aden, R., Han, M., Norander, S., Pfahl, M., Pollock, T., Jr., & Young, S. (2009). Re-collection: A proposal for refining the study of collective memory and its places. *Communication Theory, 19*(3), 311–336. http://dx.doi.org/10.1111/j.1468-2885.2009.01345.x

Buzzanell, P. M. (2015). How do C-SPAN Archives' discourse portray the Chinese Internet? Legitimization strategies around US–China relationships. In *2015 Global Communication: "China and Internet."* Manuscript submitted for publication.

Charmaz, K. (2000). Grounded theory: Objectivist and constructivist methods. In

N. K. Denzin, & Y. S. Lincoln (Eds.), *Handbook of qualitative research* (2nd ed., pp. 509–535). Thousand Oaks, CA: Sage.

Dempsey, S., & Barge, J. K. (2014). Engaged scholarship and democracy. In L. L. Putnam & D. K. Mumby (Eds.), *The SAGE handbook of organizational communication: Advances in theory, research, and methods* (3rd ed., pp. 665–688). Los Angeles, CA: Sage.

Putnam, L. L. (2009, August). *The multiple faces of engaged scholarship.* Keynote presentation to the 7th Aspen Conference on Engaged Communication Scholarship, Aspen, CO.

Rowlinson, M., Booth, C., Clark, P., Delahaye, A., & Procter, S. (2010). Social remembering and organizational memory. *Organization Studies, 31*(1), 69–87. http://dx.doi.org/10.1177/0170840609347056

CONTRIBUTORS

Ray Block Jr. is an assistant professor in the Department of Political Science and Public Administration at the University of Wisconsin, La Crosse. He received his PhD from the Ohio State University in 2006. Ray is currently working on several projects that seek to put Barack Obama's historic candidacies and two-term presidency into perspective, and he published his recent research on the First Family in the *National Political Science Review, Political Behavior, Presidential Studies Quarterly,* and *Social Science Quarterly.*

Nadia E. Brown is an associate professor of political science and African American Studies at Purdue University. She is the author of *Sisters in the Statehouse: Black Women and Legislative Decision Making* (Oxford University Press, 2014) and numerous articles focusing on Black women's politics. Dr. Brown received her PhD in political science in 2010 from Rutgers University, with major fields in women and politics and American politics. She also holds a graduate certificate in women's and gender studies. Dr. Brown's research interests lie broadly in identity politics, legislative studies, and Black women's studies. Her current research projects address the politics of appearance for Black women candidates for public office.

Kathryn Cramer Brownell is an assistant professor of history at Purdue University. She received her PhD in history from Boston University and her BA in history from the University of Michigan. Her research and teaching examine 20th-century U.S. political history with a focus on the relationships between media, politics, and popular culture. Dr. Brownell's new book, *Showbiz Politics: Hollywood in American Political Life* (University of North Carolina Press, 2014), explores the institutionalization of Hollywood styles and structures in American politics from the 1920s to the 1970s. Currently she is at work on a political history of cable television.

Robert X. Browning is an associate professor of political science and of communication in the Brian Lamb School of Communication at Purdue University. In 1987 he became the founding director of the C-SPAN Archives. He is the author of *Politics and Social Welfare Policy in the United States* and the editor of *The C-SPAN Archives: An Interdisciplinary Resource for Discovery, Learning, and Engagement.* Awarded the George Foster Peabody Award for its online Video Library in 2010, the C-SPAN Archives is housed in the Purdue Research Park and offers a window into American life.

Erik P. Bucy is the Marshall and Sharleen Formby Regents Professor of Strategic Communication in the College of Media and Communication at Texas Tech University. His research interests include visual and nonverbal analysis of television news, user engagement with media technologies, and normative theories of media and democracy. Dr. Bucy is the editor of *Politics and the Life Sciences,* an interdisciplinary peer-reviewed journal published by Cambridge University Press, and coauthor of *Image Bite Politics: News and the Visual Framing of Elections* (with Maria Elizabeth Grabe, Oxford University Press, 2009), winner of two outstanding book awards. Most recently he edited *The Sourcebook for Political Communication Research: Methods, Measures, and Analytical Techniques* (Routledge, 2013). Prior to Texas Tech, Dr. Bucy was vice president of research at SmithGeiger, LLC, a leading media research consultancy, and was an associate professor with tenure at Indiana University. He has also held visiting and research appointments at Dartmouth College (2005), the University of Michigan (2007–2008), and UCLA (2012). His research has been funded by the National Association of Broadcasters, Shorenstein Center at Harvard University, and C-SPAN Education Foundation. A former staff writer for the *Los Angeles Herald Examiner*, Dr. Bucy served as deputy press secretary and national scheduler for Jerry Brown's 1992 presidential campaign.

Patrice M. Buzzanell is a distinguished professor in the Brian Lamb School of Communication and the School of Engineering Education by courtesy at Purdue University. She also is the chair and director of the Susan Bulkeley Butler Center for Leadership Excellence and an endowed visiting professor at Shanghai Jiaotong University. Dr. Buzzanell is the coeditor of 3 books and the author of more than 160 articles and chapters. Her research centers on the everyday negotiations and structures that produce and are produced by the intersections of career, gender, and communication, particularly in STEM (science, technology, engineering, and math), and has appeared in such journals as *Communication Monographs, Human Relations, Communication Theory,* and *Human Communication Research,* as well as proceedings in engineering education and handbooks on professional, organizational, gender, applied, family, ethics, and conflict communication. Fellow and past president of the International Communication Association, Dr. Buzzanell has received awards for her discovery, learning, mentoring, and engagement.

David A. Caputo is president emeritus and professor of political science at Pace University, New York City, where he teaches courses in American government, the presidency, and electoral politics. His current research involves Massive Open Online Courses (MOOCs) and their potential role in furthering civic education. He is also completing research on how philanthropy would fare under various proposed changes to the U.S. Tax Code. In recent years Dr. Caputo has consulted extensively in the area of international education. He received his BA from Miami University (Phi Beta Kappa) and his graduate degrees from Yale University in political science. He has been a faculty member and the dean of liberal arts at Purdue University and the president of both City University of New York's Hunter College (1995–2000) and Pace

University (2000–2007). He has published various books and scholarly articles in his field and serves on the boards of Project Pericles, G-MEO, and the World Lung Foundation. He and his wife reside in Manhattan.

Bryce J. Dietrich is a visiting assistant professor at the University of Missouri. His research focuses on elite political behavior, with an emphasis on the quantitative analysis of audio, text, and video data. While his article in *Political Psychology* deals with elite personality, his dissertation considered the causes and consequences of congressional anger. Here, *anger* is defined using the text and audio from 7,453 floor speeches obtained from the C-SPAN Video Library and the House Video Archives. Ultimately he finds that the angriest members of Congress not only increase voter turnout in their districts, but they also tend to win by larger margins. Portions of this project are currently under review.

Zijian Harrison Gong is an assistant professor in the Department of Communication at the University of Tampa. His research interests include visual and nonverbal analysis of television news, strategic communication, and motivated cognition. His primary research interest concerns how different production techniques impact selective attention, message recall, and attitude formation. Practically, his research, which has appeared in *Communication & Sport* and *Journal of Literacy and Technology,* focuses on helping media practitioners enhance the persuasiveness of their messages. Dr. Gong has given more than a dozen research presentations on media psychology and message effects at competitive national conferences, including the annual meetings of the Association for Education in Journalism and Mass Communication, Broadcast Education Association, and National Communication Association. As a research assistant for the Center for Communication Research at Texas Tech, he collected and analyzed data using a variety of laboratory technologies, including MediaLab, the DialSmith Perception Analyzer System, BioPac System, and Applied Science Laboratories EyeTrac Units.

stonegarden grindlife is a doctoral candidate in political science at UCLA. Before beginning his doctoral studies, he worked as an analyst at LexisNexis Academic & Library Solutions, where he specialized in Congress, the executive and judicial branches, and governmental bureaucracy. While at LexisNexis

Mr. grindlife earned his MA in government from Georgetown University. Prior to his time in Washington, DC, at Georgetown, he served as a field director on a U.S. House race. He is also an alumnus of Purdue University.

Ernest A. Hakanen is a professor of communication at Drexel University. He received his PhD in communication from Temple University. His research interests include media policy and history, music and emotions, and content analysis. He has published in *Mass Communication and Journalism Quarterly* and *Journal of Broadcasting and Electronic Media*. His book, *Branding the Teleself: Media Effects Discourse and the Changing Self,* is available from Lexington Books, and he has edited two volumes on the Iraq War with Palgrave Macmillan. Dr. Hakanen served as the graduate director of Drexel's doctoral program in communication, culture, and media for 10 years.

Christina S. Haynes is an assistant professor of women's, gender, and sexuality studies at the University of Wisconsin, La Crosse. She received her PhD in educational studies from the Ohio State University in 2013. Dr. Haynes researches narratives of academically successful African American women who attend predominantly White institutions (PWIs) and media depictions of Michelle Obama.

Lauren Berkshire Hearit is a doctoral student in the Brian Lamb School of Communication at Purdue University. Her research examines how communication impacts economic expectations, with a focus on the intersection of economics, public policy, and organizational behavior. She has presented papers at the National Communication Association and the Midwest Academy of Management, and her first article appeared in the *Encyclopedia of Public Relations* (Sage, 2013).

Michael D. Minta is an associate professor in Black studies and political science at the University of Missouri, Columbia. He received his PhD in political science from the University of Michigan, Ann Arbor. Dr. Minta is one of the leading experts in the study of the political representation of African American, Latino, and women's interests in the United States. His book, *Oversight: Representing Black and Latino Interests in Congress* (Princeton University

Press, 2011), is a valuable guide that scholars, political leaders, and the legal community consult when assessing whether diversity in legislatures improves responsiveness to minority interests. Dr. Minta regularly teaches popular courses in U.S. government pertaining to African American politics, congressional politics, and interest group advocacy.

Christopher Neff is a lecturer in public policy in the Department of Government and International Relations at the University of Sydney. He received his PhD from the University of Sydney in 2014. Dr. Neff's research interests include theories of the policy process, policy analysis, the role of policy entrepreneurs, and comparative public policy. More specifically, he investigates policymaking around highly emotional issues such as LGBTQI politics, mass shootings, and the "politics of shark attacks." His research has appeared in such journals as the *Australian Journal of Political Science, Critical Studies on Security, Journal of Homosexuality, Marine Policy, Coastal Management,* and *Environmental Studies and Sciences.* Prior to his work in academia, Dr. Neff was a policy practitioner as a U.S. Senate staffer, lobbyist, and nonprofit executive, which included working as the first full-time lobbyist for the repeal of the "Don't Ask, Don't Tell" law and policy.

Alison N. Novak is an assistant professor at Rowan University in the College of Communication and Creative Arts. She received her doctorate from Drexel University in communication, culture, and media. Her work explores the media's representation of the millennial generation, civic engagement, and future of technology. She has previously published in *Feminist Media Studies, Review of Communication,* and *The Journal of Information, Technology and Politics.* She is currently coediting a volume on gender, race, and age in new media, available in 2016 from IGI Global.

Mary L. Nucci is a research assistant professor in the Department of Human Ecology at Rutgers University. Her research interests include public perceptions of science, the movement of science knowledge through society, and science communication in film, media, and museums. Dr. Nucci received an AB in biological sciences from Mount Holyoke College and an MS in zoology and a PhD in media studies, both from Rutgers.

Valeria Sinclair-Chapman is an associate professor in the Department of Political Science at Purdue University. Her work focuses on American political institutions, legislative politics, minority representation in Congress, and minority political participation. Broadly construed, Dr. Sinclair-Chapman's research examines how previously marginalized groups gain inclusion in the American political system. She is the author or coauthor of several journal articles and book chapters, as well as the author of an award-winning book, *Countervailing Forces in African-American Political Activism, 1973–1994* (Cambridge University Press, 2006). Her current research projects consider how legislators represent the interests of racial and ethnic minorities in Congress at various stages of the legislative process, with particular focus on why and how legislators use bill sponsorship to introduce new ideas to the national agenda.

INDEX

Page numbers in italics refer to figures.